AF394535

COASTLINE

BEN ROBINSON
COASTLINE

AN EXPLORATION OF BRITAIN'S COASTAL HERITAGE

First published in the UK in 2026 by Blink Publishing
An imprint of Bonnier Books UK
5th Floor, HYLO, 105 Bunhill Row,
London, EC1Y 8LZ

A CIP catalogue record for this book is available from the British Library.

Hardback ISBN: 978-1-78512-501-0

Also available as an ebook and an audiobook

1 3 5 7 9 10 8 6 4 2

Design and Typeset by Envy Design Ltd
Illustration copyright © Jitesh Patel, 2026
Printed and bound in Great Britain by CPI (UK) Ltd, Croydon CR0 4YY

The authorised representative in the EEA is Bonnier Books UK (Ireland) Limited.
Registered office address:
Block B, The Crescent Building
Northwood, Santry
Dublin 9, D09 C6X8
Ireland
compliance@bonnierbooks.ie

www.bonnierbooks.co.uk

*To my late grandparents, with thanks for their stories
from the past, their time and their love*

CONTENTS

Introduction

I push the throttle forward and feel the surging engine pull us ever faster. Wheels rumble and bump across the grass, then merely kiss the surface, until finally the feeling of floating and skimming over the ground takes hold. It is a sensation that begins every flight, but one that never fails to bring a smile. The aeroplane, nose up, strains to climb, until a look at the shrinking fields below and a glance at the altimeter tells me we are at a good height to level off. At 2000 feet we are high enough to see mile upon mile of patchwork landscape rolling out to the horizons, except ahead. In front of us, the gently undulating terrain ends and the flat expanse of the seemingly endless sea begins.

The lumpy, turbulent inland air that has rocked the aeroplane since take-off gives way to a breeze smoothed to an even temperature by the sea. We are above the coast now, and I bank to follow its gently curving line to the west. I am grateful for the extra pair of eyes and ears in the cockpit as my father, Peter, catches a distorted radio call and spots the glint of another aeroplane just off to port. Away from the airfield and settling into the flight, we begin to take in the coastline below.

The little seaside town of Cromer comes into view. Its large medieval church and narrow streets near the seafront indicate its ancient origins. Cromer was a renowned fishing centre for centuries and is still famous for Cromer crabs. The esplanade, clifftop gardens, terraces of villas and apartments, hotels, and the pier proudly projecting out into the sea, also mark Cromer as a Victorian seaside resort. Clusters of people, tiny colourful animated specks, are scattered along the pier and sandy beaches. A few are bobbing about in the sea close to the shore. The odd canoe and paddleboard float sedately by the swimmers and paddlers. Visitors are enjoying the fine summer weather by the sea in similar ways to generations of seaside holidaymakers and day trippers before them.

We now fly over a series of caravan parks. The neat rows of static caravans stop at the very lip of the cliffs, which we can see have been crumbling onto the beach below. It was here at West Runton in the 1990s that the eroding coastline gave up an extraordinary treasure: the near complete skeleton of a steppe mammoth. The discovery of this giant, 10 ton, 600,000-year-old beast here reminds us that the coast was not always as it is today. The coastline is by no means timeless but a constantly changing place, shaped by time.

Now we pass over Sheringham, another old fishing town that developed into a charming seaside resort. Sheringham was the recipient of some of the first aerial bombs ever dropped in anger onto British soil. From our vantage point we can see how vulnerable coastal towns were to threats from Britain's enemies across the seas. There are both great benefits and some significant disadvantages in living on the coast.

Sheringham still greets passengers from the railway line that did so much to make this part of the coast accessible in the late nineteenth century. Clement Scott, an influential London columnist, 'discovered' and popularised this part of the coast for metropolitan society in 1883, naming it 'Poppyland'. It has been a favoured getaway ever since. Part of the rail line is now run as a heritage railway. We see an engine in the station, puffing steam, and another chugging its way past the golf course towards the town.

Now the coast displays another side of its character. A long shingle spit extends westwards to the sandbank-strewn mouth of Blakeney Haven. The former port villages here appear to be almost inland, separated from the shore by extensive salt marsh. Their only access to the sea is via meandering channels, from which a maze of muddy creeks fan out into the surrounding green marshes. From above, these natural tidal channels look like gnarled old tree trunks, their denuded branches spreading out into a confusion of twisted twigs. But like a copse of old trees, this environment supports rich wildlife. Here and there we can see groups of seals basking on sandbanks, a sure sign of good fish stocks.

We have to watch our altitude now and be mindful of our engine noise. Bird reserves take in huge areas of shore and marsh here. Fifty-six miles of this coastline is designated as an Area of Outstanding Natural Beauty. But from above it is easy to see some of the tensions between giving nature space to breathe and welcoming tens of thousands of visitors. As we progress along the coast, crowded beachfront car parks start to empty and traffic jams develop in the late afternoon as people begin to head home. A few miles offshore, vast arrays of wind turbines, their blades slowly turning, stand out white and incongruous in the sea. Even renewable energy comes at some expense to the conservation of the coast, particularly where it is brought to shore and distributed inland by miles of pylons.

I turn south into the mouth of the Wash, a wide estuary of several rivers that separates East Anglia from Lincolnshire. Again the radio crackles with staccato transmissions and my father and I focus our attention on the messages being passed. We scan the skies ahead more intently. This is an area where military helicopters and jets dogfight and converge on live firing ranges on the far shore. We keep well clear of the target ships, deliberately marooned old container vessels, and the surrounding restricted airspace.

I then look down on the modern docks on the outskirts of King's Lynn, a medieval port town. Cargoes of timber are stacked on the docks waiting for onward transport inland. They have arrived in King's Lynn from Scandinavia and Baltic countries, just as timber arrived here from these places in centuries past. Modern cargoes of salt, wheat, barley and beans similarly reflect King's Lynn's ancient trading staples. A giant mound of scrap metal, waiting to be shipped out for recycling, is a much newer type of export.

We pass huge sluice gates that keep the tide from overwhelming the gentle flow of inland watercourses and surrounding fields. We are on the home straight now, quite literally. Following the familiar dead straight, parallel drainage channels for around fifteen minutes takes us directly to our home airfield. We are leaving the coast behind, but not its influence or its heritage. All the way back I can spot the tell-tale signs of a landscape reclaimed from coastal wetlands. The ghostly impressions of former tidal watercourses are visible in cultivated fields won from sea and marsh.

Down on the ground around thirty miles from the sea, as the crow or aeroplane flies, we are only three feet above sea level. This landscape still connects us to the coast. The engine gently ticks as it cools. On today's flight we have seen much of the rich heritage of this part of the east coast; a great deal that reflects Britain's history as a whole. But I know that on another flight, and in other places, I will notice different things and will be prompted to think about other aspects of our coastal history.

As a pilot, and somebody who has hitched rides in other people's aeroplanes, I am fortunate to have seen quite a lot of the British coast from the air. This is an amazing way to see history. Views from above always offer different perspectives and insights, even for apparently familiar areas. Connections between places that are difficult to read on the ground become much more obvious from above. So whether I have flown over a place before or not, I always scrutinise the aerial photographs taken by others. Huge collections of historical aerial photographs are now easily available online for armchair flyers and researchers.

Historic maps, archaeological records and old photographs are also increasingly available online. These, along with local history books and journal articles and magazine features, always make for rewarding casual background study before or after a trip to the coast. But it is always fun to explore the coast in person. Many seaside places have museums and heritage centres that display aspects of a fascinating past that would otherwise be lost to casual holidaymakers. Even the smallest of these seldom disappoints. Much coastal heritage, however, is hidden in plain sight. We are not always encouraged to look beyond the familiar to find the interesting places and features that tell different stories.

Plenty can be learnt about a seaside place by simply walking around and trying to look beyond the sometimes superficial face it presents to visitors. Finding a cluster of the oldest buildings, recognising fragments of former industrial and military structures (which are often deliberately hidden as part of the beautification of a resort), looking at the geography and geology of a place, is sure to reveal a lot about its true heritage. Different parts of Britain's coastline, and the various ways of exploring them, reveal fascinating stories and new insights into our national history. Whether from air or land, I firmly believe that seeking an understanding of the heritage of a seaside place invariably leads to a better appreciation of it, and an even more enjoyable visit.

Apart from the sheer enjoyment of looking at a place with new eyes, and understanding more of its character, why does this matter? From prehistory to the present day, the coastline has shaped Britain, not only physically but socially, economically and culturally. It has exerted an extraordinary influence on British life, regardless of how far inland and detached from coastal affairs people consider themselves to be. Far from being at the margins of national interests, the coast has been central to era-defining events, and has been at the heart of the British people's most important endeavours. For thousands of years the coastline has been both Britain's frontier and its interface with the wider world. And it is at our borders, perhaps, that we learn the most about ourselves.

My fascination with the coast began when I was very young. Living in a place called the Isle of Ely generated a childhood curiosity about landscape and history. Why is this place called an 'isle', I wondered, when it takes well over an hour to drive to the seaside? There were physical hints of the coast and clues to the former reach of its influence as far as my inland home. The river closest to my village ebbed and flowed with the tide. Occasionally, lone seals would appear for a while, their heads popping up out of the water to look at us, apparently enjoying the attention their visits generated.

At weekends and holidays I looked forward to going to our family caravan at Hunstanton on the Norfolk coast, until it was swept away in one of the periodically savage East Coast floods. Luckily for me, when my paternal grandparents retired they had moved to Hunstanton. I would look forward to staying with them at weekends and during the school holidays, with all the seaside treats and mini-adventures that entailed. My grandfather and I went for long beach walks. When I had exhausted him ('We'll have at least this far to go back you know!'), I carried on exploring the dunes, cliffs, pools, creeks and shallow edge of the sea on my own, or with any other kids who happened to be around.

This stretch of the Norfolk coast, like many other places around Britain's coastline, is an absolute treasure trove for anybody remotely interested in the natural world of the sea and shore, or ancient human history, or more recent historical events and culture. I was equally intrigued by the small darting fish and scuttling crabs in shallow pools, the flocks of wading birds, the exotic sea creatures washed up with the tide, as with the curiously striped cliffs rich with fossils, shipwrecks, the old lighthouse, ruined chapels, concrete fortifications in the dunes and jets screaming towards bombing ranges on the other side of the Wash.

It was an excellent outdoor classroom, made even more magnificent by fairground rides, amusement arcades and seaside food. No wonder that on family drives to this coast my sister and I pressed our faces to the car windows and competitively scanned the horizon to be the first to catch a glimpse of the sea.

My family is still strongly connected to this part of the Norfolk coast, and I am very grateful that we can still visit frequently. I am also privileged that work and life has taken me to many other fascinating coastal places, home and abroad, where I have explored the surprising similarities and great differences to the first coast I knew and loved. Working in archaeology and heritage, and filming *Villages by the Sea*, *Britain's Most Historic Towns* and other TV programmes, has widened my understanding and appreciation of Britain's rich coastal heritage. I have met many interesting people and heard things that have given me much cause for thought, but there is still so much more to see and do. So many coastal places still to explore.

I am sure that my own connections with the coast and interest in its heritage and future have shaped me in some ways. I am certain the coast profoundly affects, enriches and influences many of us who do not actually live and work there permanently, as well as those that call it home. I hope you will find in this book something of the hidden heritage of seaside places you know and love and be inspired to set off and explore other stretches of the coast, perhaps to discover new favourite coastal places.

The following chapters explore key coastal themes throughout history and introduce some of the most significant, intriguing and quirky places that illustrate these themes. From artefacts lost by hunter-gatherers in a land beneath the sea to bustling medieval ports, smugglers' caves, early seaside resorts, fortifications and secret bases, the coast has a rich and fascinating history to investigate and enjoy. Ancient legends, villages and towns lost to the waves, happy holiday memories and artistic expression are all invoked by places where the land meets the sea.

CHAPTER 1

SHAPING BRITAIN

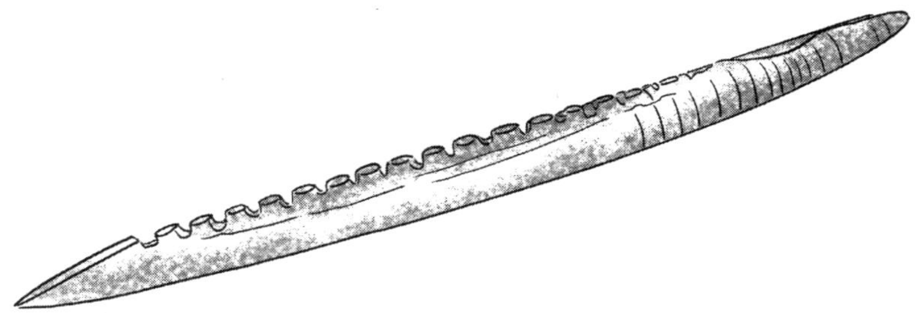

Harpoon or fish spear tip, around
14,000 years old, from Doggerland

Britain, the largest of the islands known to us Romans,
is of such a size and so situated as to run parallel to the
coast of Germany on the east and to that of Spain on
the west, while to the south it actually lies within sight
of Gaul. Its northern shores, with no land facing them,
are beaten by a wild and open sea. The general shape of
Britain has been compared by Livy and Fabius Rusticus
(the finest of ancient and modern writers respectively) to
an elongated diamond or double-headed axe. Such indeed
is its south of Caledonia, and so the same shape has been
attributed to the whole. But when you go further north
you find a huge and shapeless tract of country, jutting
out to form what is actually the most distant coastline
and finally tapering into a kind of wedge.

Tacitus, *Agricola*, c. AD 98

The curious, irregular, elongated shape of mainland Britain, which some say looks like a man with a hat riding a galloping pig (rather than a double-headed axe) is instantly recognisable on a globe or map today. It cannot possibly be mistaken for anywhere else. When viewed closely on a satellite image, the coastline is like an intricate abstract etching. It is defined by an eclectic palette of craggy cliffs, rocky outcrops and grassy headlands, islands, coves, muddy estuaries and inlets, salt marsh, gently curving sandy beaches, dunes, and the hard lines of stone and concrete sea walls, quays and promenades.

Pytheas of Massalia, in around 325 BC, was the first traveller to provide some written descriptions of Britain's geography, climate and people. Pytheas's account survives only in second, third and fourth hand in the writings of later scholars from the Greek and Roman world, but it is clear that he had obtained some grasp of the shape of the place and the main bits that jut out into the sea, such as Cornwall and the northern tip of Scotland. Later Roman writers, such as Tacitus (above), described Britain's shape a little more completely and accurately, but the earliest visual depictions of the coastline belong to a later era.

One of the earliest reasonably accurate and generally representative illustrations of Britain's shape and coastline is to be found on the Anglo-Saxon Mappa Mundi, also known as the 'Cotton Map', after the sixteenth-century antiquarian collector who owned it. This map of the then-known northern part of the world was produced in Canterbury around a thousand years ago and is now housed in the British Library.

The shape of the British Isles is recognisable in the bottom left-hand corner of the map, along with Ireland, the Isle of Man and a huge scattering of islands off Scotland. There is little attempt to illustrate the major inlets, estuaries and headlands accurately, but the general character of the wobbly and irregular British coastline is represented stylistically by something resembling the little perforations around the edge of postage stamps.

Over the next few centuries understanding and representations of Britain's coastline improved greatly. Matthew Paris's map of Britain, dating to the 1250s, is much more colourful and detailed than the Mappa Mundi version. The general shape of the British Isles is familiar on Paris's map, though somewhat compressed, as if a wet clay model has been slightly squeezed by giant hands. It shows estuaries with blue snaking rivers flowing into the sea.

The Gough Map, probably drawn in the late fourteenth century, adds far greater detail still, though Scotland projects straight up from England, rather more like a tall, stove-pipe hat than the irregular craggy shape we now recognise. The cartographer, or those who commissioned the Gough Map, seemed especially interested in watercourses. Many rivers and their estuaries are depicted, and the main islands are reasonably accurately located. Around the coast, as in the interior, settlements large and small are represented with little house, church and castle graphics.

Ever more detailed and accurate maps of Britain and its coast were produced in the early modern era, such as Christopher Saxton's atlas of England and Wales published in 1579 and John Speed's magnificent British atlas, *Theatre of the Empire of Great Britain*, in the early seventeenth century. Coastal charts to assist navigation and identify hazards to shipping became ever more numerous, accurate and informative throughout the next century. Britons were gradually learning more about the character and complexity of their coastline.

Not until the foundation of the Ordnance Survey in 1791, however, was the systematic, standardised, accurate mapping of the whole of Britain and its coastline begun. This was an initiative born of military necessity, first trialled in Scotland where suppression of rebellion required an accurate map of the highlands, and then on England's south coast, where Napoleon threatened to invade.

Throughout the nineteenth century and to the present day, the Ordnance Survey has produced series of maps of Britain that are the envy of the world. Ordnance Survey maps and the many versions of satellite imagery and vertical aerial photograph mapping now freely available through internet browsers mean that Britons have little excuse for being unfamiliar with the general geography of their coastline. But how much of the character and complexity of the coastline is actually captured in this way? How much of it do we really know?

It is a very long way round Britain's coast. The USA's Central Intelligence Agency (in its *World Factbook*) states that the United Kingdom's coastline is 12,429 kilometres (or 7,723 miles) in length. Other sources give anything from 5000 miles to a total of well over 19,000 miles if all the islands are included. The latter is nearly eighty per cent of the distance around the earth's equator. However, all these figures are problematic and a pedant's delight. The actual length of the coastline depends on what exactly is defined as the coastline, the date when it was mapped and the mapping scale. The latter is really about how pragmatic the surveyor chooses to be when confronted with lots of nooks and crannies.

It is a mathematical oddity that the more accurately you try to measure the coastline, the longer it gets. To represent the complexity of Britain's coast increasingly thoroughly requires using smaller units of measurement and taking a vast number of measurements. Larger numbers of small length measurements inevitably add up to a higher overall total distance. The wiggliness of an outline such as a coast can be expressed by something called the 'fractal dimension'. In Douglas Adams' *The Hitchhiker's Guide to the Galaxy*, Slartibartfast, the planet designer who specialises in coastlines, proudly states that he won an award for the coast of Norway. All those fjords. I am sure that the coastline of Britain would have been very high on that award shortlist. Like Norway's coast, Britain's coast has a pretty high fractal dimension.

Britain's coastline is dynamic. It remains in a state of constant flux. Erosion claims chunks in some places, while silting, reclamation and development add lengths of new coastline elsewhere. Twenty thousand years ago Britain's coastline was completely different. It was different last week. It will be different next week. Therefore the only inarguable answer to the pub quiz question 'How long is Britain's coastline?' is that it is impossible to know.

Whether the British coastline is practically immeasurable or 19,491 miles around in total, there is no doubt that this is a very long and incredibly varied, complex and fascinating strip of landscape and seascape. It incorporates glorious beauty spots, pretty harbours, understated backwaters, busy garish resorts and gritty industrial zones. It is an enticing mix of the comfortable and familiar, enigmatic and occasionally secret and sinister. From the seaside tourist hotspots that millions of people know and love, to the military, industrial and nuclear facilities that are accessible to only a few.

However, as we begin to explore Britain's coastline today, we have to understand what it was like in the past. Not only in terms of the activities that took place there, and people's perceptions of it, but in its basic shape. The British are an island people, but Britain has not always been an island.

One of the favourite walking routes for my grandfather Robinson and I was from Old Hunstanton in Norfolk along the beach north towards Holme-next-the-Sea. The most memorable of these walks took place around Easter, when there was chill in the air and the wind whipped stinging sand along the beach. Along the tide line, among the seaweed and shells and peppering the otherwise golden sands we would see large pellets of black matter. You can find them there today. They vary in size and approximate shape in the same general range as scatter cushions. They are riddled with the round holes made by burrowing sea creatures. Many have obviously been in the surf for some time, having been rounded and smoothed like beach cobbles. Others, especially after storms, are more irregular and ragged in shape.

At first I was nervous of these things, thinking that they were something bituminous and sinister; the result of some kind of industrial cargo being dumped at sea. There seemed to be a lot of news about oil tanker spills back then. This material seemed so alien to the natural shoreline debris I saw around me. It was not like the brown sandstone, red and white chalk and flint beach cobbles that come from the distinctive striped cliffs at Hunstanton. It was not like the sand, shells and pebbles on the long beach towards Holme, or the gnarled, bleached driftwood cast up towards the dunes.

I found the courage to investigate one of these mysterious

pellets further. In the time-honoured way that kids often approach the scientific examination of potentially hazardous and interesting objects, I gave it a hefty boot. The pellet flew apart, revealing fibrous innards. The 'thing' was clearly organic and incorporated identifiable plant matter, such as twigs and leaves. These were not all black, but brown and silvery, like some half-rotted garden mulch. Alongside and within the lumps, I occasionally noticed the blackened, twisted branches and stumps of trees. Coming from the Fens, and having dug around in the black soil since I was old enough to hold a spade, I had seen this sort of earth before. But where exactly had these particular lumps come from?

Fishing folk and curious travellers have long known that in various places around the British coastline the stumps of ancient trees are revealed at very low tides. Theses stumps have not been swept there from inland woodland, to roll in the surf and become buried in the sand and mud. They can be seen upright, their twisted roots fixed in place in the seabed beyond the shore. This is where the trees grew and died. The presence of these saturated remains of primordial forests was explained by folk tales, or accepted as evidence of the biblical great flood that was navigated by Noah in his ark. Early geologists and antiquarians pondered the possibility of catastrophic subsidence and compression of soils, or storms battering dune barriers down and letting the sea into formerly dry land.

Eventually it was accepted, though not widely until the first half of the twentieth century, that rising sea levels had submerged formerly dry land and its woodlands. It was apparent that plains or shelves of drowned land extended out from the current British coastline, particularly along the eastern side of England from East Anglia to Yorkshire. But how extensive was this drowned landscape?

During the nineteenth and early twentieth century, trawlers fishing well out into the North Sea frequently dragged up the bones of dry land animals that had long been extinct in the British Isles. Species such as mammoth, woolly rhinoceros, bear, wolf, hyena, bison, elk, beaver and wild horse were represented in the remains sometimes brought back to shore to fill cabinets of curiosity and museum cases. The nets also brought up wood and blocks of tough compressed preserved vegetation, peat, which mariners called 'moorlog'. This seabed debris was a nuisance to fishermen, snagging and damaging nets and creating heavy hauls without many fish to show for their efforts.

One area of the North Sea was particularly notorious for this sort of thing. Dogger Bank is an area of raised seabed here, named after old Dutch fishing boats ('doggers'). It lies around seventy miles from the British coast, and is around 160 miles long (north to south) and sixty miles wide. The finds of plant and animal remains there meant there could be little doubt that Dogger Bank, now deep beneath the waves between Britain, Holland and Denmark, had once been dry land.

In 1913, Clement Reid, geologist and Fellow of the Royal Society, published a book called *Submerged Forests*, which described and discussed the evidence for drowned prehistoric landscapes at the coast. Reid identified Dogger Bank as a place where further research on the subject would prove fruitful, and where evidence that humans had once walked this landscape might be found. He attempted to depict this drowned North

Sea landscape by creating a map using the limited evidence then available. His map showed a hidden territory extending from England to mainland Northwest Europe, complete with major river systems.

Although Clement Reid's work was impressive in its ambition, people found it difficult to accept his ideas. Further study of his barely credible theoretical landscape was severely hampered by the sheer inaccessibility of the seabed beneath the murky waters. The few archaeologists and palaeobotanical researchers who attempted to look further into the questions Reid had raised tended to be those who were already engaged in inland wetland research in Holland, the Somerset Levels and Fens. These people recognised this drowned landscape as one connected with what they saw on land, not as a separate, alien place. It was not until the 1930s, however, that the significance of this place to human heritage began to emerge.

In September 1931, an object was found that changed the perception of Britain's island history. The flamboyantly named Pilgrim E. Lockwood, skipper of the trawler *Colinda* (a small slip of the tongue away from a very unfortunate name for a boat), no doubt cursed as he found yet another large block of peat tangled in his net. Lockwood knew that one of the hazards of dragging fishing nets on or near the seabed ('bottom trawling') is the amount of debris they can disturb and collect. He was fishing in an area of sea about twenty-five miles off the Norfolk coastal town of Cromer that was particularly notable for this kind of hazard. The awkward peat block, a solid four feet square and three feet in depth, had to be broken up to make it easier to chuck back into the sea, like many others before.

However, as Lockwood hacked at the block his shovel struck something hard, which felt and sounded to him like steel. Curious, he broke the block further apart to reveal a stick-like object, about eight-and-a-half inches long (around twenty-two cm), pointed at both ends, with a barbed edge. It was unquestionably a tool made by humans, and was later identified as being made of antler. First described as a harpoon head, the find was part of a prehistoric fish or eel spear of a type that had been recorded several times before in England and Northwest Europe.

These finds usually came from former water bodies inland, and were conventionally dated to the Mesolithic period, the Middle Stone Age (around 10,000 BC to 4000 BC). A radiocarbon date subsequently gave an even earlier date for Lockwood's find (around 11,950 BC to 11,300 BC) placing it in the last years of the preceding Upper Palaeolithic period. That distinction, of course, was completely irrelevant to the prehistoric person who used and lost this implement. What is more relevant is that the character of the artefact indicated that this person was not a deep-sea fisherman, out harpooning whales, but somebody who fished in shallow water. The seabed, miles from the Norfolk coast, was once a place that hunters could visit.

Lockwood, realising he had found something notable, gave the find to the trawler's owner, who invited expert viewing and opinion. The harpoon head or fish spear was first offered to the British Museum, but they already had similar examples so declined it, probably without fully realising the artefact's significance to a very important area of study that had barely begun. Instead, it was given to the Norwich Castle Museum and Art Gallery, which looks after it to this day.

It is a delicate and beautiful object; an attractive light oak colour, shiny and polished smooth, perhaps through long and successful use. Its barbs are expertly carved and notches have been scored into its surface at one end, probably to help secure binding twine or sinew. It is known as the 'Leman and Ower Point' after the two sandbanks between which the find was made.

As technology developed, specialists extracted ancient pollen grains from the peat beneath the sea to identify the trees and plants that once grew in the area. A Dutch archaeologist in the 1970s wrote about other artefacts trawled from the area since that important 1931 find. Not until 1998, however, was a comprehensive summary of all the available evidence attempted.

Bryony Coles, who with her husband John formed a 'power couple' of British archaeological wetland research, pulled all the evidence together and wrote an influential paper in the Proceedings of the Prehistoric Society. It included a series of interpretative maps of the submerged landscape through time, adding more nuanced time depth and detail to Clement Reid's original mapping. Coles also gave a name to this lost territory: 'Doggerland'. Whatever ancient people called this land has been lost in the mists and tides of time, so Coles's name simply acknowledges the later name given to the Dogger Bank shoal.

The buried ancient landscapes beneath the sand around Britain's coast, and coastal wetlands such as the Fens, Norfolk Broads, Romney Marsh and Somerset Levels, have produced astonishing, exceptionally well-preserved archaeological evidence over the last century. Each of these areas will continue to reward archaeological attention.

However, Doggerland, beneath the North Sea, is in many ways a last frontier whose investigation, by comparison, has only just begun. Enough evidence has been seen to tease the great potential of the area. Perhaps not since the first explorers, anthropologists and archaeologists ventured to central American jungles in the middle of the nineteenth and early twentieth centuries has so much evidence for a past society lain hidden awaiting investigation. Though in those cases, a few locals at least could point the way to some of the key sites. Nevertheless, despite the enduring practical difficulties of searching deep beneath the sea, the temptation to explore one of the last lost lands of the world, so close to home, has been too great for archaeologists to resist.

In the last few decades technical advances in 'remote sensing' have placed the seabed more within archaeological reach, which has in turn heightened interest in the archaeology of the North Sea. Additionally, the pace of research has been quickened by the realisation that this submerged prehistoric landscape is under threat. This has led to enormous leaps forward in knowledge.

The seabed of the North Sea is a surprisingly and increasingly 'developed' place now. Marine planning maps show an intense web of power and communications cables, fuel pipelines, shipping lanes, sand and gravel extraction sites, oil drilling and wind turbine arrays. In fact, it is such a busy place that various competing demands are in constant danger of interfering with each other. Cables and pipelines prevent dredging and aggregates extraction. Wind farms can harm marine environments. This infrastructure and protected marine areas push trawlers into ever smaller areas of the sea.

Planning new works, attempting to share out the limited sea areas available and avoid conflicts between the various kinds of development and uses, all require surveys. This is certainly true in Doggerland.

A few years after Bryony Coles's paper was published, another great leap forward was made in visualising this drowned prehistoric world. Seismic surveys involve generating mini shock waves, which can then be measured travelling through and bouncing back from interfaces between layers of sediment and rock. The data gathered by seismic surveys builds geological profiles down through the seabed and can map these across a wide area. The oil and gas industries use this method to identify where valuable deposits are likely to be found and what has to be drilled through to get at them.

From the early 2000s, the complex raw data generated by seismic surveys has been obtained by archaeologists and manipulated to produce grainy maps of the current, undulating seabed and its earlier, buried forms. These seabed maps have been augmented with environmental evidence from hundreds of boreholes to create interpretations of the landscapes beneath the sea.

The breakthrough work of this type was carried out by a team from the University of Birmingham. Despite its home in a famously landlocked place, this university had research specialisms in subjects such as Landscape Archaeology, Geographic Information Systems, Geography, and Earth and Environmental Sciences, which are highly relevant to the exploration of ancient buried landscapes, even those under the sea. Further survey and research, by among others the equally well-qualified (albeit equally inland) University of Bradford and University of Ghent, shed even more light on this long-forgotten place.

The early research at Birmingham unexpectedly revealed a former prehistoric river almost as large as the Rhine, whose course could be traced across twenty-five miles of Doggerland. Subsequent research has revealed more rivers and creeks, lakes, estuaries and hills. The landscape beneath the sea and seabed has begun to come into focus in extraordinary detail.

Hundreds more prehistoric flint tools and bone tools have also now been found. Most of the finds derive from dredging and hoovering up the sand and gravel under the North Sea. Occasionally, archaeologists have been able to look through some of the vast quantities of material set aside by the aggregates companies in order to retrieve these elusive artefacts. Some important finds have also been made by members of the public where sand and gravel extracted from the seabed has been thrown up on beaches to help combat erosion. This adds a great deal of interest and time depth to the already fascinating pastime of beachcombing.

One sharp-eyed boy, who found an interesting looking, shiny rock on the beach at Shoreham in West Sussex, is representative of the sort of contribution to archaeological research that anybody can make on a day out. He did not know exactly what the rock was, but had cleverly noted that it looked different to the mass of other pebbles on the beach. Trying to focus on things that look different to the background mass of stones and soil is a technique employed by archaeologists when combing ploughed land for displaced artefacts that might signal an archaeological site below. This is known as 'fieldwalking'.

The boy kept his find for three years, but when he saw a similar object in a museum he realised he might have found something really special that he should get checked out. He took the object to Worthing Museum in November 2024, where it was confirmed that he had discovered a prehistoric flint hand axe.

This teardrop-shaped black stone tool is small enough to fit in the palm of the hand. It was made around fifty thousand years ago, possibly by the last of the Neanderthals to wander the region before their extinction and replacement by modern humans. The axe was not worn by years of rolling around in the surf, so might have been dislodged from beneath the seabed or shore by offshore dredging or coastal engineering works. Finding thousands of years old stone or antler artefacts from a lost world surely beats finding a washed-up toy, or a discarded piece of Lego, even for a six-year-old.[1]

Not only is it possible to find artefacts from Doggerland on a beach walk, but it is also possible to get a hint of the character of this place during a stroll around the coast. At several places around the British Isles, at low tide, you can walk out to drowned prehistoric landscapes.

---

1 Incidentally, the rarest Lego artefacts that can be found on the beach are widely accepted to be little octopus, shark and dragon figures. A cargo of Lego spilled from a container ship off Cornwall in 1997 and millions of the almost indestructible blocks have since been scattered far and wide. Tracking down the most prized pieces has become a hobby for some beachcombers, and also serves to illustrate the effects of plastic pollution in the sea. Quite what archaeologists of the future will make of these artefacts is anybody's guess. Ritual offerings to the creatures and spirits of the sea perhaps?

At Holme-next-the-Sea, a bracing walk from the beach car park, across a golf course, over the dunes and south along the beach will take you to the area where layers of black peat, similar to those that snagged fishing nets on Doggerland, can be seen in situ. It is lumps from this peat bed that my grandfather and I saw on our walks. The peat bed, which is being eroded by the sea from beneath the sand, is the remnant of a wooded prehistoric marsh, drowned by the sea 4000 to 4,500 years ago.

Breaking open one of the detached lumps of peat reveals vegetation that died and sank into the marsh all that time ago. This plant matter did not decompose, because once submerged it became waterlogged and sealed in an anaerobic environment. On dry land it would have soon been eaten away and crumbled to dust, but buried under water and sealing deposits of sand, silt and mud, there was insufficient oxygen for decomposition.

It was in this area in the spring of 1998 that beachcomber, shrimper, crabber and amateur archaeologist John Lorimer found a small bronze axe head. Drawn back to the spot again and again as the tides swept away more of the peat bed, he noticed a strange upturned tree stump that did not look at all like the other bits of wood scattered about. Even more surprisingly, it was surrounded by a ring of eroded timber posts. This discovery demanded archaeological attention, and was soon nicknamed 'Seahenge'.

After some exploratory excavations it was decided to excavate the site and remove the tree stump and timber posts, to save them from being washed away by the sea. They are now preserved and displayed in King's Lynn Museum alongside fascinating insights into the construction of the monument and its Bronze Age environment.

A wealth of information has been gleaned about Seahenge's construction. Dendrochronology (tree ring dating) has determined that its ring of split oak posts was made from trees that were all felled in the spring or summer of 2049 BC. Signature tool marks on the timbers indicate that around fifty different bronze axes were used for woodworking. Bark was left on the outward-facing sides of the posts so that when they were arranged in a circle, tight together, the effect from the outside would have been a bit like looking at one giant tree trunk or a rustic stockade. The inside of the circle would have been a private, enclosed space around 20 feet in diameter.

Seahenge is an extraordinary, enigmatic structure. Nobody can be quite sure why it was laboriously built there. If in doubt, archaeologists tend to ascribe some unknown ritual function to places such as this. One plausible theory is that the dead were left exposed to the sky on the platform created by the central upturned tree stump – this type of excarnation practice still goes on in some parts of the world. But one thing we do know for sure is that Seahenge was not the only prehistoric monument to be constructed in this area of coastal marsh during the Bronze Age. The remains of another circular monument are still there, now buried. Among the tree stumps of the prehistoric woodland and timber from shipwrecks, other Bronze Age artefacts and structures are without doubt awaiting discovery.

Holme beach is just one place where you may encounter an exposed prehistoric coastal landscape. Between Cliff End and Winchelsea in East Sussex the remains of a forest of alder, ash, birch, willow, yew, hazel and oak trees that grew between around six and a half thousand and three and a half thousand years ago can be seen at low tide. Similar remains can be seen in places around the coast at normal low tides or exceptionally low tides as far and wide as Mounts Bay in Cornwall, at Newport, Newgale, Borth and Rhyl on the Welsh coast, at Hightown just north of Liverpool, at Amble and Hartlepool in the north-east of England and at Cleethorpes in Lincolnshire.

Severe storms can temporarily expose the remains of ancient land surfaces and submerged forests, such as at Redcar in Cleveland in 2018. In fact, the dynamic character of the coastline, with its shifting currents, tides, erosion and deposition patterns, is one reason why it is enjoyable, interesting and rewarding to keep revisiting such places, keeping your eyes open.

Just over a hundred years since the landscape drowned beneath the North Sea was first theoretically depicted, it is now known for certain that Doggerland is a lost European territory as large as Britain itself. It was a complex, dynamic landscape that linked the higher land mass that became mainland Britain to mainland Europe. For prehistoric people, this was a resource-rich land of opportunity, full of the land animals, fish, trees and plants that were necessary to sustain and enrich their lives.

At times throughout prehistory its inhabitants may have had their own distinctive culture, different to those of the neighbouring territories. They may have considered Doggerland to be the centre of their world, and seen much of what is now Britain as a faraway place that was barely worth travelling to. Further research and more accidental finds will gradually illuminate their world and their lives.

From the last glacial maximum during the last Ice Age, around twenty thousand years ago, when Britain and Ireland were all joined in one chilly land mass with the rest of the continent, the sea level has risen an enormous 400 feet or so. This effect of warming conditions and melting ice gradually shrank Doggerland until it was simply islands in the North Sea. Finally, around seven to eight thousand years ago, the last island disappeared beneath the waves completely. The Channel, once merely a river or two, widened and deepened over the same period to become the expanse of seawater we see today. Mainland Britain became an island, and the course of its history thereafter has been shaped by its island status. It is interesting to ponder how Britain's story might have been different if Doggerland had not disappeared.

If the Doggerland hills had been higher or sea levels had not risen quite so much, Doggerland would still be an island in the North Sea. Who would it belong to and how would it have developed? What if most of Doggerland had remained dry land and Britain therefore had remained attached to mainland Europe? Would England, Holland, Belgium and Denmark simply have become a bit bigger, each grabbing a chunk of this low-lying land for itself and eventually settling on borders defined by one of its many rivers?

What would it have meant for the distinct history and cultures of Britain had they remained unprotected by the moat of the Channel and North Sea? Pathways through history are complicated. There are multiple social, economic and cultural factors to consider alongside geographical reality. 'Sliding doors' historical moments and random events can be equally significant. There can be little doubt, however, that the history of Britain and the British people could have been very different had Doggerland not been drowned beneath the North Sea.

CHAPTER 2
ISLAND LIFE

Lindisfarne, Northumberland

The dramatic rise in sea levels following the last glacial period caused mainland Britain to become an island, and one that has an extraordinarily long and intricate coast in relation to its land mass. Many places that were formerly attached to this land mass also became separate islands. Exactly how many British islands there are is a matter of debate, similar to the debate about the length of the coast. Anything between 4,500 and 6,000 islands is usually accepted. A quick glance at the fragmented fringes of Scotland on a map provides a clue that the vast majority of the British islands are off the west and north coasts of that country. Around 190 British islands are permanently inhabited, about half of which are Scottish.

From at least Neolithic times onwards, the people of Britain would have encountered some goods imported from across the sea, and perhaps occasionally even met people who had travelled from far-off places. Those living near the coast or on the smaller islands would have been acutely aware of their relationship with the sea and maybe knew something of what lay beyond.

Throughout the Bronze Age and Iron Age, as boat technology improved and contact with those overseas increased, there must have been a growing appreciation of similarities and differences with people and places beyond the coast, and perhaps a growing awareness of what it meant to be an island people. However, although ancient Britons left plenty of archaeological evidence about their connectedness with others, they left no written thoughts about their island lives. Nevertheless, there are some fascinating fragmentary glimpses into how prehistoric Britain and its people were seen by others.

Greeks and Romans not only recognised prehistoric Britain as an island physically distinct from mainland Europe, but also commented on aspects of its people and culture that resembled or were distinct from those on the continent. Julius Caesar only visited the south-east corner of Britain during his campaigns in the 50s BC, but he learnt about aspects of the rest of Britain directly from those who had knowledge of them. Caesar drew a distinction between the character of the native population of the south and east coast, which he wrote had been recently colonised by Belgae from northern Gaul, and the interior of Britain, which had a more indigenous population and character.

Tacitus, writing about Agricola's conquest and governorship in Britain from AD 77 onwards, agreed that the British people closest to the continent were like the Gauls. He also noted the reddish hair of the Caledonians and the contrasting darker skin and dark curly hair of the people living in South Wales.

He pontificated that the former could relate to German ancestry and the latter to Spanish ancestry.

Caesar, Tacitus and other Roman writers thought that the Britons' way of life had similarities to that of the Gauls, but they also appreciated that Britain was different as a whole, and in its various parts. The Romans noted that Britain was a land of separate kingdoms and tribes and not a single entity. The research debate continues as to whether Iron Age people at the coastal margins of Britain felt closer cultural and political ties to people just across the seas than to others on the British mainland. However, there is strong artefactual evidence of contact, trading and exchange among the sea-linked coastal communities in Britain and on the continent well before Britain became part of the Roman Empire.

'Tribes' still exist in the nations and regions of mainland Britain today. England alone has a lot of coast – let's say around 2,700 miles of it and not quibble too much. Scotland and Wales also have long coastlines (Wales less than England, Scotland very much more) and their borders with England are partly defined by estuaries and rivers. These give a sense of partial detachment between the countries, but Wales and Scotland are also firmly attached to England by sizeable land borders.

There are deep-rooted cultural differences, of course, between Wales, Scotland and England, and between various regions in these countries. I have even heard Cornish people refer to people in Devon and elsewhere as 'from England', and only the River Tamar divides that county from the rest of the country. Nevertheless, neither England, Scotland or Wales is an island in itself. Millions of Britons, therefore, share their island with other nationalities.

Nobody in Britain lives more than seventy or so miles from the sea, yet mainland Britain, with its distinct adjoining individual nations, is probably just about big enough to feel mini-continental if you do not have much direct contact with the coast on a day-to-day basis. This may be why many Britons do not appear to be as totally in touch with their island selves as they might be.

Perhaps a collective British mainland island culture appears more emphatically in the perceptions, generalisations and caricatures of others: the Royal Family, fish and chips, indifferent weather, a former empire, pubs and sports. Or perhaps it comes to the fore when Brits have to pull together to meet challenges and beat off threats from elsewhere.

If it is not straightforward to pinpoint a single, all-embracing British island culture on mainland Britain, other British islands display distinct cultural differences. Islands and archipelagos, as discrete detached geographical entities, have been particularly prone to shifting loyalties, rival claims and bargaining, changing hands or forming their own political and administrative units. Orkney, the Shetland Islands, the Hebrides and other Scottish islands were for centuries directly ruled by, or answered to, the Kings of Norway, rather than Scottish kings. A separate 'Kingdom of the Isles', incorporating the Isle of Man and islands off the west coast of Scotland, also existed as a powerful force periodically during the medieval period.

The island of Ireland, a short stretch away from mainland Britain across the Irish Sea, hosts separate countries that share a long land border. Northern Ireland is a part of the United Kingdom of Great Britain and Northern Ireland (to give the UK its full name), which has been described variously as a region, province or a country in its own right.

It is a massive and hazardous task to try to unravel and summarise the complicated, highly politically charged history that has led to the division of this island into two distinct entities. Suffice to say, many people in the north of the island have identified much more closely with the rest of the UK than with the rest of the physical island they share with the Republic of Ireland (Eire). The strong historical and cultural ties between Northern Ireland and Scotland are perhaps not surprising, when you consider that they are separated by only a few short island-hopping miles of sea.

The Republic of Ireland governs over 80 per cent of the physical island, however, and there are also very strong cultural ties between much of the population in Northern Ireland with those in the south. Mercifully, much of the extreme violence and intimidation that characterised the fight by some to unite the entire island under one Republican nation, and others fiercely to oppose the loss of their sovereignty within the United Kingdom, has abated. Nevertheless, as you travel around Northern Ireland, especially during the 'Marching Season' around the Battle of the Boyne anniversary on 12 July, the historical divisions and tensions between these island-sharing communities are palpable.

You can hear how strongly part of the population feels about retaining its own sub-island identity in the drums, fifes (or piccolos), bagpipes and fireworks, and see it in the banners and costumes. Throughout the year communities signal their loyalties with flags, murals, place names, given names and surnames, as they have done for many generations. People can create cultural islands where no physical island exists. Unhappily, here and elsewhere, there are still islands of communities living close to each other that do not mix as much as they might.

The Isle of Man, a smaller island, is far more closely knit. A self-governing British Crown Dependency, as opposed to a region of the UK, its citizens are British citizens and although they do not form a separate sovereign nation, Manx people nevertheless may consider themselves to belong to an old Celtic nation. The Isle of Man is certainly not a mini England, Ireland, Scotland or Wales, but a place with its own highly individual character and history.

Manx surnames reflect the waves of influence and control exerted over the island throughout history. The Gaelic surnames of the old Celtic population of the island were joined, from the ninth century AD onwards, by Norse surnames deriving from the ruling Vikings, and then by names from Scotland, which gained possession of the island in the medieval period. Finally, the island became a British dependency and existing names were Anglicised, or newly imported with British immigrants. Place names on the island also reflect this mixed cultural heritage, but a surprising amount of old Gaelic can be traced in both place names and surnames.

Cregneash village on the Isle of Man is the oldest open-air folk museum in the British Isles. It is also a real village, and was one of the last places that the old Manx language and traditions flourished. There you will see traditional crofters' whitewashed stone cottages. Their roofs are thatched in a distinctive Manx style, netted by ropes and weighed down with boulders at the eaves to secure them against the harsh winds. At Cregneash and in the Manx Museum at Douglas (also managed by Manx National Heritage; the National title is significant), you can learn all about the unique heritage of the island and the lives of past islanders.

However, the Isle of Man is less than three hours from Liverpool by ferry. Hundreds of thousands of visitors come every year, not least for the TT Races, the annual motorcycle road racing event, and its island culture has been far from insulated. Manx is still cherished and spoken by a few, but you are more likely to hear Scouse and a variety of other English accents on the island. Even the once common Manx cat, a tailless variety, is now quite a rare sight for casual visitors, due to a declining gene pool and cross-breeding with cats from elsewhere.

The Channel Islands, much closer to the coast of France than to mainland Britain, also have their own unique character and culture. They are also Crown Dependencies, actually two Crown Dependencies, one centred on Jersey and the other on Guernsey, the two principal islands. The self-governing detached status of the Channel Islands derives from the uncomfortable, interwoven medieval relationships between Norman dukes, French kings and the English Crown.

English is the official language of the Channel Islands, but a version of Norman-French is still spoken. Islanders do not like being lazily referred to as British, English, or simply a mix of English and French. They are tied to Britain historically and administratively, but they are also something distinct and unique: 'Curiously Brit . . . (ish)', as the Visit Jersey advertising campaign proclaimed.

Outsiders may see the Channel Islands as a single entity, but the separate cultural and administrative identities of the main islands are proudly recognised by their inhabitants. The irreverent nicknames the islanders give to each other is just one example. Jersey people call Guernsey people ânes (donkeys), because of their historic use of that pack animal and their supposed stubbornness. Guernsey returns the compliment by calling Jersey people 'beans', because of a ubiquitous traditional stew, or crapauds (toads), because Jersey has that amphibian but Guernsey does not.

Both the Isle of Man and the Channel Islands share a modern characteristic that distinguishes them from mainland Britain: they became tax havens. Low income tax and corporate tax rates, and no capital gains, inheritance or wealth taxes, have had a significant effect on the economics of the islands, but also their culture. They have attracted more than a proportionate share of 'high net worth' individuals, financial services, and trappings of wealth.

People are not only drawn to islands for earthly reasons. Many small British islands acquired a spiritual and religious identity due to their colonisation by those seeking some detachment from worldly affairs and greater focus on their faith. In some places this special aspect of island character has resonated down the centuries. These islands often had a long history of human habitation and spiritual significance long before Christianity arrived in the British Isles.

Ynys Gybi (island St Cybi, or Holy Island), for example,

barely detached from the island of Anglesey on the north-west coast of Wales, is heaving with standing stones, henges and burial chambers dating from the Neolithic period and Bronze Age. In AD 60, Roman general Gaius Suetonius Paulinus came to Anglesey to smash the refuge, shrines and sacred groves of the druids in his attempt to destroy their hold over a British population fighting against Roman colonisation.

However, it is often the quills of the early Christian chroniclers that provide the first written reference to several British islands, as it was that religion that motivated the settlement or resettlement of these places. The pioneer Christian saints of the Roman world and Middle East could wander off into the desert to live apart from society, suffer deprivations, contemplate and emerge stronger in their faith. That was not an option in early medieval Britain, but there were plenty of uninhabited or virtually uninhabited islands they could go to instead. Many islands around the coast came to be colonised by religious hermits or monasteries, or acquired lone chapels to nourish the souls of travellers.

Columba, an Irish abbot, chose Iona, an island of the Inner Hebrides, as a base to spread Christianity to Scotland. He arrived in AD 563 with twelve companions and set up an abbey that was to be the launch pad for the reintroduction of Celtic Christianity into the north of Britain as well as Scotland. Iona still hosts a Christian community. Its modern incarnation began in 1938 with a mission to rebuild the ancient monastery. The fellowship now includes Anglicans, Presbyterians, Lutherans, Quakers, Roman Catholics and others for whom the island is home, or an occasional retreat, or a place of pilgrimage.

A monk named Aidan (later, St Aidan) set out from St Columba's monastery on Iona to bring Christianity to the English. He had been invited by King Oswald of Northumbria, ruler of one of the great Anglo-Saxon kingdoms, a real northern powerhouse, to minister to his people and then spread the word. Aidan established the monastery on Lindisfarne (or Holy Island, its equally official name now) in AD 634, and the island went on to become a celebrated centre of northern Christianity.

When St Cuthbert, successor to St Aidan at Lindisfarne, wished to retire from the monastery and live the life of a hermit, he chose an even more remote spot on Inner Farne, an island a few miles south-east of Lindisfarne. This island, one of up to twenty (depending on the tide) in the Farne Islands archipelago, is about one-and-a-half miles off the Northumberland shore. People wanting to visit the holy man there had to go by boat.

I first visited the Farne Islands on a primary school trip to Northumberland. These were very different in character to the shingle spits and sandbanks of the East Anglian coast that I knew. Harsh, craggy whinstone outcrops loomed into view as we ploughed through the choppy waters in small, open converted fishing boats. We saw puffins skimming along beside us. It was an adventure. Soaked with sea spray, we landed at what seemed like a very remote place.

Many years later I took the same trip with William Sheil, the current operator of the family business that has been taking day trippers to the islands since 1918. He has a much bigger and more modern boat that accommodates dozens of people on two decks. This journey to the Farne Islands, on a beautiful day, was a bit more sedate than the one I remembered from childhood, but every bit as enjoyable. Lighthouses, a medieval tower house, medieval chapels, and a later cottage or two can be seen on the islands. Wrecks litter the surrounding seabed.

The wildlife is stunning. There are puffins, guillemots, cormorants, razorbills, and grey seals in vast numbers. Shoals of sand eels are visible in the crystal clear water of the shallows. This is a beautiful place and it seems to be in good health. Surely this was a near-paradise island retreat for a retired monk. The next day, however, a storm came in. The islands were invisible from the shore. Boat trips were cancelled. I thought of the wind and wave-lashed little islands and thought about Cuthbert's solitary life on a bad winter's day.

The Venerable Bede says that Cuthbert's chosen island retreat had no water, corn or trees and was haunted by evil spirits. It was generally considered ill-suited to human habitation. Inner Farne, like the others of the group, has no corn and no trees even today. As for evil spirits, we can only hope that St Cuthbert's exorcism carried an after-lifetime guarantee.

With some help from the Lindisfarne brethren, and a bit of divine intervention, Cuthbert made a go of the place, despite its shortcomings. Soon there was a dwelling and oratory, a well and even humble guest quarters, because people still insisted on visiting the holy man. Eventually barley grew. Cuthbert lived on Inner Farne for many years, until called back to Lindisfarne to become Bishop. It was a reluctant duty that did not last long. He returned to his small island after around two years and died there a few months later in AD 687. Other religious men followed in his footsteps. When they had long gone, the Farne Islands were home only to lighthouse keepers, and now National Trust rangers. They still retain their air of mystery and spirituality.

The smaller rocky outcrops of the Farne Islands that appear and disappear with the tides indicate the transient, equivocal nature of some islands. A number of the most fascinating of the British islands are not always islands in the way that we expect them to be: permanently surrounded by lapping waves. Other places that were once islands are no longer islands.

Lindisfarne is a tidal island. It can be reached on foot at low tide across the sands. It is also accessible to vehicles via a road causeway when the tide is out. At high tide the sea covers the sands and causeway and Lindisfarne takes on the full form of an island. The aforementioned St Aidan chose to establish his seat on Lindisfarne because it was close enough to the shore and Oswald's royal centre at Bamburgh to enjoy protection, and to serve as a convenient base for the saint's missions across the countryside. But the tidal island was also cut off enough to ensure some solitude and preserve the monastic community's ascetic way of life, without much danger of getting too entangled in the more earthy life of the royal court.

Lindisfarne's first chapter as a holy island was brought to a violent close by an infamous raid by heathen Scandinavians in AD 793. This attack, which destroyed the monastery, is widely accepted as marking the beginning of the Viking Age in Britain. A monastic community was later restored to the island, however, and Lindisfarne's priory went on to flourish throughout the medieval period. Despite closure of the priory by Henry VIII, Christian worship persists in the medieval parish church of St Mary, which is built on earlier monastic remains.

Holy Island is still a place of great spirituality and pilgrimage. I once walked across to the island with some modern-day Christian pilgrims. Feeling the sand and cool shallow seawater between my toes, distant from the traffic on the causeway, it was easy to forget the petty concerns of the day and think about the long tradition of connecting with something much greater in this place, and living by the rhythm of the tides.

However, this enigmatic, picturesque place is a tourist magnet attracting around two-thirds of a million visitors every year. They descend on the resident population of under 200, swamping the island's facilities and its cluster of genteel cultural attractions.

Visitors have to watch the tides carefully there. All too frequently hapless drivers leave it too late. A car or campervan will be submerged by the incoming tide, its occupants perhaps just having time to seek safety in the hut-on-stilts refuge built along the causeway. The vast majority of the visitors, however, are cautious and vanish before the tide rises too far. The daily transformation of Lindisfarne from bustling tourist hotspot to a virtually deserted spiritual and wildlife haven is something to behold. It is a treat to stay overnight on the island when, after the crowds have gone, you can hear nothing but the wind, waves and the haunting moans from the seal colonies.

Not all islands sought out by would-be saints or other settlers were off the coast as we recognise it today. I was born and raised in a district called the Isle of Ely. It is not situated on the coast, nor is it an island now, but it once was, or rather it was one main island (an irregular shape, about eight miles long by about eight miles wide at its maximum extents) and some smaller ones, all surrounded by wetlands.

This was a place where incursions from the sea met the swamps and meres created by rivers and streams lazily meandering into the basin-like land. It was a fluid, dynamic landscape of the coastal zone, whose boundaries had yet to be regularised by reclamation and sea defences.

An early perspective of this watery landscape is provided by the biographer of St Guthlac, a monk named Felix, who wrote in the middle of the eighth century AD, not long after his subject's death:

> There is in the midland district of Britain a most dismal
> fen of immense size, which begins at the banks of the
> River Granta not far from the camp which is called
> Cambridge, and stretches from the south as far north as
> the sea. It is a very long tract, now consisting of marshes,
> now of bogs, sometimes of black waters overhung by fog,
> sometimes studded with wooded islands and traversed
> by the windings of tortuous streams.[2]

Guthlac, Felix tells us, made his lonely home at Crowland, an island in the south Lincolnshire fens, and suffered all sorts of trials and tribulations in the general style of the pioneer saints of the Middle East deserts; albeit wetter and colder.

St Etheldreda (or Ethelthryth), daughter of King Anna of East Anglia, was another who came to this environment to do God's work. In AD 673 she founded a 'double monastery', a community of both monks and nuns at Ely. Etheldreda had been married to

---

2 *Felix's Life of St Guthlac*, text, translation and notes by Bertram Colgrave, Cambridge University Press, 1985.

King Ecgfrith of Northumbria, nephew of King Oswald, and therefore probably knew all about holy islands. Certainly, she would have been well aware of the physical characteristics of such places and the opportunities they presented.

The *Liber Eliensis*, a history of the abbey at Ely and its lands, which was compiled at the end of the twelfth century, specifically acknowledges the natural advantages of the place and the way they have been managed. It waxes lyrical about the woods, vineyards, livestock, the fertility of the ground, the abundance of wildlife and game, and waters stocked with fish, especially eels, from which the place took its name. Of the principal island the writer says:

> It is not actually an island in the sea but, inaccessible as
> it is, owing to the overflowing of ponds and marshes, the
> means of approach used to be by boat. However, now
> that a causeway has been built . . . an approach by foot is
> possible through the reed-swamp.[3]

Ely is still seen as an island a few hundred years later. It is conspicuous on the fourteenth-century Gough Map, not only because it is marked by a large church with a spire surmounted by a cross, as befits one of the most important medieval monasteries and Bishoprics in England, but also because it is shown entirely encircled by water.

The two chroniclers' descriptions of the same region, a few hundred years apart, are not just a matter of 'bigging up'

---

3 *Liber Eliensis, A History of the Isle of Ely from the Seventh Century to the Twelfth,* translated by Janet Fairweather, Boydell Press, Woodbridge, 2005.

Guthlac's saintly staying power in the face of a hostile environment, or alternatively celebrating the saintly wisdom of Etheldreda in choosing the perfect home. They also indicate the gradual de-wilding and de-islanding of the fenland region over several hundred years, long before the astonishing transformation of the landscape by drainage and reclamation from the seventeenth century onwards.

Crowland and Ely are not on islands now. These places, like all the former island settlements of the region, sit on slight rises surrounded by low-lying, but highly productive farmland. The names of the settlements often contain a clue to their island heritage. Many have names ending in 'ey' or 'ea', which is Old English for island. This Isle of Ely is now firmly inland, but it regularly reminds us of its coastal wetland heritage. Two parallel man-made rivers, dug by hand during the seventeenth century, bisect the district and take water from within and beyond the region out to the sea, keeping the area dry.

However, the wide 'Ouse Washes' between the rivers are regularly covered by flood water, and with them one, two or all three of the historic road causeways that cross them to link the east and west sides of the region. One of these, the A1101 at Welney, is known as 'the most flooded road in England'. In 2023 it was underwater for eighty-nine days. People there are faced with a twenty-two-mile diversion to reach the farms, businesses, villages and towns on opposite sides of the Ouse Washes. In Cambridgeshire, only one modern road viaduct is elevated enough to provide a reliable crossing throughout the year.

Flooding and road closures have definitely become more frequent and more persistent over the last few years. Every year, just as on the Holy Island causeway, too much trust in satnavs, impatience or bravado leads to stranded cars and lorries on the sunken wash causeways. Their drivers learn about landscape history the extremely hard and expensive way.

The former islands and raised land of the drained Somerset Levels, also once partly coastal marshland, connected to the Bristol Channel, occasionally become much more prominent during severe flooding. Just as in the Fens, medieval monasteries such as Glastonbury, Athelney and Muchelney (note the 'ey' endings) played a significant part in draining and taming this former vast wetland. The Isle of Axholme (the 'holme' in this case is an Anglo-Scandinavian version of 'ey', island) was formerly an area of island settlements in the marshes created by the Rivers Trent, Don and Idle near the end of the Humber Estuary between Doncaster and Scunthorpe. It was drained in the seventeenth century by Dutch engineer Cornelius Vermuyden, who went on to work in the Somerset Levels and Fens.

The old islands of the Fens, Somerset Levels and Axholme ceased to be islands many years ago, but elsewhere new islands have been created, either through natural processes or by artificial means, or a combination of the two.

In 2023 it was announced that a new island had formed just off the Hampshire coast. Some people think that the gradual growth of this half-acre expanse of low shingle was prompted by engineering works designed to save nearby Hurst Castle, an artillery fort first built on the orders of Henry VIII and later extended, from being washed away. These coastal defence works, it is claimed, may have subtly altered the currents in the area and displaced loose shingle. But this is a complex piece of coast in the narrowest part of the Solent between Hampshire and the Isle of Wight. Storms and naturally changing currents may well be responsible.

Two sailors visited this brand-new island to claim it for their yacht club, and a national red top newspaper sent a reporter to claim the island for its readers. These would-be colonists planted their respective flags, but with their tongues firmly in their cheeks. More significantly, however, the new island had to be added to nautical charts as another hazard for shipping to avoid.

Life on a small island is still very appealing to some people, whether they wish to live as monks, or otherwise. It is something of a niche market, but British islands are sometimes offered for sale. Drake's Island is only a few hundred feet away off the city of Plymouth in Plymouth Sound, but it has the character of another time and place. Its compact 6.5 acres comprises a limestone and volcanic rock outcrop with little sandy beaches, adorned by a verdant capping of mature trees, shrubs and grassland.

Sailing past the island reveals glimpses of old fortifications bristling with rusty cannons. It looks more like something from *Pirates of the Caribbean* than somewhere adjacent to a busy English city. This initial impression is perhaps fitting as the island is named after one of Britain's most famous privateers, Sir Francis Drake, a man who makes Jack Sparrow's piratical career look positively fourth rate. Drake is closely associated with Plymouth. It was from there that he began his extraordinary seafaring life at an early age, and on 20 July 1588, Drake famously insisted on completing a game of bowls on Plymouth Hoe before setting out to defeat the Spanish Armada.

He would have been very familiar with this little island.

Not only did he frequently sail past it on his voyages, but he probably set foot on it in his capacities as naval commander, city mayor and MP. Undoubtedly, Sir Francis Drake would have taken a close interest in this strategically situated little island's contribution to the crucial port's defences, but it was not his island, and not named Drake's Island in his lifetime. Originally the island was known as St Michael's and then St Nicholas's after the dedications to a chapel that existed there from at least the early twelfth century.

Drake's Island has had a colourful history. Fortified in Tudor times, it was a vital part of the defence of Plymouth Sound and Plymouth's naval dockyards from then until the end of the Second World War. It served as a refuge for persecuted Protestants, withstood a Royalist siege in the Civil War, became a prison and an observatory to test early maritime chronometers. In modern times it became a youth adventure centre, which John F. Kennedy Jr, son of the assassinated president, attended for two weeks in 1971, and then a squat for anti-nuclear protesters. In 1996 it was sold by the Duchy of Cornwall to a local businessman for just under £400,000, but his plans to redevelop the island as a hotel complex did not progress.

Drake's Island was sold again in 2019 to a local businessman and former Royal Navy serviceman Morgan Phillips for around £6 million. Mr Phillips has made the island available for many events and activities, from guided tours of its fascinating heritage and historical re-enactments, to corporate events, paintballing, music performances and (almost inevitably) ghost-hunting tours. At the time of writing, however, Drake's Island is back on the market.

Occasionally you might find an island listed on Rightmove or various other general property websites, but there are also companies that specialise in helping customers acquire islands for sale or rent globally. A browse through the current opportunities offered by one of these revealed several British islands that are currently on the market. Gigalum Island off Scotland's west coast, for example, is an attractive-looking nineteen acres of 'diverse terrain' with an interesting modern house based on an octagonal plan and a jetty. It is only a short boat trip to the much larger neighbouring Isle of Gigha, which is community-owned and has a far greater range of facilities.

The marketing blurb is keen to emphasise that purchasing Gigalum would place you among the exclusive rock jet set: 'Scottish private island with Paul McCartney as your closest neighbour.' The island is 'just minutes away from Paul McCartney's famous estate on the Mull of Kintyre'. Proximity to renowned single malt whisky producers on Gigha, Jura and Islay is another attraction. You will not be caught drink driving. There are no roads or even tracks for vehicles on Gigalum.

I was tempted to put in an offer, partly because I evidently missed an earlier opportunity to buy an entire archipelago. The island group of the Out Skerries Estate comes with an airstrip and a harbour served by ferries from Shetland, 'renowned and varied birdlife' and a 'thriving fishing and crafting community'. For my money I would have also got its fifteen crofts (farms), but not its school, church, telephone exchange, community hall or the thirty-nine houses owned by other members of the community. Out Skerries has now sold. It has become a mini Kingdom of the Isles for somebody who is content to be as close to Norway and the Faroe Islands as they are to the Scottish mainland.

The uninhabited islands of Faray, Holm of Faray and Red Holm, and the Inner and Outer Holmes of Stromness were still available for sale last time I looked. They are part of the Orkney archipelago, closer to the Scottish mainland than Out Skerries. These islands and their larger neighbours, at first glance, all look like very attractive places to live.

However, that has not always been so. The Scottish islands were not immune to the crop failures and 'Highland Clearances' of the eighteenth and nineteenth centuries. Landlords facing financial ruin because of the inability of their island tenants to pay rent, evicted many of them and turned to large-scale, less labour-intensive sheep farming. Many island families emigrated to the mainland, or to another country, depopulating islands and leaving behind cottages and smallholdings whose ruins are still a common sight.

There is no doubt that the scenery, wildlife, heritage and prospect of either living entirely apart from society or within a small community are compelling draws to island life for some. However, even in the modern era, where a measure of self-sufficiency can be backed up by plenty of external support, island living is not always straightforward. Island residents have to confront the same sort of issues that confront other coastal places, such as the limited availability of housing and its affordability in the face of tourism and second-home pressures, community vitality, the viability of schools, services and amenities, limited employment opportunities, and so on.

They also confront issues brought about by an obvious fact.

An elderly island resident once told me that they had enjoyed a lovely life on their relatively large and populous island, but also said: 'People don't realise that living on an island means that almost everything has to be brought in, from a pin to a bus.' Their point was that all islanders depend on what can be brought by sea or flown in. Failure of these connections inevitably results in inconvenience or even disaster.

Living on an island gives some measure of independence and self-reliance, and can foster a sense of belonging and distinctiveness. But island life also depends on engagement with the world beyond the island shores. It is the interactions with others that partly defines the character of an island. With all their geographical, ethnic, cultural and political complexity, the islands of the British Isles, large and small, from the Shetland Islands to the Channel Islands, have played immensely important roles in British history and culture.

CHAPTER 3

TRADING, SMUGGLING AND SAVING LIVES

Old Flamborough Lighthouse, Yorkshire

On Wednesday, 25, the stewards met at St Ives, from the western part of Cornwall. The next day I began examining the society, but I was soon obliged to stop short. I found an accursed thing among them; well-nigh one and all bought or sold uncustomed goods.[4] *I therefore delayed speaking to any more till I had met them all together. This I did in the evening and told them plainly either they must put this abomination away or they would see my face no more. Friday, 27. They severally promised so to do. So I trust this plague is stayed.*

John Wesley, *The Journal of John Wesley*, 1753

Few people living and working deep in the countryside, or living in cities such as Manchester or London, would probably put coastal concerns very high on their agendas, and yet both of these places were formed by their relationship with the sea. Their success, and the success of many firmly inland places right across Britain, still relies on association with the coast. Port cities, towns and villages were not just places where goods

---

4 Goods that did not pass through customs – i.e. smuggled.

were loaded and unloaded; they also connected Britain to the wider world and its partners across the seas. The earliest sea ports and estuarine ports were simply places where boats could be readily beached to unload goods directly to shore markets or wherever else they were required. The most promising natural harbours, havens, coves and anchorages were sought out, and these gradually generated activity and facilities to service the shipping of goods. They attracted people who could find livelihoods for themselves and their families. These people created settled coastal communities, establishing villages and towns where none had existed before, bringing hitherto obscure places to prominence.

Roman writers described Britain's exports of tin and other mined metals, including silver and gold, along with staples such as wheat and other goods as diverse as woollen garments, hunting dogs and slaves. In turn, coinage and luxury products from the Roman Empire reached Britain long before the Roman conquest. Britain was already connected to the known world by sea, but the Romans established new ports to facilitate conquest and trade, which greatly expanded under Roman rule.

When their rule ended in the early fifth century, urban life disintegrated and the maintenance of key coastal ports was severely hindered. Tintagel in Cornwall was exceptional as a place where international trade thrived in the immediate post-Roman period. Eventually port towns were reinvented at estuarine and coastal locations. For example, early international trading centres called 'wics' were established from the seventh century at Ipswich (Gipeswic), London (Londonwic) and Southampton (Hamwic).

The gradual construction of quays, jetties, slipways and hard standings improved the convenience and resilience of ports throughout Anglo-Saxon and medieval times at London and several other places, making loading and unloading goods more convenient. But many significant ports and harbours seemingly did without much infrastructure at all. The Bayeux Tapestry[5] depicts something of the character of an early medieval harbour. Early panels of the tapestry show the ill-fated King Harold II and his party going into a church to pray, feasting in a hall and then going out to a waiting boat. They wade knee-deep in the sea with their trousers and tunics rolled up, believe it or not.

It is a look that is reminiscent of seaside photographs from Edwardian times to the 1970s, when many people (especially older generations) arrived at the beach in Sunday-best attire in a way that did not suggest paddling would form any part of the day's activities. At least Harold was not wearing a knotted handkerchief on his head.

The place depicted is Bosham, not far from Chichester in West Sussex. It is a village that overlooks a wonderful natural harbour, which the Romans knew well, and is a busy leisure sailing centre today. King Harold had an estate there where he kept his fleet. It was an established setting-off point for cross-channel voyages. Bosham has obviously changed a lot over the almost one thousand years since King Harold left, but remarkably, in addition to the topography of the harbour itself, there are other features he might recognise.

---

5 Famously misnamed, as it is not a tapestry but embroidered cloth, and probably not made in Bayeux, but displayed in the cathedral there – Bayeux Museum. *see* https://www.bayeuxmuseum.com/en/the-bayeux-tapestry/.

Bosham church, though much altered subsequently, is still there overlooking the shore. Archaeologists believe that the site of Harold's hall, where the parting feast took place, has now been definitively located too – by identifying the remains of the toilet. Only very high status premises had built toilets at this time. Skipping forward a few metres of story, the Bayeux Tapestry comes to show William the Conqueror's invasion fleet crossing the English Channel, and then the unloading of horses and troops on the shore at Pevensey Bay. Again, they waded through the surf. No signs of port infrastructure were depicted there.

Throughout medieval times and well into the industrial era, it was quite common practice for even quite large cargo vessels to come in on the tide to beach and unload, then be hauled and floated off at the next high tide. There are lots of wonderful old paintings and some early photographs showing large boats seemingly stranded on wet sand and often listing heavily to one side. Their skippers knew what they were doing and the boats' hulls were built to withstand these rigours, but nevertheless stormy seas and unhelpful tides could make these places hazardous or impossible ports of call. The growth of many port towns and villages was therefore prompted by harbour improvements: building breakwaters to shelter beached boats, and piers and jetties to allow them to stay afloat to load and unload.

Building substantial structures from the shore out into the sea is difficult and expensive. It requires a long-term commitment if the benefits are to be fully realised. Harbour works required a wealthy landlord or consortium to finance construction, and then to periodically repair and maintain these sea-battered edifices.

A breakwater was probably first built at Clovelly in Devon during the late fourteenth century under the auspices of manorial landlord Sir William Cary. This structure was formed of huge boulders retrieved from the base of the cliffs.

In the second half of the sixteenth century, Sir William's descendent George Carey invested a colossal £2000 in building a beefed-up version along with cellars (probably fish cellars) and warehouses. The Pier, as it is now called, has been periodically repaired, heightened and extended, such as in 1826, and was augmented with concrete in the twentieth century. The Careys and their successors' investment in this structure was a calculated one. The unpromising little patch of sand at the base of steep cliffs at Clovelly, battered by Atlantic rollers, became the only safe and reliable haven on a long stretch of Devon coast.

A harbour village developed and thrived at this unlikely place. The original focus of the settlement was set well back from the shore, a quarter of a mile from the top of the cliffs, where the medieval church and the eighteenth-century successor to the old manor house, Clovelly Court, can still be seen.

Clovelly's harbour breakwater and pier, built largely of roughly dressed stone rubble, still shelters Clovelly's little fleet of fishing boats and leisure boats. It also looks the part. Its flights of steep steps, ladders, tall timber rubbing strips, crow's nest navigation light, and bollards made from old cannons (reputedly from the Spanish Armada), add a good deal more character and charm to an already interesting place. Goodness knows how many tourists have meandered along the pier over the years and how many paintings and photographs feature this structure. When the tide is in, children swim in the clear waters of the harbour, reassuringly sheltered by the pier, like a large outdoor pool.

The growth of a port has always drawn people from well beyond its immediate hinterland to work and live in the area. Working on boats around the coast led some mariners from the different home nations and across the seas to live temporarily in a new place, or maybe to settle and make it their permanent home. Therefore ports have tended to be more cosmopolitan places than many inland villages and towns.

King's Lynn started to develop as a significant east-coast port around nine hundred years ago. The town was literally formed on salt. The waste from salt production and other rubbish from the growing settlement was used to fill in the tidal fringes of the 'linn' or 'lunn' (a Celtic word for pool, which also contributes to the name Lincoln). It was a deliberate move to raise ground levels and it pushed the waterfront further out into the estuary. Trade from Lynn (which became Bishop's Lynn, then King's Lynn) along the coast and across the North Sea was brisk. Series of merchants' houses, warehouses and yards were built during the fourteenth and fifteenth centuries, many of which survive today. One of these mercantile complexes is especially significant in showing a key aspect of Lynn's maritime history and international reach.

You can find Hanse House by following one of Lynn's ancient winding streets to the Minster Church of St Margaret. An elegant mansion dating to the middle of the eighteenth century now occupies the place where the original living quarters of the trading complex stood facing the street and church. However, down a narrow, cobbled lane that runs down towards the quay, there is the original, late fifteenth-century warehouse. This is a huge building range that runs almost the entire length of the lane. The jettied, timber-framed structure has a ground floor faced with old red brick. The upper floor has red brick nogging in a herringbone pattern between the close-set, blackened timber studs.

Fishing boats are moored at the quay near the back of the Hanseatic complex. This is still a working quay; still as vital to the town today as it has been for several hundred years. An entrance in the sixteenth-century, red brick back range of the complex leads to an enclosed courtyard. There can be seen the north warehouse range, parallel to the timber-framed one on the lane. It is also of late fifteenth-century date, but built in brick. The courtyard is a lovely space, totally enclosed by these buildings and secure.

During one of King's Lynn's Hanse Festivals, you might see some costumed musicians there playing medieval tunes on a variety of authentically reconstructed instruments. They will transport you back to life in this ancient enclave. This would have been a hive of activity and serious business in the late fifteenth and sixteenth centuries, but there must also have been some time for music and celebrations.

Goods would have been loaded and unloaded from ships on the quay, which was then even closer to the rear of the property. Batches, bales and barrels would have been checked, counted, and then trundled and hoisted into the warehouse, or sold there and then; tokens counting out the prices, coins changing hands. The foreign merchants brought things such as timber and wooden goods, pitch, tar, wax, iron, furs, flax, hemp and fish. The King's Lynn merchants, in common with those from much of the east of England, specialised in wool and woollen cloth, but also sold items such as hides, beer and cheese.

The premises now known as Hanse House developed in the 1480s with the permission of the king, on land identified by Lynn's leading merchants. It was specifically for use by German merchants. However, as early as 1271, the merchants of the organisation known as the Hanseatic League had a presence in Lynn, and were given special privileges, including the right to their own premises, rather than lodge with townsfolk as most foreigners were required to do.

The Hanseatic League started as a confederation of north German trading towns, but gradually took in about two hundred trading settlements from the Netherlands to Norway and Estonia. It was never a strong, centrally controlled organisation, but it offered recognition, protection and assistance to members and became a highly significant and influential force in the development of European trade. The Hanseatic League had a presence and facilities in several British port towns, including London, York, Newcastle, Hull, Boston, Norwich, Ipswich and Bristol. Their bases were called kontors (which loosely translates as 'office') or steelyards (from the old weighing apparatus used in them). Cannon Street Station was built on London's Steelyard. Only at King's Lynn has one of these properties survived.

I know King's Lynn quite well, but on every visit I find myself marvelling at the exceptionally rich heritage there. The range and quality of its medieval, post-medieval and Georgian architecture is amazing, and I come away astonished that King's Lynn is not more widely known and visited. I suspect that most people bypass the town on their way to the seaside resorts, or merely call in at the outlying industrial estates or shopping centre. Here is a tip: take some time to visit and walk around the streets leading off the Tuesday Market place and Saturday Market place and the quay. You will be stepping back into the history of what was once one of Britain's most renowned North Sea ports.

Historic trading ships occasionally moor up at the quay for visitors to board and explore. *Lisa von Lubeck*, a faithful reconstruction of a fifteenth-century Hanseatic caravel, sailed there from Germany in 2009. The *Kamper Kogge*, a reconstruction of a fourteenth-century Hanseatic trading ship from Kampen in Holland visited in 2015. Boarding these vessels gives a marvellous impression of how skilled and bold medieval mariners had to be. It was no mean feat to navigate the seas and treacherous coasts with valuable cargoes and then manoeuvre ships like these into port in whatever the weather threw at them.

The ships were well-built and sturdy, but there was very little assistance available to the crews. They relied on their experience of reading the skies and waves, feeling the tension and slack in the rigging and watching gusts in the sails. The crew of the *Kamper Kogge* gave me some schnapps when I went on board to explore their vessel in 2015 and I do not remember much else about that afternoon. A new Hanseatic League was instituted in 1980 to help foster cultural and economic links between member towns, which now number around two hundred in sixteen northern European countries. King's Lynn finally (re)joined the Hanseatic League in 2005.

From the Elizabethan period onwards, Britain's international trade networks expanded and intensified. Colonisation created new commercial opportunities. In medieval times, northern European countries were Britain's main trading partners, so the ports on the south and east coasts were dominant. As the 'new worlds' of the Americas and Asia opened up, west-coast ports with their easier access to the Atlantic became increasingly significant. When the industrial age dawned and maritime engineering became more advanced, the development of ports became ever more ambitious.

In 1715 the world's first commercial wet dock was opened at Liverpool. It was totally enclosed by walls, controlled by lock gates and held water regardless of the tides. The additional convenience this brought was soon recognised by shipping companies, and a string of similar, interconnected docks surrounded by warehouses was constructed. This type of development eventually extended along a waterfront of nearly eight miles. Liverpool became one of the most advanced and busiest ports in the world, able to handle shipping all around the clock.

The original 'old dock' of 1715 is now buried under a shopping centre, though you can catch a glimpse of part of its structure in the basement level, or through a small viewing window built for the purpose in the pavement above. To get an even better idea of the city's historic maritime importance, head out of the city centre and cross the busy multi-lane road (A5036, Strand Street) that now marks a boundary between the city centre and south docks. This area became quite derelict after wartime bombing and post-war industrial and commercial decline. It was increasingly irrelevant and forgotten as larger container ports were constructed elsewhere.

However, regeneration from the 1980s onwards brought the historic docks back from the brink. I think the Royal Albert Dock is by far the most impressive success of this regeneration campaign. Its vast rectangular pool of water is enclosed by ranges of elegant red brick, multi-storey warehouses. They are symmetrical and all of similar height. Their ground floors are set back so that colonnades of red iron Doric columns create a covered walkway around the dock side. When the Merseyside weather is kind, the buildings reflect in the water to create an effect like walking into a Canaletto painting.

A bold architectural statement was certainly made there, but the design was also extremely practical. Moored ships could load and unload directly into the adjacent warehouses. These buildings were structurally iron-framed and faced with brick with iron-clad roofs, which reduced weight and increased resilience to fire. Not long after opening in 1846, the Royal Albert Dock introduced the world's first hydraulically-operated cranes.

Operating such a port and staffing all the associated industries, commercial services and administration that grew with the port's increasingly global activities required a massive workforce. During the course of the eighteenth century, Liverpool grew from a somewhat ramshackle old town of around 8000 people to a modern metropolis of around 80,000 people. By 1900, the population was around 700,000. People were drawn to Liverpool from the inland environs of the city, from across Britain, and from much further afield. In the middle of the nineteenth century, following the Irish famines, Irish immigrants made up around twenty per cent of Liverpool's population. Some people made a very much greater journey there.

Not far from the Royal Albert Dock, within the grid of streets that were laid out as the city grew, you can find another astonishing piece of architecture. At the top of Nelson Street is a paifang arch. It is the largest multi-span traditional arch of its kind outside of China, and it is a genuine Chinese example. It was gifted to Liverpool by the city of Shanghai and assembled there in 2000. The lavishly ornamented and painted arch is the gateway to Liverpool's Chinatown.

Liverpool claims the oldest Chinatown in Europe, dating back to 1834 when the first Chinese merchant ship arrived at the docks. Chinese seamen were employed by Liverpool's shipping owners and increasingly settled in the city from the 1860s. Originally the Chinese community was rooted in the dock area, but the focus of the community shifted to the present site after wartime bombing. Around 20,000 Chinese workers were employed at the docks in the middle of the twentieth century. Chinese people and people of Chinese descent still comprise the largest single, non-white ethnic community in Liverpool.

One of the Royal Albert Dock warehouses has been converted to the Mersey Maritime Museum and International Museum of Slavery. Though closed for a major redevelopment at the time of writing, I visited several years previously and saw how the museum had chosen to represent the city's heritage. The first part of the museum conveyed the enormous importance of Liverpool to Britain's maritime endeavours, and the second reminded me that part of the city's success, like so many others around the world, was built not only on innovation, entrepreneurship and hard work, but also on exploitation and suffering.

In the second half of the eighteenth century, Liverpool was by far the largest slave trading port in Britain, having eclipsed London and Bristol. The slave trade also influenced maritime developments at places around the coast other than the three ports most directly involved. Britain's entry into the transatlantic slave trade followed the already well-established Spanish, Portuguese and French models of transporting and selling African slave labour to agricultural plantations in their colonies in the Americas and West Indies. In 1807, however, it was made illegal for a British ship or British citizen to engage in slave trading. In 1834, slavery was abolished in most British colonies.

Physical reminders of these aspects of Britain's coastal heritage are not always obvious, but there are some exceptions. A well-tended, poignant grave of a young boy believed to be a slave or servant of African descent can be found at a windswept spot at Sunderland Point in Lancashire. The former port village there received products from the plantations of the West Indies. A huge, lavish memorial to Thomas Clarkson, a leading abolitionist, is prominent in Wisbech, Cambridgeshire, the historic port town of his birth and upbringing.

In many other coastal places there are statues or memorials to more controversial figures connected with this traumatic episode in history. Some argue that it is necessary to remove their presence and names totally from the public domain. Others point out that this would misrepresent the complexities of history, and paradoxically take dialogue about the legacy of slavery and empire further away from public consciousness.

SMUGGLERS

Trading in people and goods produced by their extreme exploitation was for a long time not only condoned by the state, but legitimised by the state. Other forms of coastal trading were not. Smuggling, or what was euphemistically called 'free trading', has been around as long as taxes have been levied on imported and exported goods, and at least since medieval times. In fact, since anybody wanted to import something without the authorities being aware. Despite determined efforts by governments over hundreds of years, coastal smuggling has never been entirely stamped out, though the illicit goods themselves and methods of conveying and concealing them have changed with the times.

Smuggling is a significant part of the rich heritage of the British coast. You will be hard pushed to find a historic seaside village or old coastal inn that does not claim to have been the notorious epicentre of smuggling, nor a remote beach, sheltered cove or dark cave that is not said to have been the secret landing place and hideaway for contraband. It is probably fair to say that there are not many seaside communities who were not engaged or complicit in smuggling at some point in history, particularly in the eighteenth and early nineteenth centuries when spirits, tobacco and tea were heavily taxed. Smuggling was an important part of the economy for many impoverished fishing communities.

This shady, black economy became much blacker still when gangs of 'wreckers' quickly descended on stranded ships to hack them apart and take their cargoes, or so it is said, deliberately took to luring ships into danger. Wrecking was at its height in the age of sailing ships and expanding global trade from the sixteenth century well into the nineteenth century.

From the late seventeenth century, the Board of Customs had ships patrolling the coast between Bristol and Yarmouth to intercept smugglers. On land, 'Riding Officers' rode the coastal routes on horseback looking for suspicious activity. The size of this meagre force, which came to be called the 'Land Guard', was eventually increased and patrols were intensified in particularly notorious smuggling hotspots. Nevertheless, it must have been a lonely, dangerous and somewhat frustrating occupation for the officers, since there was no quick away of summoning help to confront smuggling gangs. If a smuggler's boat was spotted offshore, there was no ready-made provision to go out and challenge it.

To plug the gap between the shore and the larger anti-smuggling patrol ships known as 'Revenue Cruisers', small coastal patrol boats were brought into commission in 1809. Known as the 'Preventive Water Guard', their crews lived in watch houses near the shore and each crew covered a stretch of coast. These three lines of patrol – the Revenue Cruisers, the Preventive Water Guard and Riding Officers/Land Guard – were amalgamated to form the 'Coast Guard' in 1822. At that time around three thousand men were employed in its anti-smuggling operations.[6]

---

6 *H M Coastguard: Our History*: https://hmcoastguard.uk/history.

A few years later, formal instructions were issued to the service that included sections on lifesaving and the use of lifesaving equipment. Saving lives at sea was still very much a secondary function, however, as the Coastguard was also designated as a reserve force to assist the Royal Navy when required. Today, search and rescue is the primary role for HM Coastguard, but it still has a role in sharing information to counter maritime security risks, such as organised crime and terrorism.

Despite the government's efforts to restrict smuggling, there were still ample factors that led to many coastal inhabitants turning to this way of life. In the seventeenth and eighteenth centuries, goods such as wine, spirits, tobacco, spices, silk and tea were subject to such heavy import duties that smuggling became almost ubiquitous. Healthy profits could be made by avoiding this tax, but there were severe punishments if caught, including the death penalty. Smuggling was not a bit of fun on the side, a chance to make an extra bob or two, but an occupation, and often one that was a matter of life and death.

Two gravestones in Old Hunstanton village churchyard recall the very high stakes those engaged in smuggling and those tasked with preventing it were risking: The epitaph of the first reads:

In memory of

William Webb

Late of the 15 L[igh]t D[ragoo]ns who was

Shot from his Horse by a party of Smugglers

On 26 Sep 1784

Aged 26 years

I am not dead but Sleepeth here

And when the Trumpet Sound I will appear
Four balls thro' me Pearced there way
Hard it was I'd no time to pray
This stone that here you Do see
My Comerades Erected for the sake of me

The second reads:

Here be the mangled remains of poor
William Green
an Honest Officer of Government who
in the faithful discharge of his duty
was inhumanely murdered
by a gang of smugglers in this parish
September 27, 1784, aged 37 years

Green and Webb lost their lives in the same incident. They belonged to detachments of revenue officers and dragoons who had been tipped off about an illegal cargo arriving from Dunkirk.

On that September night, they lay in wait to ambush the smugglers on the beach. Several of the smugglers were immediately captured and their goods seized as they landed their contraband from a small boat, loaded from a lugger anchored just offshore. Others got away, including the leader, William Kemball.

Kemball (also spelt Kimbell) was the captain and owner of a lugger named *Lively*. His vessel was of a type widely used for fishing and coastal trading of all kinds. This working boat would not in itself attract attention plying along the coast there, which undoubtedly assisted Kemball's cover. But he was already a notorious, seasoned smuggler to those in the know.

On this occasion, Kemball was bold enough to try and retrieve the barrels of spirits and sacks of tea seized by the customs officials and soldiers. Later that night he went back to shore with a small armed band of accomplices to find them. The goods had been taken to a farmhouse under guard, and it was while the smugglers approached along a lane that they encountered again the small government force. A shoot-out ensued, resulting in the immediate death of William Webb, the fatal injury to William Green, and serious injuries to others.

Kemball was captured and along with two crewmates, Andrew Gunton and Thomas Williams, he faced trial and the death penalty. Williams gave evidence against his old boss to spare his own fate, but two separate murder trials in 1785 ended in not guilty verdicts. It was said that no Norfolk jury would find them or other smugglers guilty! Kemball was then taken to London to face the lesser charge of failing to pay import duty. He was found guilty, but paid bail and off he went.

Kemball was nothing if not persistent. The rewards of smuggling were very high at the time, and his clash with the authorities and brush with death had clearly done little to discourage his nefarious activities. The following year he was intercepted off the Norfolk coast, but this time taken to Hull, where he disappears from history.

Smuggling aside, the sea occasionally delivered unexpected bounty to coastal communities, such as cargoes of wine, whisky, cotton bales, timber, in fact anything that was traded across the sea and dislodged from ships in storms. It still does. A consignment of BMW motorbikes in shipping containers was washed up on a Devon beach in 2007. In an act reminiscent of the wreckers of old, dozens were spirited away before the authorities could intervene. In 2020, beaches in South Wales got a much less welcome, widely distributed cargo of nappies (mercifully unused).

On a recent visit to Cornwall, I went poking about in a cave off a beach only to be told by a local that a load of cocaine had been found in there a few days previously. He said the first person to come across the stash, which had washed in from the sea, was pondering what to do when a second person arrived walking their dog. This was a magistrate and any lingering doubts about the right course of action were quickly settled! Smuggling is still a serious concern to the authorities today, of course, but I am confident that smugglers find much less support in coastal communities than they did in the eighteenth century.

Then, as John Wesley found out, in some places virtually everybody in the community was implicated in one way or another. Almost anybody would be prepared to help shift and hide contraband, look out for approaching officials, act as 'muscle', provide an alibi, turn a blind eye for suitable remuneration, or knowingly buy contraband. Coastguards, customs officers and other officials were by no means immune from temptation themselves. They were often closely embedded in the communities they policed through family members and home life, and often worked without much supervision.

Association with smuggling is one reason for the reputation of lawlessness, roughness and apparent loose morals that clergymen, reformers, commentators and travellers often ascribed to out-of-the-way coastal villages and towns in the eighteenth and nineteenth centuries. Living and working in a harsh, unforgiving environment with the ever-present dangers of the sea was surely another factor in shaping the character of these communities. However, this also brought out more humane collaborative approaches to their endeavours: saving those in distress.

SHIPWRECKS

Britain's growing number of ports became larger and more busy from late medieval times and into the modern era. The shipping routes became increasingly crowded. The diverse and treacherous nature of the British coastline, with its rocky outcrops, islands, sandbars and unpredictable weather, inevitably led to a huge number of mishaps in this heavy flow of traffic. There are around 37,000 recorded shipwrecks and known ship losses in English territorial waters alone, up to 20,000 more in Scottish waters, and around 6000 around the Welsh coast.[7]

Many shipwrecks occurred far off the coast in deep water, but they also happened agonisingly close to the safety of the shore. You do not have to be a diver to get a glimpse of these sobering reminders of the inherent dangers of Britain's maritime endeavours. Shipwreck remains can be seen and visited on foot today in many places around the coastline.

The first historic wreck I ever saw, and one that is still

---

7 National Marine Heritage Record; www.scottishshipwrecks.com: Royal Commission on the Ancient and Historical Monuments of Wales.

visited by many thousands of people each year, lies beneath the cliffs at Hunstanton. It is ironically close to Hunstanton's tall, cylindrical, rendered and whitewashed lighthouse on top of the cliffs. However, the presence of the lighthouse could make no difference to the outcome of this particular coastal mishap.

The wreck is exposed when the tide goes out, and was a favourite destination on my childhood explorations. I will not say 'playground', because although I find wrecks fascinating, I have always found them quite a morbid experience too, and of course many still present dangers to casual visitors. It is a long walk to the wreck along the beach at the foot of the cliffs and one that has to be timed with some care, because the tide can cut you off from reaching the steps at either end of the cliffs. They are vertical cliffs, and not ones that you can scramble up to safety above.

The familiar low profile of the wreck comes into view as I approach, dark and incongruous, lying on the sand among the sea-worn boulders. Closer still, I can see the rusting steel of its hull, and the ribs within, or poking jaggedly out of the sides. It is reminiscent of the carcass of some giant, rotting sea creature. Only the lower part of the hull survives.

As I child I could not work out why the bottom of the hull held a solid mix of concrete, broken bricks and granite paving setts. I now know that was fixed ballast to help stabilise the vessel when unloaded. Trying not to cut myself on the harsh, barnacle-encrusted structure, I would try to net the little fish stranded in the pools of water within the hull. I knew nothing about the history of the wreck, but when I asked my mother about it, she drew me a sketch of how it looked when she was a child. She drew a substantial vessel with a complete hull, cabin, tall mast and funnel.

This is the wreck of a steam trawler named *Sheraton*. She was built in 1907 and worked out of Grimsby as part of that town's world-renowned fishing fleet. In the First World War, *Sheraton* was requisitioned, along with around eight hundred other working boats from Hull and Grimsby, to undertake minesweeping and anti-submarine patrols. In the Second World War she was again requisitioned by the Royal Navy, and fitted with a gun as an armed patrol vessel. She ended her service much less valiantly, but much more conspicuously, painted yellow as a target ship in the Royal Air Force ranges in the Wash. In 1947, a mighty storm broke her moorings and *Sheraton* went on her last unmanned, silent voyage to her final resting place at the foot of the cliffs at Hunstanton.

There is slightly less of the *Sheraton* than there was when I was child, though there are still small darting fish in the remnants of its hull. She still provokes thoughts about the other wrecks that lie hidden around the coast and the stories they have to tell.

The lighthouse at Hunstanton, like the thousands built around the British coast, had an important job to do, and has a long history. It is probable that the medieval chapel of St Edmund's close by, now a ruin, had the multiple roles of not only commemorating the traditional landing place of King Edmund of East Anglia, marking the coastal terminus of the ancient Peddars Way route and ministering to travellers on land and sea, but also guiding ships into the Wash. It was undoubtedly a landmark, and may have also housed a simple lit beacon.

In 1663, King Charles II granted the merchants of King's Lynn in Norfolk and Boston in Lincolnshire permission to build two towers with lights at this spot, the highest for many miles around. Candles and a coal-fuelled brazier provided lights in the two stone towers constructed there. Over the next hundred years, fire and decay necessitated renewal and replacements, until around 1776 a new wooden tower was constructed. This is said to be one of the first substantial lighthouses to use oil lamps instead of coal fires, and the first in the world to use a parabolic reflector to concentrate the light it emitted, though there are other claimants to this particular record.

This wooden structure was replaced with a brick tower lighthouse, which first sent its light out over the Wash in 1840. It was built by Trinity House, an organisation founded in 1514 to assist navigation on the Thames. Over the years Trinity House acquired more duties, much further afield. The frequent loss of colliers on the all-important Newcastle to London route, for example, led to its construction of a lighthouse at Lowestoft, Suffolk, in 1609. In 1836, Trinity House was given powers to take over the remaining individually and privately operated lighthouses around the coast, and that led to the rebuilding of the Hunstanton lighthouse. However, like many other historic lighthouses, this no longer beams a light out over the sea. It was sold in 1921 and is now a characterful holiday let.

Trinity House is still a charity, and as a statutory duty holder designated as the 'General Lighthouse Authority', still manages over seventy lighthouses and light vessels around the English and Welsh coast. These are now automated, the last lighthouse keepers having been relieved of their duties in 1998. Trinity House also has the duty to deploy Emergency Wreck Marking Buoys in the event that its other marine safety functions have failed to prevent a sinking.

Trinity House still manages the lighthouse at Flamborough Head on the Yorkshire coast. It was built in 1806. Nearby is its privately funded and built ancestor. Set further back from the cliffs on the edge of a golf course is a tall octagonal tower of four storeys. It is built of the chalk that outcrops in this area, and its rough, weathered walls tell of centuries of exposure to the North Sea-flavoured elements. There is a single pointed-arch doorway on the ground floor, with small rectangular windows in the floors above.

This structure was built in 1669 by Sir John Clayton, who had to get permission from King Charles II to do so, like the merchants of King's Lynn and Boston. Sir John actually obtained permission to build a chain of lighthouses around the coast. However, there is considerable doubt that the light of the Old Flamborough Lighthouse was ever lit. It proved impossible to extract the necessary fees from the boats and ships that were supposed to benefit. I am sure there must have been a technical legal reason for this, rather than it being an observation on old Yorkshire attitudes to parting with money.

The tower did find a use in the nineteenth century as a marine telegraph station, relaying shipping reports down the coast. When I visited I was not allowed to ascend the stairs to take in what I assume must be a superb view from the top, but I found scratched into the chalk walls of its ground-floor room evidence of its uses in later history. Graffiti including military ranks and units suggest that this imposing tower was used as a lookout in the Second World War.

The Old Flamborough Lighthouse is one of the oldest to survive in Britain, but it is a mere youngster compared to the earliest British lighthouse still standing. The Pharos within the circuit of Dover Castle was built not long after Emperor Claudius invaded Britain in AD 45. It guided Roman ships across the Channel and along the Kent coast. Its miraculous survival is due to the tower being converted to a belfry for the adjacent thousand-year-old church of St Mary sub Castro. The octagonal tapering, stepped lighthouse structure is classically Roman in construction with bands of thin red brick levelling courses at intervals in the stone rubble walls. Only the highest of its four storeys is a medieval addition.

In England alone, over one hundred historic lighthouses have been designated as listed buildings or scheduled monuments. Even when they no longer function, many still serve as landmarks and navigation aids, as well as being important reminders of Britain's coastal heritage. Is any seaside scene completely satisfactory without a lighthouse in view?

Happily, there were no casualties in the wreck of the *Sheraton* at Hunstanton, but countless lives have been lost around Britain's coast. Memorials to ships and crews and the graves of seafarers are all too common landmarks in coastal towns and villages. It is fascinating but saddening to read what they record of each tragic incident and the roles the vessels were undertaking at the time.

There is an exceptionally elaborate monument in the churchyard at St Aidan's Church in Bamburgh, Northumberland in the Decorated Gothic style. It looks like the tomb of a manorial lord, lady or bishop. In fact, its canopy supported on little spiralled bronze columns protects a recumbent effigy not of a magnate, but of local girl Grace Horsley Darling.

Grace Darling was the daughter of lighthouse keeper William Darling, and lived on the Farne islands. This cluster of islands, one-time refuge for saints, presented a monumental hazard to shipping coasting through the area. The rocky outcrops lurk among the waves like a horrendous jagged trap. There had been a series of beacons and lighthouses on the Farne Islands, and a proposal for one by Sir John Clayton, which again stalled due to the inability to raise income from Northumbrian merchants.

The Darling family first lived in the lighthouse on Brownsman Island, but in 1836 moved to the newly built lighthouse on Longstone Island, a little further out into the North Sea. Early in the morning of 7 September 1838, Grace looked out of an upper-storey room and saw a wreck and survivors clinging to the rocks of a nearby island. Realising that the weather was far too rough for boats to set off from the shore, William and Grace set out in their small rowing boat to rescue them. Sea conditions were awful. The relatively short journey was made more tortuous by having to go a long way round to make use of the little leeward shelter offered by the low rocks.

Grace took the oars to keep the boat as steady as possible and avoid getting dashed on the rocks while William grappled five survivors on board. William, already exhausted, made a second journey with three of those rescued previously, and retrieved four more survivors. Both William and Grace received awards for their bravery and admirers sent money and gifts for their rescue of the survivors of the SS *Forfarshire*, but it was Grace's role in particular that caught the public's attention. Grace was widely feted as a model of Victorian female selflessness and heroism. She inspired prose, poems, plays and paintings. When she died from tuberculosis only four years later, a monumental cenotaph was built to accompany her simpler grave in the parish churchyard.

This famous event certainly shone a spotlight on Britain's formative coastal rescue services. The Royal National Lifeboat Institution (RNLI) was founded in 1824, with the less snappier title the National Institution for the Preservation of Life from Shipwreck, to which 'Royal' was soon added. At least the name on the tin conveyed most of the institution's purpose. This included establishing lifeboats around the coast, providing equipment that could project rescue lines from the shore, and even offering medals and financial reward to rescuers. Traditionally, mariners would try to come to the rescue of fellow seafarers in trouble, and in some places, individual private or subscription-funded lifeboats had been established for some time.

On the beach at Formby, partially buried by sand, you can find the sandstone blocks and setts of the slipway of what is claimed to be the world's first lifeboat station. It was established in the 1770s. Historic lifeboat stations, essentially big stone or brick barns near the shore, can be seen in many seaside towns and villages. Many have been converted to museums, having been replaced by newer lifeboat facilities nearby. The oldest surviving lifeboat, the *Zetland*, can still be seen in an old lifeboat and coastguard station at Redcar in Cleveland, where it entered service in 1802. There are rival claims about who invented the first 'unsinkable' lifeboat, but in the 1780s Lord Crew's Charity commissioned the conversion of a local fishing boat to an 'unimmergible' lifeboat. It was based at Bamburgh Castle.

The RNLI celebrated its 200th anniversary in 2024. It now has well over four hundred vessels operating from over two hundred stations, a few of which are hovercraft. These cope better with shallow water, sandbanks and the mud of some estuaries. It is an interesting sight and sound to see RNLI hovercraft out on a practice, skimming along the coast. The RNLI is still a charity and 97 per cent of its crews comprise volunteers: local people who are prepared to risk their lives to save others.

The state, of course, also has responsibilities and a key role to play in maritime safety. The Coastguard slowly developed as an organisation and expanded around the coast. Terraces of historic former coastguard cottages and lookouts are a common feature of both coastal towns and villages and remote coastal places. Though the Coastguard service gained its life-saving remit as something of an afterthought, this particular role increased over time. Today His Majesty's Coastguard is the primary agency responsible for coordinating all maritime search and rescue endeavours in the UK. HM Coastguard receives 999 calls and 'mayday' distress calls and then decides which services to deploy. It has its own rescue teams and Search and Rescue helicopter fleet and can call on the services of other organisations.

Some people find it odd that the two key organisations tasked with warning of coastal danger and with rescuing people if they succumb to it, Trinity House and the RNLI, are charities and not state-run and financed. Perhaps it is something to do with the old British spirit of self-help, of getting on and doing it, rather than waiting for officialdom to take the lead, that particularly manifests itself at the coast. Of course, this independent, resilient 'let's just do it ourselves' approach applied by coastal communities to establishing and running lifeboat services is not that dissimilar to the 'let's help ourselves' approach they took to 'free trading'.

CHAPTER 4

LEGENDARY COAST

The Old Man of Hoy, Orkney

*Against sea-beasts my body armour hard-linked and
hammered, helped me then, this forge-knit battleshirt
bright with gold, decking my breast. Down to the bottom
I was plucked in rage by this reptile fish, pinned in his
grip. But I got the chance to thrust once at the ugly
creature with my weapon's point: war took off then the
mighty monster; mine was the hand that did it. Then
loathsome snouts snickered by me, swarmed at my
throat. I served them out with my good sword, gave them
what they asked for: those scaly flesh-eaters sat not down
to dine on Beowulf . . . Daylight found them dispersed
instead up along the beaches where my blade had laid
them soundly asleep; since then they have never troubled
the passages of travellers over that deep waterway.*

Anon, Beowulf

The coast, our frontier with the forbidding expanse of the
oceans, has always been a place of wonder and mystery. Gigantic
and strange creatures lurk in the depths offshore. Strangers from
unfamiliar lands arrive with the tides. The sea and salt wind
sculpt rock into shapes that seem to defy rational explanations.

It is not surprising, therefore, that the coast has been a rich source of legends, fables, tall tales, myths and superstition. Some coastal legends are inspired by real history, others are just wild stories that pass down through the ages.

Archaeology has occasionally revealed solid evidence of some grains of truth in stories and places that hitherto had been firmly wrapped up only in enigma and legend. One such place where fact and fiction intertwine is Tintagel on Cornwall's north coast. Archaeological investigations there have demonstrated that this was the site of an exceptionally sophisticated settlement from the fifth century AD and throughout the course of the next few centuries. This was the period after the Roman governance of Britain had ended in chaos, an era that used to be universally referred to as the 'Dark Ages'. Over the last few decades, however, archaeological work has shed much light on this fascinating period, and has provided crucial insights into the character of the unique site at Tintagel.

The Dark Age settlement at Tintagel sat on a rocky promontory, almost totally surrounded by the breakers of the feisty Atlantic sea, but attached to the shore by a narrow neck of land. The natural defences of the promontory were augmented by the excavation of a deep, wide and dry ditch on the landward side. The old Cornish name 'Tintagel' means something like 'fort of the constriction'.

Excavations carried out there since the 1930s have shown that many of Tintagel's buildings were substantial and made at least partly of stone. This is unusual. At this period most settlements across Britain had only timber buildings. The artefacts found there are also unusual. Exotic glassware and pottery indicate strong trading links with the Mediterranean. Sherds of amphorae, vessels to transport wine or oil that originate from as far away as Turkey, have been found at Tintagel. Pottery typically found on other sites of this period across Britain is very home-made indeed.

Many settlements and graves of early Anglo-Saxon England contain items such as amber and glass beads that indicate a level of international trading. The vast majority of this material indicates that the cultural influences and trade networks focused on Northwest Europe, not the Mediterranean Roman heartlands. The food remains found at Tintagel suggest that the diet there was richer than on most settlements of the period. And, again unusually for this period, excavations have revealed writing. Celtic, Latin and Greek words are etched on to artefacts.

The conclusion drawn from the excavations in the 1930s was that Tintagel was not an everyday settlement, but an early monastery. However, in 1983 a fire burnt off much of the vegetation over the site and this revealed the foundations of many more buildings than had been discovered previously. This was clearly a more extensive and long-lived settlement than had formerly been thought. Archaeologists began to question the monastery interpretation. From 2016 new excavations confirmed that Tintagel was indeed unlike other monastic sites of the period, and reinforced the theory that there was something very special there, not seen before.

All of the current evidence suggests that Tintagel was a specialist trading emporium and/or a royal settlement. It may have been the centre of a regional Romano-British kingdom that survived well after Roman rule ceased. It certainly was a place that contrasted greatly with the settlements and culture of the Anglo-Saxon people sweeping across Britain from Northwest Europe. But as with many examples of coastal heritage, elements of factual history are tightly wound with something much less tangible but as culturally important.

Tintagel has been associated with Arthurian legend for hundreds of years. It is said to be the place where the future King Arthur, folk hero of British resistance against the invading Anglo-Saxons, was conceived by a mother deceived by Merlin's magic. The story goes that a British king, Uther Pendragon, fell madly in love with the wife of one of his nobles, Ygerna. The suspicious noble hid Ygerna away at the Tintagel stronghold, which was robust enough to withstand siege and attack by the king's forces. Trickery was the only way in. Merlin the wizard came up with the idea of using a magic potion to turn Uther into the likeness of Ygerna's husband so that he was able to fool the guards and the good lady.

Arthurian stories were widely known in medieval times. King Arthur and his knights were much admired chivalric figures and formed a central part of the culture of the elite classes. Arthurian festivals and re-enactments were held in Britain and across Europe. Artefacts too were imbued with Arthurian legend. King Edward I had a huge wooden round table made (probably in 1290) in homage to King Arthur's round table.

In the sixteenth century this table was painted and embellished with the names of King Arthur's knights. A big Tudor Rose was painted in the middle, and what is almost certainly a portrait of King Henry VIII as King Arthur was added. King Arthur was someone that even great English kings from later periods aspired to be. This round table has resided in the Great Hall of Winchester Castle for over seven hundred years to remind kings, dignitaries and others of Arthur and his knights, and the chivalry to which they too should aspire.

Richard, Earl of Cornwall (brother of King Henry III), was so keen to associate his own dynasty with the legendary King Arthur that he acquired the promontory at Tintagel by exchanging other land at a financial loss. By then, the place was deserted and had no real strategic, commercial or military value. Nevertheless, Earl Richard built a castle there in the 1230s. Richard's construction was really just a show castle, almost a theatrical stage set, built at a place that had a widely understood special meaning.

Tales of King Arthur have been enduringly popular down the ages and have lent names to many much older, prehistoric monuments and natural landscape features right across Britain. None of these can be proven to have anything to do with King Arthur, if indeed he ever existed. At Tintagel, however, an archaeological excavation in 1998 uncovered a piece of stone inscribed with a dedication including the personal name 'Artognou'. This was interpreted by some as an early version of the name 'Arthur' and it caused a media sensation. Finally, this was proof that an important 'Arthur' existed at Tintagel during the time of the legend's Dark Age setting. Or was it?

'Artognou' does not necessarily translate to the name 'Arthur' first mentioned in medieval literature. In ancient Britain and beyond there were several names beginning with 'Art', similar to this one. Even if Artognou is the direct ancestor of the name Arthur, the Tintagel find only means that somebody with that name, probably quite a common name in that era, lived at

Tintagel at about the time the Arthurian legends are set. Never mind, lack of solid facts and irrefutable evidence has in no way diminished belief that Tintagel was Arthur's home. Tintagel's connection with the legendary king has continued to inspire building projects in the modern era, just as it inspired Earl Richard's castle in medieval times.

Frederick Thomas Glasscock was a Victorian custard and jelly magnate. He and his wife Esther took holidays in Tintagel and, like others who visited the place, evidently took a great interest in its association with Arthurian legend. The romantic, adventurous, character-building, nation-forming tales struck a chord in Victorian Britain and King Arthur and the Knights of the Round Table became very popular again.

Glasscock retired from the firm he co-founded around 1920 and with time on their hands and considerable wealth at their disposal, the couple moved to Tintagel permanently. The historic village that had grown up away from the deserted rocky promontory was actually called Trevena, but the village took the name of Tintagel at some point in the middle of the nineteenth century. This was probably an entirely conscious decision to make the village more widely identifiable with King Arthur.

Here, in his Trevena/Tintagel village house in 1927, Glasscock founded the Fellowship of the Knights of the Round Table. It was a society that was intended to foster the medieval values of chivalry, virtue and honour in a rapidly industrialising and modernising world. British and international branches, or chapters, were quickly established and Glasscock set about turning his home into the world-wide headquarters of the movement. This genteel, sizeable but otherwise unexceptional

Victorian house was transformed into a ceremonial venue, resplendent with early twentieth-century Arts and Crafts interpretations of medieval architecture and iconography. It is now known as 'King Arthur's Great Halls'.

Glasscock knocked through the rear wall of the house and built a massive extension, a great hall that occupied the entire plot. It is a real surprise to walk through the current gift shop/foyer and into a stone-lined, tunnel-like corridor that feels like the intra-mural passageway in a medieval castle. The biggest surprise, however, is to turn from the corridor into the great hall. There you will be confronted with a sight that would not be out of place in a royal castle or palace. At one end, raised on steps and beneath a stone canopy supported on piers, is a giant throne flanked by two smaller ones. In front of this is a large stone round table, naturally.

At each end of the hall and high in the side walls there are round-arched and lunette windows that throw stained-glass-dappled light into the august space. The windows and everything else are laden with Arthurian symbolism. High on the walls are seventy-two shields of polished Cornish granite and other Cornish stone. Glasscock seems to have spared no expense in fitting out the great hall, showcasing Cornish craftsmanship and getting exactly the character and atmosphere he sought.

King Arthur's Great Halls has been designated as a grade II* listed building because of its architectural and historical significance. The star is important and means that it has a similar level of recognition and protection as real medieval great halls, which is no mean feat for a building that is only around a hundred years old and based on a story.

Back outside, it is obvious that the village has been transformed by Arthurian legend. Perched alone on the cliffs is a large and striking hotel. Opened in 1899, King Arthur's Castle Hotel, as it was then known, is a square four storey building designed to resemble a medieval castle, with battlemented corner towers and a central entrance tower. Some tourists are so convinced by the grand appearance of this building that they think this is the medieval castle they have come to see, rather than the ruins on the nearby headland. The hotel and the village were due to benefit from the extension of a railway line, but this didn't materialise. Nevertheless, guests were brought to the hotel from the nearest station by horse and carriage and later arrived by motor car. The hotel was very popular and welcomed famous people in its heyday: Sir Winston Churchill, Noel Coward, J.B. Priestly, Edward Elgar, Ava Gardner, among them. It suffered a decline but in 1999 it was bought by John Mappin of the Mappin and Webb jewellery dynasty. It is now his family home, but also a hotel once more. Renamed The Camelot Castle Hotel, it has welcomed some starry guests in recent years.

And there is more to be seen in the village's centre. Coastal resort villages sometimes have more pubs, restaurants, cafes, guest houses, B&Bs, shops and pay-and-display car parks than most large inland towns could sustain, but Tintagel is rammed with them. Arthurian names and references abound. There is even a 'Sword in the Stone' car park. The village is exceptional also in the number of shops selling goods with a 'mystic' and New Age vibe. You will not have any trouble finding a special crystal, dragon figurine, replica Excalibur or dreamcatcher in Tintagel. People often go there searching for something mystical and spiritual, perhaps without knowing quite what they are searching for. Many seem to think that something otherworldly resonates in this special place.

King Arthur may or may not have been a real person. Emphatically real historical figures, however, have inspired other coastal legends. On 28 January 1596, the swashbuckling and somewhat controversial life of the archetypal Elizabethan explorer and privateer, Sir Francis Drake, drew to a close. Succumbing to dysentery while anchored off the coast of Panama, yet another Spanish possession that he had set about attacking, he entrusted his dying wishes to his shipmates.

Drake asked to be dressed in full armour to meet his maker, and specified that his drum, which had accompanied him on his voyages around the world, should be returned to England. He is said to have promised that if the drum was ever beaten, he would return from the grave to fight in defence of England. The drum, a snare drum decorated with his coat of arms, was indeed taken back to Buckland Abbey, Drake's grand house in Devon, a few miles north of Plymouth. Sir Francis was buried at sea in a lead-lined coffin, at a site that has never been located.

Throughout the ages since, unexplained drum rolls are said to have been heard at various times, usually connected with momentous maritime events and the city of Plymouth. Legend has it that the drum was heard in 1620 when the *Mayflower* left Plymouth on its way to America, at the arrival in Plymouth of Napoleon as a prisoner, at the start of the First World War, and during the Second World War evacuation of Dunkirk.

The drum was temporarily removed from Buckland Abbey for safe keeping in 1938 because of a fire. However, a few years later, during the war, Plymouth was heavily bombed. An old prophecy was remembered that the city would fall if the drum was ever removed from its home. The drum was hastily returned to Buckland Abbey. The last time I looked, Plymouth was still there, so Drake's drum is clearly doing its job.

The Giant's Causeway on the north coast of Northern Ireland is probably the most famous and striking example of a natural coastal feature that has generated rich folklore. This outcrop of basalt rock, lining the craggy shore and jutting out into the sea, looks bizarre and out of place. The exposed, close-fitting columns seem to be far too regular and purposeful to be explained by natural processes. They are mostly hexagonal in section and these strange building blocks combine to form platforms, steps and chimneys. There are even formations that have been compared to giant church organs, with arrays of pipes pointing skywards.

This extraordinary place was a source of wonderment and puzzlement to visitors until the age of enlightenment explained it as the quirky result of lava flows cooling and cracking around sixty million years ago. In fact, when you stop to think about it, the hexagonal shapes seen in the fossilised lava of the Giant's Causeway are similar to the surface patterns seen in the dried mud of a drought-diminished pond or river bed.

The mundane comparison with dried mud, however, was nowhere near romantic enough to satisfy or inspire the early observers of this astounding place. Instead they came to think of it as the work of the legendary Irish figure, Finn McCool (or Fionn mac Cumhaill). McCool, it was said, built a causeway across the sea to better get at his Scottish antagonist, the giant,

Benandonner. The Scot came off second best in the encounter between the two rivals and ripped up the causeway to prevent McCool following him to Scotland, leaving just this fragment on the coast of Northern Ireland.

An alternative story has McCool falling for a Scottish girl and building the causeway across the sea so he could visit her more easily. His grandmother did not like the idea though, so she kept destroying the causeways he repeatedly built by conjuring up ever more ferocious storms. Eventually the exhausted McCool fell dead into the arms of his girl. The grandmother was so remorseful that she turned to stone, thereby becoming another of the local rock formations. Another of the distinctive stones on the shore is said to be McCool's lost boot.

It was not until the late seventeenth century that the Giant's Causeway came to more than local attention. It took another hundred years for the scientific theory of its volcanic origins to be committed to print, but the science did not dampen the wonder of the place one bit. It became a must-see destination for those who had the means to travel. The attraction was opened to mass tourism in 1887 when a hydroelectric powered tramway (a world first) began a service to the site. The Giant's Causeway is Northern Ireland's only World Heritage Site and is now largely in the care of the National Trust. It is visited by around one million people a year, which poses some problems for the ongoing preservation of the site.

Footfall alone causes gradual erosion, but some visitors have also been indulging in a practice that resonates with the ancient mystery and spirituality of the place. Increasingly, people have been leaving coin offerings wedged in the cracks between the basalt columns. But this type of offering is harmful to the preservation of the site. The coins rust and expand in the salt environment, which opens up the cracks, shatters the rock and accelerates natural erosion. The National Trust has appealed to visitors to stop doing this, and has had to pay £30,000 for specialist stone conservators to remove the coins.

Across the sea, on the little Scottish island of Staffa, is an array of similar basalt columns, some of which form the magical Fingal's Cave. This place is also associated with the legendary Finn McCool. Once it was brought to wider attention in the late eighteenth century by the eminent naturalist Sir Joseph Banks, Fingal's Cave, like the Giant's Causeway, became an attraction sought out by the great and good. The sight and sounds of this legendary place inspired Mendelssohn, who visited in 1829, to write *The Hebrides*, or *Fingal's Cave*, overture. In 1969, prog rock giants Pink Floyd wrote a somewhat eerie and off-putting instrumental piece also named after the place.

There are many other locations around Britain's coast where quirky geology has inspired not only enduring folk tales, but artistic endeavours and heightened tourism interest. Some of these formations have taken their eccentric shape in relatively recent times.

The Old Man of Hoy in Orkney is a pillar-like stack of red sandstone rock that stands approximately 450 feet high. It separated from its headland only around 200 years ago, and has been further shaped by wind and waves since then. It once had an arch at its base, giving an appearance of stumpy legs, which inspired its name, but that part of the formation has now been eroded away.

The 'Drinking Dinosaur' at Flamborough Head in the East Riding of Yorkshire is another highly distinctive coastal geological formation. As its nickname suggests, it probably attained its current form in relatively modern times. The spur of land projecting into the sea has a sea arch that gives shape to its neck and head. It is attached to the cliffs by its tail. Topped by greenery, it is reminiscent of a dinosaur that has emerged from a slimy primeval lake to take a drink in the shallows. The peculiar shape of the formation is the product of the differential erosion of the chalk that outcrops in the area. If it had looked as it does now many centuries ago, before dinosaurs had been recognised as such, it would surely have been called the Drinking Dragon or Lolling Lizard.

The Old Man of Hoy and Drinking Dinosaur have become very popular features for tourists to visit and photograph and paint. People are drawn to the intrigue and romance of these strange places, despite knowing exactly how geological processes have formed them. The appetite to infuse the coast with an air of mystery and legend is enduring.

FOLK TALES, SUPERSTITIONS AND CUSTOMS

There are stories about mermaids all around the British Isles, but the village of Orford in Suffolk is associated with a medieval 'merman'. The story of the villagers' encounter with the merman was documented by Ralph of Coggeshall, a monk and abbot of the Cistercian abbey at Coggeshall in Essex. Ralph's account, written in the early years of the thirteenth century, relates a story that was told to him about something that happened perhaps fifty or so years earlier, in the reign of Henry II.

He included this curious episode in his sweeping historical work *Chronicon Anglicanum*, which summarises national history from 1066 onwards. The inclusion of the merman tale, in some detail, indicates how significant it was in terms of the history of the region. Many medieval chroniclers, Ralph emphatically included, found quirky incidents, supernatural phenomena and freaks of nature almost as important as the affairs of state and religion, and so equally worthy of recording for posterity.

The tale goes that fishermen caught a 'wild man' in their nets, which they took to the local seat of authority, Orford Castle. Here the castellan (the governor of the castle and surrounding area) Bartholomew de Glanvill took the strange being into custody. It is clear from the story that neither Bartholomew nor anybody else knew what they were dealing with. It was something like a man, but not quite a man.

The merman is described as naked and hairy, with a long beard and limbs like a man. We are told that the merman always went to bed at sunset and rose at sunrise. He ate the things that were brought to him, including raw fish, though he only ate these after squeezing all the moisture out of them with his hands. But he did not speak, despite being induced to do so by being hung upside down and tortured. He was taken to church, but did not show any signs of recognition or reverence. He was once allowed to go back into the sea, guarded by circuits of fishing nets, but was such a good swimmer that he dived down beneath them and swam free, taunting his captors. He then voluntarily returned to shore and captivity, but after two months escaped again and never returned.

It is an odd story, but one that I cannot help feeling could contain some grains of truth. Presumably, something notable was caught by the fishermen of Orford, but who or what was it? Ralph of Coggeshall speculates that it was some kind of spirit in the body of a drowned man, or a fish in human form, or perhaps just a 'mortal man' after all. Was the Orford merman merely a man who was very good at swimming? If so, this person was sufficiently different from his captors not to be described simply as some kind of foreigner who did not understand the locals.

In Orford's impressive medieval church, St Bartholomew's, there is a fine, decorated stone font. It dates to the fifteenth century and around its base are carved effigies of bearded, hairy men holding clubs. These are often said to be depictions of the Orford merman. However, these sorts of figures are quite common across Britain. The ancient folk character, the 'wild man', 'green man' or 'woodiwiss' is a spirit of nature, invoked to represent the wild, pagan realms that contrast with good Christian society.

It is not beyond the realms of possibility that the Orford Merman was a real man living wild, outside society, taking sustenance from the land and sea, and without language skills. Stories of feral people, usually children, wandering into society abounded across medieval and early modern Europe.[8]

---

8 For example, the Wolf Boy of Hesse, Wild Peter of Hanover, Valentine and Orson of France, Victor of Aveyron, Jean of Liege, and the Green Children of Woolpit (also in Suffolk).

This is something to ponder as you look at the Norman architecture at the ruined east end of the church. Did the merman gaze upon those same piers and arches as bemused as his captors when brought here to satisfy their curiosity? Entering the magnificent Orford Castle keep with its hidden dungeon below and great hall above also prompts thoughts about the confusion of the locals and the brutal interrogation of the merman.

Could the Orford merman have been some kind of ape, a highly exotic but not totally implausible ship's mascot that had been lost overboard? The people of Hartlepool, further up the east coast of England are still disparagingly called 'monkey hangers', because of their supposed encounter with something simian from the sea. During the Napoleonic Wars, the town's authorities reputedly hanged the sole survivor of a French shipwreck, after a summary trial, because they thought he was a spy. The 'French spy' is said to have been identified as a monkey dressed in a military tunic, though nobody can verify the story.

Curiously, Hartlepool has worn this less-than-enlightened lapse of compassion and the subsequent derision with some pride. In displays of questionable taste, Hartlepool Football Club has a mascot called H'Angus the Monkey and local rugby club logos feature monkeys being hanged. There are modern monkey statues in the port town, one of which at least is a collection pot for charities. A similar story is also told about places in Scotland and Cornwall, but it has really stuck in Hartlepool.

It seems easy to rule out the possibility that the Orford merman was a seal. Seals are often assumed to be the source of mermaid sightings, but these animals are plentiful around the British coast and a familiar sight up close. No seafaring or coastal people could possibly mistake a captured seal for a person. Or could they?

In Scotland, selkies (or selkie folk) are mythical creatures that can change between seal and human forms. Both male and female human forms of selkie were very attractive to humans, and there are tales of people who took a 'selkie wife', compelling her to stay by hiding her seal skin somewhere. This was invariably discovered eventually, and the selkie wife would return to the sea, leaving any offspring behind. I have seen plenty of seals from boats and from the shore. Their heads bobbing up can look surprisingly dog-like or even human at a distance, or with a fleeting glance, but surely close up could not be mistaken for selkies, mermaids or mermen? People seem to want to experience encounters with mysterious coastal creatures, rather than accept more mundane explanations.

The sight of whales thrashing in the waves and breaching (propelling themselves upwards and crashing back into the sea) could have been mistaken by some as monstrous, legendary sea creatures. Pods of dolphins swimming along in an undulating motion, their backs and fins rhythmically breaking the waves in turn, occasionally could have been mistaken for huge sea serpents. Natural phenomena half-glimpsed in poor light and turbulent seas undoubtedly gave rise to many stories of mythical sea creatures.

Cornwall has 'Morgawr', a serpent-like monster that is said to have been seen in the sea off Falmouth Bay. Some people claim it is the same creature as the huge, unidentified crocodile-like beast that a German U-boat captain claimed he saw on 30 July 1915. He had just torpedoed a British ship, which then sank and exploded under water. The explosion sent debris towering into the air, and with it a gigantic writhing beast that neither he could identify, nor his comrades in the conning tower who also witnessed the sight.

Peculiar, unexplained things have also come ashore. As I child I was captivated by the TV series *Arthur C. Clarke's Mysterious World*. Clarke was a science-fiction writer, whose show considered various unexplained phenomena and strange creature sightings from around the world. One of the many featured cases that intrigued me was about a huge, strange, dead creature that washed up on the shore of the Firth of Clyde in 1942.

It was brought to the attention of the Borough Surveyor and Sanitary Inspector, Mr Charles Rankin, because of the terrible smell its rotting body was emitting. Rankin could not identify the creature, so called the Royal Scottish Museum, but they were not very interested. He could not photograph the creature, because this was wartime and the Navy would not let him bring a camera into a restricted area. The British Home Fleet was based there.

Nevertheless, he described the curious carcass. It was about twenty-eight feet long and up to six feet in depth at the broadest part of its oval or round body. It had a long tapering tail and a long neck. Its small head, a bit like a seal's head, had large pointed teeth in its jaws. Its body was covered with bristles, and apart from a backbone, he described bone or cartilage fan-like structures only in the four flippers and tail.

The thing was cut up to be disposed of, during which (and this adds a whole new level of creepiness to the story) a fragment of knitted woollen clothing and a piece of woven cotton with tassels was found in its stomach. These, thought Rankin, were probably part of a seaman's jersey and something like a table cloth. Yikes. The chopped-up bits of this festering monster were quickly buried in the grounds of Gourock town's rubbish incinerator, which later became a school playing field.

Several sea-life experts have concluded that this creature was in fact the decomposed remains of a basking shark. Basking shark carcasses have washed up in a similar-looking state elsewhere. Like most sharks, they have a largely cartilage skeleton, which is not as durable as bone. Fins and much of the body mass rot away. The lower jaw also disappears leaving the snout and backbone looking like a head on a long neck. Many of the features Rankin described are present in basking sharks, but what about those large teeth? Basking sharks do have rows of teeth, but they are tiny. Perhaps it was some other kind of giant shark? Or was it something previously unknown to science? Or even something thought to be extinct? That is not totally beyond the realms of possibility.

Coelacanths, a type of large lobe-finned fish, are known from fossils. It was thought that they had been extinct for over 60 million years, but in 1938 a living coelacanth was hauled up in fishing nets just off the coast of South Africa. The coelacanth looks exactly like a prehistoric monster fish. Is it at all possible that strange survivors from prehistory have somehow escaped scientific attention around the heavily fished waters off Britain's coast?

Rankin intended to excavate the remains of his 'sea monster' after the war and find out once and for all what this creature was, but he moved away from the area and never got the chance. It would be fascinating to locate exactly where the bits are buried and dig up and examine anything that remained.

It is not surprising that folk living on the threshold of the wide, deep expanse of dark and threatening seas, populated by monsters, have often resorted to folklore to explain a phenomenon that seemed otherwise inexplicable. Indulging in superstition to help ward off natural and supernatural threats from the dangerous sea is entirely understandable.

Fishing is still an occupation fraught with hazards and occasional terror. Before radio, global positioning systems and super-computer weather forecasting, fishermen routinely confronted exceptional danger to bring in a catch. The sudden appearance of violent storms or unexpected reefs and rocks could seem like acts of displeasure meted out by a displeased God, or episodes of simple wickedness conjured up by malevolent spirits. All the hard work and risks of a fishing voyage could turn out to be for nothing if the catch was poor. All too often the absence of fish in the nets was totally unfathomable. Perhaps coming up with some form of explanation for bad luck, however otherworldly, provided a little comfort.

Fishermen, therefore, have been among the most superstitious of people. Their superstitions and customs are legion, though shared with many other seafarers. Several fishing superstitions and customs are common right around the British coast, with assorted local variations. Most have obscure origins that are still debated today. Some superstitions apparently derive from interpretations of Christian belief, others are much older.

The widespread custom of avoiding launching a boat, or

even starting a serious voyage or new venture on a Friday may be associated with Good Friday and the crucifixion of Christ. Some fisherman would cast out nets only after saying 'over for the Lord', to invoke help for a good catch. However, many fishermen did not want to draw too much attention to their Christian faith while at sea, because of the fear that they might offend pre-Christian gods and spirits. Clergymen were often not welcome on board and not appreciated when met incidentally on the way to the boat. On some parts of the coast even mentioning a minister or the church while on board was considered to prompt bad luck.

Once, when I was deep in conversation with the skipper of a boat, he used a term that he then realised I did not understand. 'You know,' he said, 'like a P.I.G.' He would not say the word 'pig' out loud on board. Anything to do with pigs, even mention of pigs, is still studiously avoided by some mariners. The use of pseudonyms, such as 'long-nosed fellow' or 'curly tail', can apparently mitigate the harm. Mariners' strange dislike of pigs may have something to do with the biblical story of Jesus casting demons from an afflicted man into some swine, who promptly jumped into the sea and drowned.

Casual references to rabbits, cattle and sheep could also cause some fishermen concern, though it is not clear why. Cats were helpful in keeping down vermin on board, but other-wise somewhat wayward in terms of their contribution to fate on the seas. Meeting a purring cat could signal a forthcoming good catch, having a black cat climb aboard could also be a good omen. However, in Scotland particularly, cats could be considered very unlucky.

Practices around food and drink are similarly steeped in superstition. Washing the nets and blessing them to help purify them evokes Christian faith. 'Wetting the nets', having a drink and pouring some on the fishing nets before setting off, is in the same tradition as the libations offered to ancient and classical gods. The practice of tossing coins over the side, or placing them in slits in cork net floats, is also an echo of pre-Christian religious practice. Depositing offerings of coins and precious metal items was very widespread across society in prehistoric and Roman times.

Any tin of food accidentally opened upside down, with its connotations of an upside-down vessel, is still immediately thrown overboard by some mariners. The stipulation to make sure that eggshells are holed at the bottom or completely broken up after cooking is a bit more obscure. It was supposedly to prevent witches using half eggshells as mini coracles to get out to sea and make trouble.

Infamously, the superstitions surrounding women and the sea have been long-lived and, in many cases, fatal – although not necessarily in the ways one might predict. According to Shakespeare, it was believed that witches were perfectly capable of sailing in sieves, never mind half eggshells. One of Macbeth's tormentors boasts about doing just that to take revenge on the master of a ship called *Tiger*, which was on its way to Aleppo in Syria. The witch intended to conjure up a storm. Shakespeare, always conscious of the political mood, was probably nodding to King James I's belief that witches had tried to frustrate his union with Anne of Denmark, and indeed tried to drown them, by conjuring up North Sea storms.

Anne was meant to have made the voyage to Scotland in 1589, but a series of accidents to her ships and bad storms had frustrated those plans, and she had taken refuge in Norway to wait out the bad winter weather. James (then James VI of Scotland) set out with his retinue to rescue her and bring her home. However, this expedition was also plagued by fierce storms. The couple did not arrive back in Scotland until late April 1590. Many people might have blamed plain bad luck, or ruefully regretted failing to read the warning signs in the weather and wished they had delayed their journey. King James, however, came to a different conclusion.

In Denmark, witch-hunts were under way and James was told that witchcraft was responsible for his maritime mishaps. Rather than blaming his own bad judgement or luck, the king was convinced this was true. Once home, fuelled by paranoia and suspicion of widespread witchcraft, he wasted little time in launching vicious witch-hunts. These went on to rage across Scotland and England for the next century. The denouncing of thousands of innocent people as witches, usually by their neighbours, and the interrogations, torture, one-sided trials and horrific executions by the authorities that followed, is one of the saddest and most shameful episodes in British history. And it was all set off by the North Sea weather and a paranoid king.

Suspicion and prejudice resonated down the years. To some mariners, having a woman aboard, witch or not, meant certain disaster. In Scotland, even seeing old women before reaching the boat, or especially a group of old women in a circle, meant abandoning the fishing expedition. More understandably it was commonly frowned upon to allow loved ones to watch as the menfolk departed for their work at sea, since a fond lingering look might turn out to be the last. And the men would not whistle as they disappeared from view, since it was thought to raise storms. Singing aboard was not so dangerous, but widely thought to cause poor catches.

Particular ornaments, charms or even clothes could either avert trouble, or encourage it. Seafarers, like some others, were suspicious of the colour green, possibly because it was considered to be an ancient, natural colour that rightly belonged exclusively to the earth goddess. No green clothes would be worn aboard. The colour white also posed problems, being associated with death. White-handled knives and white stones were thought to be particularly unlucky. However, stones with holes through them (sometimes known as 'adder stones', 'serpent's eggs' or 'hag stones' among other names) were used as lucky charms.

In past times, it would be highly unusual to see any man other than a gypsy or sailor wearing an earring. Gold earrings were a way of keeping some currency very close to the person, and therefore safe, when even the most carefully hidden portable wealth was liable to pilfering and loss. Wearing a gold earring was also thought by some to enhance eyesight, which would be very useful at sea. Belief that piercing the ear and wearing gold close to the skin would improve eyesight, ward off seasickness and other illnesses may relate to ancient principles of Chinese acupuncture.

Certain times of the year have special spiritual meaning across the country and around the coast. Christmas is a time of year marked by customs, many of which were inherited from a pre-Christian past and either adapted or tolerated by the Church. Coastal communities, of course, observe many of the seasonal customs that are common across Britain, though often with a seaside twist. Some customs, however, are unique to coastal places. Winter could be a very hard time for coastal communities. Prolonged periods of bad weather could make fishing and trading impossible. Stores of preserved food could run dangerously low during the long winter months.

This was exactly the crisis that is said to have faced the Cornish village of Mousehole at some point in the sixteenth century. Fearing that the village would starve, a fisherman called Tom Bawcock volunteered to brave the awful seas in the hope of landing a catch. He managed to bring back enough fish to feed the entire village. The legend goes that the much-needed food was shared out by baking the whole catch, comprising seven different types of fish, into one large pie.

The current 'Tom Bawcock's Eve' festival is held on 23 December in Mousehole, and includes the parading of a large 'Stargazy Pie' through the village, before eating it. The curious name of the pie, which is a fish, egg and potato recipe, derives from the fact that fish heads are left poking out of the crust, as if gazing to the sky. The tale relates that this was done to prove to everybody in the village that fish were indeed present in the pie. Presumably, though grateful for Tom Bawcock's efforts, the villagers were a bit suspicious that some kind of less appetising, though more easily procured sea-sourced ingredient might have been used instead.

In its present form, this distinctive festival dates back only to the 1950s. It was a clever idea by a pub landlord to boost activity at a lean time of year outside of the traditionally busy tourism periods. In that way, the modern festival resonates with its original meaning. Subsequently the custom was popularised by Antonia Barber's 1991 children's book, *The Mousehole Cat*. It is now a thriving, popular fixture in the Cornish calendar. This curious celebration may ultimately derive from an ancient winter festival, possibly observed long before the sixteenth century, which also included a feast of different kinds of fish. There is no evidence that a 'Tom Bawcock' ever lived in Mousehole. The name may be an attributed one, like Robin Hood, given to some long-forgotten hero, or folk character.

The winter celebrations at Mousehole also include illuminating the harbour with a colourful display of Christmas lights, a tradition started in 1963. The display of Christmas lights is of course very well established in other villages, towns and cities across Britain. At the seaside, though, the tradition often gets a maritime makeover. At Wells-next-the-Sea in Norfolk, a Christmas tree built of crab pots and adorned with lifebelts and buoys, as well as lights, was first built in 2020. When Covid restrictions threatened to prevent the more traditional and official Christmas lights being installed on the quayside, fishermen donated the materials and a group got together to build an alternative festive feature. Such is the way traditions form. The Wells crab pot tree is now a firm Christmas fixture.

In Filey, North Yorkshire, the lighting up of the 'Fishtive Tree' (their name, not mine) made of crab and lobster pots and surmounted by a leaping salmon has become a very popular part of the town's celebrations. In its seventh year at the time of writing, the event draws in visitors from far and wide, and has raised thousands of pounds for the town.

In many places around the coast people assemble to go for a Christmas Day, Boxing Day or New Year's Day swim in the sea. A dip in the icy water of say, Porthcawl in Wales, Sunderland in north-east England, Queensferry in Scotland's Firth of Forth (where it is called a 'dook'), Felixstowe in Suffolk, Folkestone in Kent, Boscombe in Dorset or Newquay in Cornwall, is an invigorating alternative to the numerous walks and runs that also take place around the coast on these days. Now considered traditional, the earliest of the seaside mass dips seems to date only to the 1960s. Many of these events raise money for charity. Fancy dress is usually optional, but sometimes wetsuits are not allowed!

Local coastal traditions at other times of the year have also grown from a fusion of ancient custom and modern enthusiasm. In November 2005, I was staying with friends in Kent and they suggested we popped down to the old port town of Rye in East Sussex for Bonfire Night. We arrived in the town in daylight and wandered around taking in its charms. I noticed that several shops and houses had hastily drawn notices tacked on to them saying things such as 'Do not stand on this window ledge'. Some of the window sills with these notices were at chest height. I could not work out why on earth such a specific warning would be required in a quiet, genteel town such as this. I found out that evening.

From being virtually deserted, the town filled until the main streets were jammed with people all straining to get a look at the unfolding event. An extraordinary parade appeared out of the darkness. Teams of semi-historically costumed and exotically costumed drummers thrashed out marching beats, hundreds of similarly attired torchbearers filed past, their flaming torches swirling embers and smoke above them, collection buckets swinging. Bangers went off, trumpets blew, people cheered, clapped and screamed, and followed on through the narrow streets, where watching crowds pressed against the buildings. Now I understood.

It all ended with a fireworks display and a huge bonfire, on which a massive effigy of Napoleon Bonaparte was set alight. That year was the 200th anniversary of the Battle of Trafalgar. I had never seen anything quite like it.

Rye Fawkes Night has a history that goes back to well before the Guy Fawkes celebrations with which it now coincides. Rye was a key south-coast port in medieval times and was frequently targeted by the French, who looted and burnt properties and took any useful ships and boats they found. There is an old local saying, 'Rye burns its boats', which many believe derives from the practice of Rye townsfolk setting fire to their own boats before the French could capture them.

This is explained in an old rhyme, part of which goes:

> Ryers angry but distraught,
> rather than have their vessels caught,
> set them alight by their own hand,
> and watched them burning off the Strand,
> flames engulfing higher, higher,
> the gallant vessels funeral pyre . . .

A strange self-destructive tradition developed. On one unruly night of the year, people would gather to drag burning boats through the town, just for fun. The festival got increasingly violent in the eighteenth and nineteenth centuries, with the 'Bonfire Boys' taking possession of the streets, not only targeting boats but sometimes their owners and the authorities. Town dwellers had to barricade themselves in their homes. In expectation of trouble, extra police had to be drafted from the wider area. Things have calmed down in recent decades, and much money is now collected for various charities on the night, but it is still a far wilder, more bacchanal spectacle than you might expect to find in an English seaside town.

The coast will continue to generate mysteries and inspire legends to add to those of earlier centuries. It does not seem to matter that the modern world can find scientific explanations for virtually any phenomenon, there is still a lingering doubt, even a desire that some things remain mysterious and governed by the supernatural. Modern 'urban legends' can be generated almost anywhere, but nowhere is the boundary between the visible and known and the hidden and unknown more acute than at the edge of the sea. This is where imaginations can run wild.

Today's reinvention of old celebrations and the invention of totally new ones is still about binding coastal communities together. But it is also about attracting visitors and creating more economic resilience, especially at times of year when tourists would otherwise be very thin on the ground. Even the most ardent sceptic would have to agree that the future success of many coastal communities still depends more than most places on a little mystery, folklore, tradition and custom.

CHAPTER 5

FISH AND SHIPS

*Fishing boats with crab and lobster pots
at Aldeburgh, Suffolk*

They produce on the sea the appearance of the shadow of
a dark cloud. This shadow comes on, and on, until you can
see the fish leaping and playing on the surface by hundreds
at a time, all huddled close together, and all approaching so
near to the shore, that they can be always caught in some
fifty or sixty feet of water. Indeed, on certain occasions,
when the shoals are of considerable magnitude, the fish
behind have been known to force the fish before, literally
up to the beach, so that they could be taken in buckets, or
even in the hand with the greatest ease.

Wilkie Collins, *Rambles Beyond Railways*, 1851

Fishing and fish processing, building and repairing boats and ships, are the industries that are most associated with the coast. Fishing boats moored on quays or drawn up on to shingle beaches still characterise many seaside places today, even though the fishing industry is not what it was even a few decades ago. Shipyards and boatyards are still prominent in some places around the coast, though the industry is also much less extensive than it once was. Nevertheless, both of these industries are still highly important to the coast, and to Britain as a whole. And in addition to the influence of their modern evolving forms, these industries have left a huge, enduring physical heritage, social and cultural legacy,

The oldest fishing implement found in England, the Clacton Spear Point, dates back around 400,000 years. It is a simple wooden stick, sharpened to a point. The Leman and Ower Point that was dragged up from Doggerland in 1931, at around 13,000 to 14,000 years old, is much more sophisticated. These finds indicate that fishing has a very long history in the British Isles and that fishing technology gradually improved.

However, these objects and those like them are not evidence of deep sea fishing, but river fishing or estuarine fishing. It is highly likely that even with the advent of log and sewn-plank boats, prehistoric people would not usually have ventured too far from shore to obtain a catch. Throughout Britain fish bones are quite rare on most late prehistoric sites, though this may be as much to do with preservation characteristics as the availability of fish. Sites close to meres and sea show that where fish were abundant, prehistoric people caught and ate them.

Fish bones, scales, fragments of possible fishing net, weight and a float recovered from the astounding Late Bronze Age Fenland settlement at Must Farm near Peterborough show that fish were definitely on the menu. The fantastically well-preserved eel traps and wooden hurdle fish weirs found buried in a river channel nearby (along with several log boats) show the lengths that people were prepared to go to catch fish in the Bronze Age c. 1500–600 BC. But this site was at the far reach of tidal influence, and the fish caught there were freshwater (or more accurately muddy fen water) species.

A coastal Bronze Age site at Brean Down in Somerset and archaeological sites in north and west Scotland are among the very few that have produced evidence of sea fish consumption in pre-Roman Britain. The remains of Neolithic and Bronze Age wooden fish weirs have been found in the tidal zone at the Isle of Wight and Severn Estuary. Evidence of shellfish consumption, however, is more common at prehistoric coastal sites. Archaeological evidence for sea fishing in Roman Britain is also sparse, even though we know Romans ate plenty of fish and loved fermented fish sauce (*garum*). They certainly imported this 'acquired taste' condiment and may even have made a British version. Oyster shells, however, are a very common and abundant find on Roman sites throughout Britain, so there was clearly a well-developed industry able to harvest, possibly cultivate, and trade this shellfish well inland.

Oysters were also very widely eaten in medieval Britain, and became so common in the nineteenth century that they were an everyday staple for the masses everywhere. In many places around the coast you can still find clusters of disused oyster pits. These were shallow seawater ponds, often lined with wood and later concrete, where oysters were fattened and kept before onward sale. Emsworth Harbour in Hampshire is one such place where evidence of a once extensive oyster industry can be seen. Unfortunately oyster farming there suffered a notorious set-back in 1902 when guests at a banquet became ill after eating Emsworth oysters. The Dean of Winchester died, and with him went the previously good reputation of Emsworth oysters.

However, oysters are still cultivated or harvested in several places around the British coast today, from Lindisfarne in Northumberland, to West Mersea in Essex and Whitstable in Kent, around the south coast and Cornwall and up to Kyle of Tongue (a sea loch) on Scotland's north coast.

The Domesday Book, completed in 1086, gives the impression of being incredibly thorough about the assets of manors in every place in England. Every plough and every pig seems to have been counted. But it is curiously silent about fishing in many coastal places where it must have formed some part of daily life and the local economy. In Cornwall, for example, no fisheries are mentioned. This is clearly a massive oversight in an area of the country that is largely defined by its coast and where fishing has such a long heritage.

William the Conqueror's unprecedented Domesday survey was carried out with significant inconsistencies across the country. It was not about counting subsistence-level assets, but rather things that amounted to wealth which could be taxed, sold or given by the king. Nevertheless, hundreds of fisheries inland and on the coast of England were recorded in the Domesday Book. Some of those produced tens of thousands of fish for annual rent payments made by a tenant to a lord or king. Dunwich, for example, was counted on to provide 60,000 herrings a year at the time of the Domesday survey, though over time monetary payments increasingly substituted for quantities of fish.

Despite generally understating the extent of fishing around the coast, the Domesday survey and other records do provide evidence of the growing importance of the industry throughout the medieval period. As boat technology improved, fishing fleets were not only able to fish coastal waters more intensively, but go far out into the deep sea.

Fish was very significant in the medieval diet. The Catholic church stipulated that meat could not be eaten on Fridays and Saturdays, over the weeks of the Lent period and during other important Christian festivals. Dolphin and porpoise were considered fish for the purpose of this rule, and were occasionally served up at the highest status tables. Strangely, seal was also considered a fish, and was a rare high-status delicacy. Unsurprisingly, evidence for the consumption of sea fish is abundant on medieval archaeological sites, and a varied diet of several species can be represented at any one site.

Hundreds of years before the Norman Conquest and throughout the medieval period many fish weirs were constructed in the tidal zones around the coastline. Typically, these were v-shaped arrangements of posts and stakes around which low wattle walls were woven. Fish were trapped by the tide and funnelled into a net or baskets at the point of the 'v'. If you are lucky, you may come across the stumps of fish weirs at exceptionally low tides or after storms.

You do not need luck to find the medieval fish weirs in Strangford Lough, Northern Ireland. Many are wooden, but some were built of stone and are easily visible today. They were built similar to dry-stone walls in upland areas, stone stacked upon stone without mortar bonding, and at about the same height. Giant 'v' shaped, tick-shaped or 'L' shaped arrays of rubble foundations between 165 and 980 feet in length can be seen on the sandy bed of the Lough when the tide goes out. The weirs there were built between the eighth and thirteenth centuries.

The later ones may have been operated by the Cistercian monks at Grey Abbey.

These weirs, which have been described as medieval 'fishing machines' by the archaeologists who have investigated them, were an extremely efficient way of extracting fish from the Lough. The weirs would have required a lot of effort to construct and maintain, but scooping up the huge and varied floundering catch when the tide went out was very much easier and more productive than venturing out into the open sea with a boat and nets.

Herring fishing was incredibly important for hundreds of years, especially along the east coast of Britian. The growth of the herring fishing industry up to its peak in the early twentieth century had a profound effect on the social history and fabric of seaside towns and villages from the Scottish islands, right down to East Anglia. Tens of thousands of boats were involved in herring fishing. Harbour and railway infrastructure were extended or newly built to cope with the demands of the industry. Extensive new processing facilities had to be established in coastal villages and towns.

Until the eighteenth century, Seahouses on the Northumberland coast was just a farm and some cottages by the sea. These buildings were outliers to the village of North Sunderland, which lay inland. They were known as North Sunderland's sea houses. Tellingly, the parish church of St Paul is situated in the middle of North Sunderland, not in Seahouses. During the eighteenth and nineteenth centuries, Seahouses developed as a busy fishing centre, as an agricultural and industrial port, and later as a resort. Its growth outstripped the old village.

Natural disadvantages had to be overcome for the port to develop there. Initially, boats had to thread their way between rocky outcrops to land at a beach. The construction of a small breakwater or jetty was instrumental in the development of the harbour at Seahouses in the eighteenth century, but rock had to be cleared to extend the harbour and lessen hazards to the increasing size and volume of ships using it. There is a tiny little building about the size of a garden shed perched on a rock promontory just out of the harbour. It is made of stone, with a barrel roof, no windows and a single doorway. It could be mistaken as the primitive cell of a hermit, such as St Cuthbert. In fact, it is an explosives store and dates to 1886. Rock was blasted away to create the harbour we see today.

Day trippers to Seahouses tend to ignore the old village of North Sunderland completely and instead flock to the shops, pubs, fish and chip shops and attractions along the coast road. Or they stroll along the harbour wall where they can watch the comings and goings, or take a trip out to the Farne Islands. The part of Seahouses up on the low cliff to the south of the harbour is quieter and less frequented, but it is there that much of the fishing history of the place can be found.

The regular grid of streets there indicates planned greenfield development rather than centuries of gradual growth within an existing old settlement. The street plan incorporates several large enclosed squares or courtyards. Now converted into residential courts, these are former herring yards. The wide cart entrances to the yards can still be seen, and the old cobbled surfaces of the yards survive in one or two cases. Walls around the yards have evidence of blocked former openings, which are too low for windows and too small for doors. These are hatches where cart loads of herring could be tipped into the yard, ready for processing.

Herring are a fatty fish that will go off quickly. Huge numbers of the fish had to be gutted, salted, packed in barrels and carted off to the railway as quickly as possible. Teams of 'herring girls' laboured swiftly and skilfully with sharpened knives at benches in these yards, or out in the open at harbour sides. They turned the catch into a preserved product for hungry markets at home and abroad. It was hard and unappetising work: long cold hours up to the elbows in fish guts, and prone to getting salt-stingingly wounded hands.

Strangely to us, perhaps, it was also said to be something of a liberating job. The herring fleets followed the migrating herring shoals around the coast during the year, and the herring girls followed too. Lasses from the islands and coastal villages of Scotland would progress south, ending up in places such as Great Yarmouth and Lowestoft in the autumn. It was quite an adventure for teenage and unmarried women and gave them an independent income and opportunities that very few women of the era could hope for. Married women brought children with them. Hard work though it was, there was also companionship, and even sometimes a little time for fun.

Tucked away in the back streets of Seahouses near the herring yards is a business that is still successfully carrying on a fine British culinary tradition. This is the historic premises and smokehouse of Swallow Fish Ltd, which has operated since 1843. I last visited in 2024, when I met the proprietor, Patrick Wilkin, a big man who appeared at the door with a big dog.

Both appeared quite gruff and intimidating at first, but after they had checked me out, all was fine.

Patrick is a busy man and an enthusiastic advocate of his craft. He takes great pride in using the traditional method of smoking fish. No artificial flavourings, colourings, or any modern technology is used. It is all about the quality of the fish and judging the right smoking conditions, he explained. Little heaps of oak shavings on the floor have to burn at exactly the right intensity to smoke the fish suspended from racks in the small smoke chamber. The walls of the chamber are coated in a thick, black tar that has accumulated over generations of smoking. There are little openings at the eaves of the building to draw out the smoke, but no cowls or chimneys to rotate to help get the right draw. Salmon and haddock are smoked there and sold in the adjacent shop, but the premises is mainly known for its kippers.

The origin story about how the humble herring was first transformed into the popular kipper is somewhat obscure and the subject of lively debate. Some accounts say that it happened by accident when somebody left herrings too close to the fire and they got smoked. Others say that kippers were invented when the place where herring were being stored burnt down. The main contenders for the credit of discovering or inventing kippers include a fisherman from Great Yarmouth in the sixteenth century and a man named John Woodger either at Seahouses, or at his inn at Newcastle in the 1840s.

Whatever the case, herring businesses and harbour owners, such as the Craster dynasty a few miles south of Seahouses, started to create smokehouses for kippers, often adapting their existing herring yards for the purpose. The Robson family's

Craster kipper business, which begun in 1906, is thriving today in its historic premises, a former herring yard and smokehouse of the 1850s.

Neil Robson, just like Patrick Wilkin, is as much an enthusiast as a business owner. The care with which he cures and curates his products was evident as he talked me through the process and explained what makes Craster kippers special. The herring were at their fat and oily best as they passed the Northumbrian coast on their way from the north of Scotland to East Anglia, which placed the region's kipper producers at an advantage. These days herring have to be sourced from Norway, but choosing the right fish is still key.

Craster kippers and Seahouses kippers have become internationally renowned, and rightly so, because they are delicious. Unlike a lot of specially recognised and famous artisanal foodstuffs, these kippers are not only very good for you, but are still very good value indeed.

If the herring was once king, or at least 'silver darling', in various places around the coast of Britain, the pilchard (a smaller relative of the herring) was once premier in Cornwall. The heyday of the pilchard fishing industry was between the middle of the eighteenth and the late nineteenth centuries. It was an industry that had a profound effect on coastal communities, and shaped many of the historic Cornish harbour towns and villages we celebrate today.

Taking and processing the pilchard catch was a whole community affair at the smaller harbours. Lookouts called 'huers' were posted on clifftops to watch out for the approach of the shoals of pilchards as they migrated around the coast. The huers would cry out and wave foliage or white spheres as a signal for the fishing boats to launch, and then give directions towards the shoal. Typically the fishing method, known as seine fishing, was to surround as much of the shoal as possible with a huge horseshoe-shaped net that was manipulated by two boats, then use another net to close the loop.

All this took place near the shore, so the seine net could be hauled towards the beach and tightened. A smaller net (a tuck) would then be deployed in the centre of the seine net by four more boats, bringing the fish to the surface so they could be scooped up. It all required close coordination between the various boat teams, which rowed their boats into place, and the people on the shore. Once the fish had been landed, the next job was to prepare them for curing. This was done in 'pilchard cellars' or fish cellars, which were also sometimes referred to as 'pilchard palaces'. They typically comprised stone barn-like buildings or open-sided roofed sheds and storerooms arranged around a courtyard.

There the fish were stacked between layers of salt in a great heap. The curing process took several weeks and nothing was wasted. The mess of blood and offal that seeped out of the heaps of pilchards was collected to be sold as fertiliser. Oil that drained out was also retained and sold for lamp fuel and for the lubrication of machinery. The fish were then washed and packed in barrels. Weighted poles or beams, acting as great levers, pressed down on the barrel lids, squeezing the pilchards flat and pressing out more oil. A hogshead barrel, the standard measure of the industry, contained 3000 to 4000 pilchards.

Virtually all of the Cornish pilchard catch was exported

in hogsheads to Catholic southern Europe. Some pilchards were retained for local consumption, of course. Swiping a few between shore and pilchard cellar to feed hungry mouths was more or less expected. The author Wilkie Collins described the frenetic scenes at one pilchard fishery in the middle of the nineteenth century. He noted that a boy with a long cane had been employed to fend off other boys attempting to pilfer pilchards from barrows as they were trundled to the cellars.

At the height of the industry the sizes of the catches were extraordinary. Cornwall could produce up to 50,000 hogsheads of pilchards (probably 150 million to 200 million fish) each year. In the record year of 1868, Newlyn alone produced over 30,000 hogsheads. But it could not last. The pilchards stopped coming in such huge shoals. A more individualist form of drift net fishing took over from collective seine fishing as catches drastically reduced, until finally the industry collapsed.

Pilchards are still caught in Cornwall today, however, following a limited revival of commercial fishing. The fish has been rebranded as the 'Cornish sardine'. Whatever it is called, it is best eaten fresh and simply grilled.

The pilchard fishing boom resulted in a lot of investment in fishing communities, with landowners and entrepreneurs building pilchard cellars, buying boats, improving harbour capacity and facilities and hiring locals for the work. Houses were refurbished and newly built on the proceeds. Many coastal settlements grew and changed in character. It can still be discerned today, even though most of the historic Cornish fishing villages and towns have largely become sanitised places of tourism and second homes.

Pilchard cellars survive in whole or in part in many Cornish harbours. They have found all sorts of new uses, from art galleries, shops and restaurants, to garages and dwellings. One, in Newlyn, is now a cinema. Some are still in use by fishermen. Even surviving fragments of cellars that have been mostly demolished or incorporated into other buildings can be spotted by their thick granite and slate walls and the tell-tale slots (often subsequently blocked) for the weighted poles that pressed out pilchard oil.

In his account of a pilchard fishery Wilkie Collins commented that in the pilchard cellar were '. . . assembled all the women and girls in the district'. He then made some distinctly non-feminist comments about the 'variety of the female type' therein and the hubbub they generated, which I will skip over. However, he also noted just how hard they were working. This is something I have heard time and time again when chatting to people about the fishing heritage of their town or village. They are keen to stress how important women were to the whole enterprise.

Women may have been excluded from the boats and under-represented in documents about business ownership and operation, but comments such as '. . . but the women worked the hardest', 'the women did everything else', 'and the women managed it all', or 'the women had the hardest lives' are derived from first-hand or handed-down family knowledge of what really went on in a place. In addition to running the household (often a very large household) and all the domestic management and chores that involved, women were relied upon for bait collecting and preparation (collecting shellfish and small fish and putting them on the hooked lines in huge numbers), mending nets, ropes and pots (to catch crab and lobster) and making and repairing clothing.

The fisherman's jersey, the 'gansey', was a crucial home-produced garment throughout Britain's fishing communities. This densely knitted woollen jumper was carefully designed to be warm and water resistant. It had a gusset in the armpit to allow freedom of movement and slightly shortened sleeves that would keep the hands free and not easily snag on gear. Patterns of cables, diamonds, ladders, and so on, in each gansey were associated with particular families and communities. Folklore has it that these distinctive patterns would help to identify the bodies of drowned fishermen washed up on the shore, but the truth is probably more to do with tradition and local pride.

You can find machine-made imitations of ganseys everywhere now, but acquiring a real hand-made gansey often requires patience (they take a long time to make, and there are usually waiting lists) and a few hundred pounds. But it is a precious garment for life.

Women often had to carry boxes and baskets of wet fish on their heads, and on one part of the North Yorkshire coast, this gave rise to the 'Staithes bonnet'. The bonnets were made of cotton. They had an in-built sunshade peak at the front and covered the neck at the back, to divert dripping seawater. Up until the twentieth century, every woman and girl in Staithes wore one of these traditional bonnets.

In a few fishing communities around the coast it is claimed that part of the women's work was to roll up their skirts and carry their husbands out to their boats. It sounds ridiculous and unreasonable to us, but a fisherman who was already wet and cold before starting a fishing trip would only get much wetter and colder at sea, and this was risky. A good sturdy lass was sought after in these communities.

GREAT GRIMSBY

The industrialisation of the British fishing industry in modern times is exemplified by Grimsby, on the Lincolnshire side of the Humber Estuary. Approaching the town from the edge of the Lincolnshire Wolds, along the A46, provides a glimpse of an extraordinary building. Long before the rest of the town comes into view, there in the distance is a tall, thin tower that seems to have been plucked from Renaissance Italy. It has in a way, since this tower was based on the famous bell tower of the Palazzo Pubblico that characterises Sienna's central square. But why is it there?

The tower stands at the sea lock entrance of Grimsby's Royal Dock. Built of red brick and standing over 300 feet tall, 'The Dock Tower' is one of the major and most visible clues to Grimsby's rise and dominance as a North Sea fishing port. Like many Lincolnshire places founded or taken over by the Danes, Grimsby has an Anglo-Scandinavian name deriving from a personal name, *Grimr*, combined with *by*, meaning settlement or village. Well before the Norman Conquest, Grimsby was noted as a ferry crossing point of the Humber. In medieval times it grew as a significant sea fishing and trading port.

The notable size and fine thirteenth- and fourteenth-century architecture of Grimsby's Church of St James, now designated as Grimsby Minster, gives some impression of the importance and location of the medieval town. Grimsby's other medieval parish church has long since gone, and there are few buildings that pre-date the middle of the nineteenth century. But there are many buildings that indicate a boom in commerce and civic pride thereafter. Wandering around the town today reveals a place entirely replanned, rebuilt and vastly expanded from Victorian times and into the twentieth century.

The Church of St James and the Dock Tower are not the only elegant and striking structures in Grimsby. The huge red brick silo tower of the Victoria Flour Mills looms over Alexandra Dock, a body of water built from the canalised and widened River Freshney. A great deal of care was taken to ensure that this enormous industrial building, in its highly prominent waterside location, was easy on the eye. It looks similar to the early American skyscrapers, which were being built about the same time in the late Victorian period.

The walk, cycle ride or drive from the town centre to the Port of Grimsby is made slightly more off-putting by busy roads and much less interesting architecture, but the reward is the discovery of another part of Grimsby, almost another town. Much of the modern port area is out of bounds to curious members of the public. However, it is possible for those with a legitimate reason to visit businesses in the docks, or those attending periodic open days, to gain access and take a closer look.

To do so you must carry on past the imposing Victorian dock offices, surmounted by a clock tower, with its statue of Prince Albert at the front. A huge building, again in the red brick favoured in Victorian and early twentieth-century Grimsby, immediately draws attention. It has seen better days, but like

Victoria Mills, this building has considerable presence and grandeur, with architectural details that give it some flourish. Large pedimented frontages, pilasters, turrets, domes, large square and arched windows and blind panels, and dentilled cornices are all features that eighteenth- and nineteenth-century stately homes or grand public buildings might have employed to accentuate their elegance and communicate their importance.

But the lettering on one elevation gives away the purpose of this building: 'The Grimsby Ice Company Ltd'. This is the Grimsby Ice Factory, basically a massive freezer and ice-vending machine. The huge quantities of ice this factory was able to produce, up to 1,100 tons per day in the 1930s, together with the output of smaller ice factories established there, was crucial to the success of Grimsby's fishing fleet. Grimsby trawlers, formerly reliant on sporadic local supplies of ice and imported Norwegian ice, could now get as much ice as they wanted and therefore venture out further for longer.

The Ice Factory complex is curiously split into two main blocks by an oblique gap between the buildings. This is another clue to Grimsby's success. A rail line ran there and when the Ice Factory was extended in 1907 the second block was built just to the north of the rail lines. There are remnants of rail lines elsewhere across the dock. With much foresight, the chairman of the Manchester, Sheffield and Lincolnshire Railway Company urged the purchase of the existing dock company at Grimsby and from 1846 set about building what was probably the first modern rail-integrated dock in Britain.

This required a massive construction programme on the salt marsh and mud flats, requiring huge coffer dams to keep out the tide. The foundation stone for the new Royal Dock was laid by Prince Albert in 1849 (which is why his statue is prominent in front of the dock offices) and the dock's opening was celebrated three years later. Trucks of Grimsby fish on ice could now be loaded up and speedily conveyed on the rail network throughout Britain. A market and fishing port once limited by the perishable nature of its products to regional significance became nationally and internationally important. In fact, Grimsby became the world's premier fishing port.

The Dock Tower is an architectural expression of a place well on the way to success and full of confidence for the future. It is an enduring icon, a symbol of Grimsby, and seen on supermarket packets of frozen fish. It is even modelled in plastic bricks at Legoland Windsor, along with Victoria Mills, the Dock Office and Corporation Bridge, in a miniature recreation of a classic working port. The Dock Tower is not just a monument, however, but another crucial piece of port infrastructure. Completed in 1852, the tower is actually an innovative hydraulic engine, and the largest hydraulic tower in Britain. It was built to power the dock's sea lock gates. A much smaller hydraulic tower was built alongside in 1892, which was itself superseded by an electrical system in 1980.

Cutting-edge Victorian engineering and technology is all very well, but it also took a lot of people to run a port such as this. In 1801 Grimsby's population was just over 1,500, but by 1871 it had grown to over 20,000. By 1901 it was nearly 37,000. That explains the prevalence of mid-nineteenth-century and later housing, commercial premises and public buildings in the town. However, the businesses and people working in the port also needed services close to hand, as well as the distant town centre.

At the heart of the port is an area that came to be known locally as 'The Kasbah'. The name derives from the bustling maze of streets that developed there. There were shops, banks, a post office, cafes and pubs alongside smokehouses, sailmakers, rope works and other nautical gear makers and suppliers. It was almost a mini self-contained town in its own right.

The Grimsby dock complex continued to grow throughout the late nineteenth and twentieth centuries with the construction of huge new dock basins. In the 1930s, 85 per cent (by weight) of the fish landed in England and Wales came through Grimsby, Hull, Fleetwood and Milford Haven, but already there were warning signs about the sustainability of industrial-scale fishing. Fish stocks started to dwindle.

The 'Cod Wars' with Iceland in the 1950s and 1970s, which were heated enough to require Royal Navy protection of British trawlers, were a result of the fierce competition that had developed to exploit what remained. During the 1980s Grimsby's fishing fleet suffered a catastrophic decline. This all but ended ways of life that had existed for hundreds of years at Grimsby and had huge social consequences for the town. Today, according to the Government's published Indices of Multiple Deprivation, Grimsby has some of the most deprived neighbourhoods in Britain.

However, this was by no means the end of the port. Work has pivoted to the processing of seafood caught elsewhere, often globally. The port still houses businesses that collectively process around 70 per cent of the UK's seafood, supporting around

6000 jobs. But this is just one activity that the Port of Grimsby and its sister port of Immingham, a few miles to the north, now specialises in. These ports are a major handler of imported vehicles, of agricultural, forestry and construction products, and a hub for offshore wind farm servicing.

The fishing heritage that built Grimsby has not been forgotten. After years of decline, dereliction and demolition, the historic buildings of the Kasbah are gradually being rescued and fitted out for new leases of life. Historic smoke houses, such as Alfred Enderby's, carry the tradition forward to great culinary acclaim. Traditional Grimsby Smoked Fish is in fact a legally recognised and protected food type,[9] similar to Stilton, Scotch Whisky and Champagne. The Ice Factory awaits new uses for alternative industries, and conversion as a venue for live events and exhibitions, offices and research space.

Ross Tiger, a unique surviving example of a 1950s diesel trawler is moored outside Grimsby's Fishing Heritage Centre, in Alexandra Dock.

A tour of *Ross Tiger* and the heritage centre brings home the enormity of the fishing industry at its peak, and its all-encompassing effects on the communities of this Lincolnshire coastal town. Adjacent to the *Ross Tiger*, a few exposed timbers and red poles mark the resting place of *Esther*, a Grimsby fishing smack launched in 1888. It went on to ownership in Great Yarmouth, the Faroe Islands and Iceland before returning to Grimsby after more than a century of service.

In 2012 *Esther* sank at its mooring. For many people the fate

---

9 Department for Environment, Food and Rural Affairs, Protected geographical food and drink names.

of this historic vessel and the slow disintegration of the Kasbah and the Ice Factory symbolised the decline of Grimsby itself once its fishing industry had collapsed. The apparent lack of solutions to these losses reflected the despair that any form of regeneration of the town and recovery of its reputation was possible. Now the Kasbah and Ice Factory are being looked upon as something far more energising than the decaying backdrops for apocalyptic films, which they have both been. The repair of Corporation Bridge and the salvage, repair and relaunch of *Esther* will also be important milestones in the future of this fascinating coastal town.

SHIPBUILDING

Fishing, trading and fighting at sea requires boats and ships, which gave rise to a long tradition of coastal boat-building. Vessels capable of cruising around the British coast, crossing estuaries or even shuttling back and forth across the Channel were built during the Bronze Age, well over three thousand years ago, and probably much earlier. It is obvious from traded goods and Roman writers that Britain's coastal waters would have been increasingly busy leading up to the Roman period. Contact with the Continent and Roman world was well-established long before the Roman military expeditions and conquest of Britain in the first century BC and first century AD.

Britain's absorption into the Roman Empire would have greatly increased maritime traffic and the sophistication of seafaring vessels in British waters. It is reasonable to assume, for example, that many of the ships of the Roman navy fleet of the British Isles (*Classis Britannica*) would have been built and repaired here. In fact, tiles made and stamped for the *Classis Britannica* have been found at iron production sites in the Weald of south-east England, suggesting that the navy had some role in the production of this raw material, which then as in later times was crucial to shipbuilding.

However, direct archaeological evidence for boatbuilding in Roman Britain is frustratingly sparse. Of the handful of Roman seagoing vessels found in the British Isles, two are London finds. One of these was a Mediterranean type, but definitely built using English timber.

Evidence of shipbuilding in the Dark Ages is equally tantalising. The most famous British ship of this period is the one revealed at Sutton Hoo in Suffolk in 1939. This ship was part of the most extraordinarily lavish, early medieval burial site ever discovered. It was in effect the sarcophagus for a great king and all the spectacular treasures and possessions his retainers thought fitting for his afterlife.

The most likely recipient of this spectacular burial is King Raedwald of East Anglia, who died around AD 624. His huge ship had to be hauled up from the tidal reach of the River Deben to a promontory overlooking the river. There it formed the centrepiece of what was undoubtedly a magnificent funeral ceremony, before being covered with an earth mound. Only the ghostly impression of the ship's timbers punctuated by lines of iron rivets (clench-nails) survived the acid soil conditions, so information about the origins of its construction materials are limited. There is no reason to believe, however, that this ship was not built in Raedwald's East Anglian kingdom.

A ship just like this one is being built just across the Deben in Woodbridge today. The Sutton Hoo Ships Company is using authentic tools and techniques to make a full-scale replica (around 90 feet long) that can navigate the Deben and coastal waters, and even sail across the open sea, as its ancestor probably did. A huge amount is being learnt about early shipbuilding in the process. You can visit the Sutton Hoo Ships Company premises to see the progress of this astounding construction and research project. If you are very lucky you may even see an earlier half-length replica, the *Sae Wylfing* ('Sea Wolf Cub') out on the river under sail or oar power, conjuring up the spirit of Anglo-Saxon maritime endeavour.

Evidence for other boats of this period, usually in the form of rivets and clench nails, has been found in dry land contexts such as burial sites. Only a few finds of woodworking tools hint at a handful of possible shipbuilding sites in Britain. No definite shipwrecks dating from the end of the Roman period (around AD 410) to the twelfth century have been found on the seabed, but the remains of a few seagoing vessels have been found in estuarine locations. Mostly these are only fragmentary: a rudder or some planking discarded or reused in a waterside wooden structure.

One remarkably intact ship, however, has been found. It was accidentally revealed when cutting a drainage ditch in the Graveney Marshes on the north Kent coast in 1970. This is a clinker-built vessel, probably originally more than 45 feet long, dating to around AD 900. There was evidence it had been hauled out of the water onto a hard or platform, perhaps for repairs or cannibalisation. Analysis of its timber indicated that it was almost certainly built in south-east or eastern England. Its hull held the remnants of a cargo or ballast that included fragments of continental pottery, lava quern stone and hops, implying that it was involved in international trade. Again, a half-length replica of this vessel was built and this is now operated by Faversham Creek Trust.

Anglo-Saxon kings following Raedwald were able to build and requisition considerable numbers of ships, and according to the *Anglo-Saxon Chronicle* even occasionally beat Vikings and Danish fleets. For example, King Alfred the Great commissioned new, improved warships to beat the Danes, twice as long as existing models, faster and more stable, some with more than sixty oars. There was obviously a skilled workforce of shipwrights and sufficient capacity, in Wessex at least, to carry out his order. In AD 911, Alfred's son, King Edward the Elder, was able to raise a fleet of about a hundred ships on the south coast. And apparently this was only as a deception to allow his land forces to sneak up on the Danes invading Mercia.

King John was another monarch who was keen on strengthening the navy and its supply ships. Dozens of galleys, some of sixty oars or more, and other ships were commissioned. They were primarily built and repaired at south-coast facilities. King John's investment eventually paid off, because in 1217 after his death, a French fleet was defeated off the Kent coast, preventing an invasion.

Shipbuilding technology moved forward in the medieval period with the development of a greater variety of larger vessels, and eventually the introduction of 'carvel' or skeleton construction. Clinker-built ships have overlapping planks to form the hull. In carvel construction the planks join edge to edge and are secured to a timber skeleton framework. Ships were typically of one mast and sail in the early medieval period, but came to be equipped with two, and then three masts and secondary sails, which greatly improved their handling.

The shipbuilding industry seems to have remained relatively small, however, and somewhat artisanal. Given the highly skilled, labour-intensive, materials-hungry process of building a sizeable ship, it seems strange that the documentary evidence suggests there were a few small shipyards scattered around the coast, rather than a concentrated effort in highly developed shipbuilding centres. These small shipyards did not comprise much in terms of permanent infrastructure and facilities, and so have not left much archaeological evidence. A stable place at an estuary tideline was probably sufficient in most cases, with supplies of iron and wood fairly close to hand, a temporary work camp, and a shallow scoop in the mud for a berth.

SHIPYARDS AND 'WOODEN WALLS'[10]

Medieval ships were built on the East Sussex coast at Rye and at Winchelsea. Now well inland of these places was another shipyard whose national significance is belied by its size and situation today. Small Hythe is a charming Kent hamlet. As its name implies, this was never a large port. It once stood on the

---

10 This term for fighting ships comes from a 1635 speech by Thomas Coventry, lawyer and politician: 'The dominion of the sea, as it is an ancient an undoubted right of the crown of England, so it is the best security of the land…The wooden walls are the best walls of this kingdom.'

tidal reach of the River Rother, whose estuary gradually silted and was reclaimed along with much of the Romney Marshes. Limited archaeological investigations at Small Hythe have revealed ironwork and timbers from ships and shipbuilding, evidence of smithing, large hollows that formed berths or slipways, and part of a wharf.

Documentary evidence tells us that several famous and remarkably large ships were built there. These include *Marie* (of 100 tons) built 1409–11, *George* (120 tons) and the huge *Jesus* (1000 tons) both built in 1416. *Jesus* was one of King Henry V's four 'great ships' that were completed between 1415–17 and formed the nucleus of his navy. King Henry himself visited Small Hythe in 1416 to see work progressing. Of the other 'great ships' only *Grace Dieu*, which was built at a specially constructed dock at Southampton, was larger than *Jesus*. *Trinity Royal* and *Holy Ghost* (a captured Spanish ship) were about half and three-quarters respectively of *Jesus*'s tonnage.

The 'Keeper of the King's Ships', Robert Brigandyne, lived at Small Hythe, another clue to the large significance of this little place. It was there that the timbers for *Henry Grace a Dieu* (or 'Great Harry') were prepared before its construction at Woolwich in 1512. This was the ship that carried Henry VIII on his diplomatic expedition to the Field of the Cloth of Gold and is depicted in the famous picture of the expedition fleet. Henry VIII's *Grand Mistress* and *Great Gallyon* were also built at Small Hythe in 1545–6. In greatly building up his navy, Henry VIII gave work to shipyards large and small. Inevitably, this meant dockyard facilities had to develop for building ever larger ships, fitting them out, repairing and provisioning them. The

Small Hythe shipyard suffered from silting of the River Rother, which hindered larger ships reaching the sea and fell out of use in the later sixteenth century.

What was probably the world's first dry dock had been established at Portsmouth in 1495 under Henry VII. Over the next century naval dockyards and bases were developed at places such as Chatham, Erith, Woolwich and Deptford on the Medway and Thames, and in the Colne Estuary and at Harwich in Essex. Scottish naval bases clustered along the Forth at places such as Leith, Newhaven and Airth. Nevertheless, the expansion of British sea power meant that some surprisingly small, tucked away and apparently obscure places still came to play significant roles in shipbuilding.

In 1722 John Montagu, the 2nd Duke of Montagu, was appointed Governor of St Lucia and St Vincent in the West Indies. He spotted a business opportunity to develop sugar plantations and identified a place on his vast Hampshire estate that would form a key part of the plan. The place was called Buckler's Hard. The last part of the name refers to a firm place on the generally marshy banks of the tidal Beaulieu River where boats could be landed. There the Duke planned to build 'Montagu Town', a brand-new port town that would service the plantations in the West Indies.

A prospectus for investors and tenants was drawn up, together with a plan showing the intended layout of the place. This town plan can be seen in nearby Beaulieu Abbey. It depicts a square-shaped development by the river formed of rows of terraced buildings and yards. The plan was based on four quadrants separated by two wide streets that intersected at a central market square. The all-important quays on the river are marked as 'Keys' on the plan. At least 240 properties are shown.

However, Montagu was unable to develop his West Indian estates, not least because the French quickly booted out his English settlers. Only a handful of the proposed houses had been built at Buckler's Hard by the 1730s, and the grand plan for a new port town was in tatters. In the 1740s, however, the Navy Board was looking for more shipyards and selected Buckler's Hard as a suitable place where civilian contractors could fulfil Navy contracts. The surrounding New Forest could supply plenty of timber and the yard was only a short sail up the river from the Solent.

Things began to really take off when Master Shipbuilder Henry Adams was sent from Deptford in 1744 to oversee the construction of a warship named *Surprise*. Within a few years he married a local girl, Elizabeth Smith, and took the tenancy of the Buckler's Hard shipyard. Adams was very good at his job. He went on to build many warships and carried out infrastructure improvements such as lengthening the launch ways.

Buckler's Hard grew during this period, though never to the extent envisaged in the proposed 'Montagu Town'. The basis of the plan, however, is apparent in the form of the village today. A wide central green separates the two facing terraces of neat red brick and plain tile houses that gently step down towards the river. This pretty and distinctive place has been a popular tourist destination since the 1890s, when steamboats brought day trippers up the river from the coast.

The tranquil atmosphere of the village and river today is in stark contrast to the hive of manufacturing activity it would have been in its shipbuilding heydays. The tinkling of rigging wire, flapping of sails and pennants, hum of outboard motors, and jolly greetings in the crowded yacht harbour do not quite evoke the sights, sounds and smells of ships being built for war. A highly detailed model in the museum does convey the enormity of the enterprise there. The central green, paddocks, in fact every spare open space, is filled with piles of timber in various states of preparation. Carters haul, sawyers saw, smiths smith, and there on the slipways are two warships under construction. The huge ships, surrounded by scaffolding, loom over the buildings of the village.

Buckler's Hard produced three of the Royal Navy warships present at the Battle of Trafalgar in 1805. One of these, HMS *Agamemnon* (of 64 guns), was Admiral Lord Nelson's favourite ship. Her crew struggled with pronouncing the name from Greek mythology and referred to her as 'Eggs and Bacon'. Nelson was her captain for three years before he went on to higher appointments and national hero status.

The end of the Napoleonic Wars saw the end of warship building at Buckler's Hard. The Adams family continued building merchant ships there until 1847, when they gave up the tenancy of the shipyard and the place slipped back into obscurity. However, Buckler's Hard was pressed into naval service once again during another time of great national need. In the Second World War, tucked away from the vulnerable south-coast ports and surrounded by camouflaging woodland, the old shipyard made significant contributions to the war effort.

Motor torpedo boats and minesweepers occupied the berths built for eighteenth-century warships. Dummy wooden landing craft, part of a grand D-Day deception plan, were built there and all manner of other craft crowded the river awaiting the landings themselves. A little way downstream from the village a dock was created to build concrete pontoons, called 'Beetles'. These were a crucial element of the transportable, floating 'Mulberry Harbour' that would be so crucial to the Normandy landings. An experimental floating concrete dock that could be towed across the Channel was also built there. The navy and army personnel and civilian workforce accommodated in the area (which by now was understandably well out of bounds to leisure boating and tourists) included 600 Irish workers.

It is easy to miss the traces left by this frenetic activity when cruising down the river today. Understandably, most of the wartime paraphernalia has been swept away as part of the post-war beautification of the leisure destination. A muddy inlet with iron sheet piles and concrete at its entrance could be mistaken for some piece of decaying modern industrial infrastructure, but for the Union Flag and Stars and Stripes flying from flag poles as a memorial. This was the dock created to build elements of the crucial floating concrete D-Day harbour. Nearby, on the river's east bank, an abandoned wooden landing craft is barely visible at low tide in the marsh, but its skeletal remains are readily apparent from above.

Back at the village, only some short lengths of concrete track near the slipways are recognisable to enthusiasts such as myself (or 'saddo', as I have heard some people close to me uncharitably say) as the type of concrete laid down at airfields, army camps and naval bases during the Second World War. Other traces are even more evocative of the wartime hands that worked at Buckler's Hard. On the wooden beam of a fireplace in the Master Builder's House Hotel (formerly Henry Adam's home and headquarters) is a roughly carved inscription: 'D-Day, Royal Navy 1944–45'. This graffiti has the appearance of being done spontaneously during a boozy celebratory session to mark the end of the world war, and Buckler's Hard's role in the victory.

Elements of Britain's coastal heritage made at Buckler's Hard have even found their way to foreign shores. Second World War concrete pontoons made there undoubtedly still lie on the French coast and the wreck of the *Agamemnon* has been located off the coast of Uruguay.

The small shipbuilding yards dispersed around the coast were suited to earlier times, and helpful in distributing risk in times of wartime emergency, but the industrial era demanded very much larger facilities and a larger workforce. When we talk about British shipbuilding over the last century or so, we probably think of the great centres of the industry such as the Tyne, Wear, Mersey, Clyde, Thames, Aberdeen, Bristol, Belfast and Barrow-in-Furness. These places built ships not just for Britain, but for the world. During the nineteenth and early twentieth centuries, shipbuilding towns expanded massively to accommodate huge populations of workers and their dependants, and a wide range of service industries and facilities.

Modern shipbuilding required vast infrastructure and has left both a distinctive built heritage and rich social legacy in many places around the coast. However, the practices and products of British shipyards had implications and influence well inland and beyond these shores. The British military and merchant fleet dominated the seas of the world.

British shipbuilding was eclipsed by other nations during the latter half of the twentieth century, and the industry was largely nationalised in 1977, before being privatised again in the 1980s. The near total collapse of profitable shipbuilding from the 1960s had serious social and economic consequences for places such as Glasgow, which had come to be defined by the industry. However, shipbuilding is still a significant employer in several of its historic centres and is set for a mini-boom as defence spending is set to increase once more.

Many small coastal towns and villages that were once gritty, hard-working centres of trade and industry have been transformed into picturesque holiday destinations over the last hundred years or so. But even in the most picturesque seaside spots you can still find traces of formerly extensive historic industry, and therefore get a better appreciation of their true heritage.

CHAPTER 6

INDUSTRIOUS COAST

Mine engine houses near Botallack, Cornwall

The creaking and groaning of timber, the stress on the machinery, the grating of the brake, the rattling of the huge links, the clash of the hammer against iron bolts, and the thundering crash of the coal falling through the bottom of the wagon into the hold of the vessel, are all sounds that excite the senses and rivet the attention [. . .] and yet, after all that, the whole establishment altogether is but as a speck in the balance, compared with the vast, incessant shipments that cross the bar of the Tyne, whose banks on either side, the whole distance from Newcastle, are studded with chimneys. These vomit into the air a dense mass of smoke, till nature herself seems, as it were, forced to take again under her special charge, in the form of one huge, black, unbroken cloud, the noxious particles and effluvia rejected by the saturated atmosphere.

Sir George Head, *A Home Tour
Through the Manufacturing Districts of
England in the Summer of 1835*

In 1999, two treasure hunters armed with metal detectors surreptitiously approached a prominent hill in the Ziegelroda Forest, not far from Leipzig. They were unlicensed and should not have been there, but the area is well known for its prehistoric monuments and the lure of loot had proved too great. Sure enough, they got a signal and their spades soon revealed ancient artefacts. Most of what they uncovered was fairly typical of Bronze Age hoards across much of Europe and Britain: bronze swords, axes, a chisel and dress items, there in the form of armbands. One object, however, was unique.

Happily the German authorities were eventually able to rescue the artefacts from the black market, convict the looters, and thereby bring this hoard, and one extraordinary item in particular, to public attention. The looters had struck (actually struck with their spade) the world's earliest depiction of astronomical phenomena. The Nebra Sky Disc, as it has become known, is circular and around 1 foot in diameter. It is made of bronze, with gold studs and inlays that seem to map stars, a full moon or sun, a crescent moon, a graduated arc (one remaining of a probable pair) to help mark the solstices, and another mysterious arc whose purpose is more obscure.

This is a world famous but mysterious object whose exact use is not known for certain. Science, however, has provided much information about its origins. It has been dated to between 1800 and 1600 BC and was periodically modified from a simpler, original form. The copper necessary to make the bronze disc came from Austria and some of the gold came from the Carpathian Mountains. Remarkably, however, the gold used for the first phases of the design came from Cornwall. So did the tin that was added to the copper to make the bronze disc. It is astounding to think that Cornish metal was being extracted and exported to the Continent in the Early Bronze Age.

When people think of the Cornish coast today it is probably the blue seas pounding against rugged cliffs, sandy coves, little fishing harbours and cream teas that first come to mind. Perhaps also traffic jams in peak tourist season. On a recent trip back from filming in Cornwall I dropped in to an airfield out of curiosity, and persuaded an instructor to take me for a flight along the coast. My curiosity had been aroused by seeing his aeroplane going overhead during the previous few days. I had recognised it as the type of motor glider that I first learnt to fly and in which I did my first solo flight as a teenage air cadet.

It was a nostalgic flight as I felt my way back into the controls and characteristics of this machine, but I also had time to look at the coastal landscape below. The sandy bays and coves, where I had seen swimmers, surfers and walkers enjoying the delights of the natural environment, are in fact enveloped by a vast former industrial landscape, scarred and pitted by centuries of prospecting, quarrying and mining. Nature is reclaiming the denuded industrial landscape, and this makes it additionally difficult to appreciate on the ground.

The contrast between how coastal Cornwall is perceived by visitors on the sand, and what the view from above tells us about its heritage, is incredible. In fact, large parts of the coast (and large areas inland) are designated ('or inscribed') by UNESCO as the Cornwall and West Devon Mining Landscape World Heritage Site.

The presence of varied and valuable minerals in Cornwall

and Devon is an accident of geology, which saw magma pushing up through earlier sedimentary rocks, changing them, causing mineralisation and then cooling to form granite deposits. These very specific and localised events millions of years ago meant that the region is rich in deposits of cassiterite (tin ore). Nobody knows how people first learned about the ore and how to turn it into a useful metal, but probably as early as 2000 BC a craft or industry had begun there. Cornish tin was known to the Greek and Roman world in the centuries before the birth of Christ. Pytheas of Massalia (a Greek colony in Marseilles), a geographer, explorer and astronomer, reportedly travelled around the coast of Britain in about AD 325 and noted this important Cornish product.

At first, mining was not necessary. Rivers and streams did the job of scouring out ore-rich deposits. Tin ore was sifted from the sand and silt and smashed from the rocky debris deposited by the watercourses. It is a technique called 'streaming'. Then people began following likely looking seams into valley sides and cliffs, first quarrying out scoops, then digging as far as possible before air supply and drainage problems became insurmountable.

Incredibly, at times in the medieval period the tin produced in Devon and Cornwall provided most of Europe's total supply. Bronze, pewter and other tin alloys were in demand for all sorts of fixtures and fittings, tools and instruments, tableware, decorative items and coinage.

So valuable was the industry in Devon and Cornwall that special concessions in law and tax affairs were granted by the Crown. Areas of devolved jurisdiction, 'stannaries', were created. Each had a stannary town, such as Helston, Truro, Launceston and Lostwithiel, where tin quality was assured and tax was collected.

Originally, rocks containing ore would have been pounded into fine sand in something resembling a large kitchen pestle and mortar. Then eventually a distinctive machine was developed: a stamping mill, or Cornish stamp. Tucked away in a little valley leading down to Trevellas Cove on Cornwall's north coast is an extraordinary survival: a working, water-powered Cornish stamp that is still used to produce tin.

It is a marvellous piece of kit, based on very ancient and simple technology. A water wheel turns a large shaft or cylinder with tooth-like metal protrusions arranged around it (the camshaft). These catch lugs on an array of stout wooden posts (stamp stems), which rise and drop rhythmically with the turning of the wheel. It looks rather like a giant vertical version of those little old music boxes that produce a tune when you crank their handle.

The stamp stems are shod with iron and thump away at a small water-filled trough into which lumps of ore-rich rock are tipped. The rock is gradually crushed and the resulting mix of sediment and water is channelled into a circular pit called a 'buddle'. Next, arms adorned with brushes made of heather rotate to rake the sediment gently and separate out the finer, ore-rich grains. Further washing and separation is required to get even finer particles that can be smelted to produce molten tin. Mark Wills runs the whole operation there at Blue Hills Tin Streams, from gathering ore washed out on the shore in the ancient streaming fashion, to producing tin jewellery, gifts and commissions specifically made to order.

This is a quiet and lovely spot now, but the scars and spoil on the sides of the valley and cove, though now partially hidden by vegetation, hint at a very busy industrial scene. Imagine cartloads of rock being hacked from scoops and tunnels by miners. Nearby 'Bal maidens', female workers ('bal' is a Cornish word for mine) would be breaking up rocks into smaller lumps with sledgehammers. A series of stamps down the valley would be pounding away. Buddles, supervised by 'buddle boys' would be continually rotating, and smelters would belch heat, flame and smoke.

Close to the stamping mill are the ruins of another piece of technology that transformed the mining industry in Cornwall, and across the world. The engine house of the former Blue Hills Mine, solidly built of local Killas stone rubble, rises majestically above the scrub like the tower of a huge, medieval fortified house. The interior is empty of machinery now, the building is a big roofless rectangular cylinder, but this was where the crucial mine pumping engine once relentlessly chugged away.

Flooding was a continual problem in mines. Digging adits (near horizontal tunnels) as drainage conduits worked only as far as gravity permitted. Using manual or horse-powered chains of buckets allowed mines to go a little deeper, but it was steam pumps that allowed mines to be deepened and extended to hitherto unimaginable depths and lengths. Steam engines propelled the Cornish mining industry to global significance.

The first experimental steam engines were designed in the seventeenth century, but it was the Newcomen 'atmospheric engine', which used condensing steam to create a vacuum to power a piston, that became the first to be widely rolled out.

First used in Black Country coalmines, by 1715 it was employed in Cornish mines. Newcomen's design was improved by James Watt, the celebrated steam engineer of the industrial revolution. Subsequent developments, notably by Richard Trevithick, a Cornish mining engineer, resulted in the much more powerful and efficient, high-pressure 'Cornish engine'. The basic 'beam engine' principle, however, endured and the demand for steam power only increased.

Around 3000 engine houses, similar to the Blue Hills one, were built across Cornwall and west Devon. The remains of around a tenth of these survive. Because the engines worked on the same principle, the classic engine houses that characterise the south-west coast follow the same basic design as the Blue Hills example. They all have one wall that is notably thicker than the others. This wall, the 'bob wall', supported the great weight of the engine's beam. Very close by the bob wall was a deep shaft (hopefully now protected by capping or filled in) into which the pump rods extended. There was usually a pond nearby to store water for the steam engine.

The Blue Hills engine house has one variation in format, in that its tall chimney is situated some distance away up the valley side instead of being right alongside the engine house as most of them are. At Blue Hills, the chimney top had to be raised well above the floor of the valley to get sufficient draw and disperse the fumes. A conduit fed the smoke from the engine house up to the chimney. Steam engines were used not only for pumping, but also for winding up ore, to power primitive elevators for miners, and for running ore-processing machinery.

Engine houses and their chimneys have become instantly

recognisable icons of the Cornish coast, the 'Tin Coast'. In places such as St Agnes Head, Rinsey Head and Botallack they cling to the cliffs, lashed by the sea's salt spray. This is because the mines they served went right out under the sea. Levant Mine, where a working 1840s Cornish winding beam engine can still be seen, went down nearly 2000 feet below sea level, and extended around a mile out to sea. It often took a very long time for miners to climb down ladders and get to the working face. This was an exhausting, precarious, non-productive hour before the real work began. The heat and air quality this far underground was terrible. Falls, accidents with explosives, collapses and flooding added to the daily dangers.

In 1919, thirty-one miners were killed at Levant Mine when the 'man engine' (a primitive lift) broke and plunged down the shaft. By this time the Levant Mine was already in decline, but in its heyday it had been a 'champion' mine, capable of producing huge amounts of both copper and tin. Many mines could extract both metals, which greatly improved their resilience to changing markets. In the late eighteenth century, Cornish mines supplied the majority of the world's copper. Already vital for engineering in the early industrial age, copper became even more in demand for electrical engineering in the nineteenth century.

Tin, which had long been extremely useful for all sorts of applications, found another huge demand from the second half of the nineteenth century when canned food moved from becoming a niche market to a global household staple. It was not just these metals that the mines produced. Silver, zinc, lead and wolfram (tungsten ore) were also extracted to lesser degrees. However, another extremely useful, though notorious, metalloid became especially important.

On top of the cliffs at Botallack, not far from the Levant Mine on Cornwall's north coast, is a ruined, wide stone arch that leads to a rectangular courtyard. Rows of little barrel-vaulted stone chambers line both sides of the courtyard. It looks like a primitive prison, or perhaps a large cellar complex of some kind, but there is a tall chimney at one end, and it sits among the remains of other industrial structures. This is a calciner complex. There mined ore was heated to produce vapour that was then circulated in the 'labyrinth' of chambers. The vapour cooled in the chambers leaving a powder residue on their walls: arsenic.

This is a highly poisonous material that is fatal in tiny doses. I was going to look up quickly the exact size of a fatal dose, but I did not want that in my internet search history. The arsenic residue was scraped from the walls of the condensing chambers by labourers. Their only protection was to smear their arms with wet clay, stuff cotton wool up their nostrils, and wrap handkerchiefs over their nose and mouth.

Arsenic is actually a very versatile substance. It was not only helpful for Agatha Christie plots, but was a widely used pesticide, employed as rat poison and sprayed on crops as an insecticide. In carefully measured doses it also treated various illnesses, and was an early Botox-like makeup ingredient. It was also used to put vibrant green colours into wallpaper and dresses. Arsenic production was therefore a very good source of extra income for mines when copper and tin prices fell. In the 1870s a few mines in Cornwall produced half the world's total supply of arsenic.

The Cornwall and West Devon World Heritage Site inscription emphasises the period between 1700 and 1914, which was the most transformational and globally significant height of the region's mining history. The remains of the mining industry are very widespread, not just within the World Heritage Site boundaries. Even where physical traces of a mine have gone, or are difficult to make out now, the placename 'wheal' is an indicator of its presence. It is a word derived from old Cornish and means something like 'workings', but is specifically applied to mine names, hence 'Wheal Coates', 'East Wheal Rose', 'Wheal Kitty', 'Wheal Button', and others.

It was not just the mines themselves that transformed the coastal landscape. Vast quantities of coal to power the engines, building materials, and other vital goods such as timber for pit props had to be brought to the region as cost-effectively as possible. The products of the mines, of course, had to be shipped out. Before railways, the sea was the only feasible import and export option.

In 1791, landowner and businessman Charles Rashleigh commissioned the renowned engineer John Smeaton to build a new harbour at an obscure fishing hamlet called Porthmuer (or Polmear) on Cornwall's south coast. The plan was to export copper from nearby mines, but the construction of a suitable facility there required considerable ingenuity. An innovative wet dock was constructed, controlled by lock gates, so that large ships could be brought in and loaded while afloat. The dock had to be topped up by fresh water from specially constructed reservoirs above the harbour, which themselves had to be fed by a conduit that brought water from a valley seven miles away.

Ships were pulled in and out of the narrow harbour entrance from the open sea by a winch system. The new harbour was a success, handling the export of china clay, pilchards, copper ore, stone and the import of coal and many other things necessary for industry. The substantial village that was built around the harbour was named Charlestown. The harbour exported china clay until 1999, and then closed as an industrial facility. At one time it was said that one half of the harbour was white, coated in china clay dust, while the other half was black with coal dust.

Charlestown is now celebrated as one of Cornwall's most attractive historic harbours and a major tourist destination. Its remarkably intact Georgian character has led to starring roles in many period dramas. Heritage tall ships are still based in the harbour, and it is an impressive and evocative sight to see them berthed there or going out to sea, much as they did in Rashleigh's time.

Cornish mining technology, expertise and the miners themselves were exported around the world. It was widely said that the definition of a mine was 'a hole with one or more Cornishmen at the bottom'. The Cornish diaspora is perhaps less famous and less celebrated than those of the Irish and Scots, but Cornish people either went to work temporarily or emigrated to North America, Central America, South America, South Africa, Asia, Australia and New Zealand.

That is why you can find pasties in California and Mexico, where there is even a museum of pasties. Ironically, it was partly this exported expertise that helped fledgling mining industries in other countries to grow and finally undercut and drive Cornish mining out of business. Emigration of Cornish families increased as the mines at home became less viable and closed down one by one.

Much of the Cornish coast and a good part of its moorlands were once raw, post-industrial, heavily polluted landscapes. The scars of quarries and mines were like open wounds. Mounds of spoil were left to settle, toxins percolated into the ground. Filthy, contaminated mine water drained into the sea. The metamorphosis of this battered coast into a tourism hotspot and the transformation of the rusting infrastructure of industry into romantic ruins is not simply a matter of time and nature softening and disguising the man-made wreckage.

Much thought, effort and money has gone into the clean-up and conservation. A dangerous, collapsing, scrub-covered engine house, adorned with decaying 'keep out' signs is not as romantic as one that has been carefully consolidated and managed in the same way as many castle ruins. So successful and celebrated has the Cornish coast become for nature, leisure, culture and heritage that it is almost impossible to think of renewed mining as even a remote possibility in its future, rather than a chapter from its past.

However, the most innovative technology of today and tomorrow is still very heavily reliant on what can be extracted from the earth. The same geological richness that saw Cornwall become internationally important for its tin, copper and arsenic has another sought-after element in its mix. Lithium is useful for all sorts of applications, but it is the metal's use in rechargeable batteries that has led to it becoming the 'white gold' necessary for global transition to renewable energy.

Cornish Lithium Plc claims that Cornwall has the largest

lithium deposits in Europe and that it can extract these in an environmentally friendly manner, from underground water and from rock in old china clay workings. A demonstration site to prove the concept received planning permission in April 2025. Time will tell if this leads to another, unexpected Cornish mining boom in the middle of the twenty-first century.

CHEMICALS AND COAL

Britain's coast has had a very much greater influence on the history of farming than might be first supposed. A vast amount of formerly marshy coastal land has been turned into productive arable land. Ports have facilitated the export of agricultural produce and therefore have encouraged farming for more than just the home market. Ports also handle imports that compete with British farm produce, and therefore force home farming to take different directions and strive to become evermore efficient. They import agricultural equipment and materials, too, such as tractors and fertilisers.

In a surprising number of pretty locations around Britain's coast you can find the remains of a once very widespread industry that was vital to both the farming and building industries. The Romans appreciated the qualities of lime as a key constituent of building materials. The building boom in medieval times relied on huge quantities of the stuff for mortar to bond stonework and for renders, plasters and limewashes to coat both stone-built and timber-framed buildings. Lime was also increasingly used as an agricultural dressing to reduce the acidity of soils and allow a greater range of crops to be grown.

All over Britain, wherever limestone or chalk outcrops, you can find evidence of historic lime quarrying and lime burning. It is perhaps more surprising to see this evidence at the coast rather than inland where the vast majority of the product was used, but the coast played a highly significant role in the industry.

In the famously attractive Devon coastal village of Clovelly, among the buildings overlooking the little harbour, is a structure that should invite some curiosity. It is a large construction built of coursed stone rubble, with a curving wall. Attached to the curving section of wall is a short length of straight wall that has a large, pointed arch opening in it. The steps that take you up the village's incredibly steep single street adjoin the structure and give access to its top. There is a large central shaft (now protected by railings for safety) that tapers to the bottom of the structure. It all looks like the base of some massive medieval tower built to defend the harbour. It is in fact a limekiln, and probably dates to no earlier than the nineteenth century.

What on earth is it doing there in what otherwise looks like a little fishing village? The answer is that producing lime relied on bulk materials, large quantities of limestone or chalk rubble, and lots of coal and brushwood. Clovelly is a notoriously difficult village to bring goods into by land. Donkeys previously hauled supplies up and down the main street. Locals still use sledges to bring furniture, household equipment and groceries to their houses. Heavy cargoes of limestone and coal could be brought in much more easily by sea, and the manufactured lime taken up the hill or away by boat.

Lime burning generated a lot of heat, which might have been

nice for nearby residents in winter, but it also created toxic fumes and smoke, which in this location at the foot of the village would have been bad at any time of year. However, a village that already had to put up with the guts and gore from fishing and fish processing, and had a cholera-inducing open sewer running down its centre, was probably resigned to having this latest acrid addition to its business.

A huge bank of limekilns forms the centrepiece of the harbour side at Seahouses in Northumberland. Again, I suspect that many people enjoying a trip out of the harbour mistake them for some kind of ancient fortification or storehouses. They do now act as stores. The seven regularly spaced, large, round-arched entrances to the limekilns have long been furnished with double doors, allowing harbour-related equipment to be stored in the limekiln chambers. The open tops of the kilns have been sealed and now form a grass terrace on which patrons of the Bamburgh Castle Inn can enjoy food and drink at picnic tables while they look out over the harbour.

These limekilns were a large part of the impetus for the development of the industrial and commercial harbour at Seahouses. Not far away, to the south of Seahouses at the little harbour of Beadnell, is a huge free-standing, castle-like array of limekilns. This was begun by one Richard Pringle in 1798 with the expectation of producing more than a thousand cartloads of lime per year. The enterprise was successful, so two more limekilns were added on and lime was shipped from there to other English and Scottish harbours.

A few miles to the north of Seahouses, on the tidal island of Lindisfarne, in the shadow of Lindisfarne Castle, is yet another well-preserved bank of limekilns. This was built by a Scottish lime merchant in 1860, and again much of the lime produced there went to Scotland. Thirty-five men were employed at the lime works there, enough to spark the development of a new little hamlet around the quarry not far away on the island. These limekilns, just like Lindisfarne Castle, are designated as a scheduled monument, and like the castle are an evocative, physical reminder of an important chapter in the island's past.

Evidence of chemical industries can be found right around Britain's coast. A long time ago I attended Teesside Polytechnic, and due to a shortage of accommodation I was billeted with lots of other students in a large Victorian hotel on the seafront at Redcar. The daily train ride I took every day to Middlesbrough seemed to wind through mile upon mile of steaming industry, and I distinctly remember seeing, right alongside the tracks, people in protective spaceman-like suits prodding at various hatches from which flames leapt.

Later, while living in Middlesbrough, there were occasional leakages from chemical factories, and advice over local radio to keep doors and windows closed until potentially poisonous gas clouds had dispersed. There was no escaping the fact that Teesside was a place steeped in the chemical, iron and steel industries. It was everywhere you looked. I played cricket for a good local team with the poetic sounding name of Billingham Synthonia. It was a team founded at the ICI chemical plant and its name is simply a contraction of 'synthetic ammonia', which is what the plant produced.

Much like other areas of the coast, the landscape itself bore tell-tale scars of a long industrial heritage. Roseberry Topping, a hill of around 1000 feet that overlooks Teesside, was named by the Vikings. This was the childhood adventure training ground for Captain James Cook. But the highly distinctive half-conical, Matterhorn-like summit that I approached on my hikes is not quite the one the young Cook would have known. Its current shape is a result of a landslip in 1912, when mining exacerbated a geological fault. Sandstone was quarried here, and there are ironstone workings beneath the hill and across the district. Salt was also mined in the area. The beloved natural landscape of this edge of the North Yorkshire Moors is in fact a former industrial landscape.

Huge quantities of coal, mined not far away, were handled at a new railway-serviced port built on the Tees in the first half of the nineteenth century. All this industry caused massive growth. In 1801, Middlesbrough was a farming community of around twenty-five souls. In 1835 Sir George Head reported:

The town of Middleborough . . . has not yet, generally speaking, been laid down on the maps; nevertheless, in addition to the coal wagons from the Darlington pits, of which frequently not less than three hundred may be seen together at the staithes, a communication by steam for passengers has been also established with Stockton, from whence trains of carriages have departed and returned thither, for these twelve months past, regularly six times a day.

By 1871 Middlesbrough had a population of nearly 40,000, and had already been a chartered borough, with a mayor and councillors, for nearly twenty years. By 1901 it was a bustling and sprawling 'modern' industrial port town of over 90,000 people.

Another industry was instrumental in establishing this area as a hub for chemical production, and this too has left its transformational and striking mark on the coastline. A long walk south along the Cleveland Way from the small seaside village of Skinningrove (with its neighbouring modern steel plant and 'Land of Iron' mining museum) takes you through an extraordinary clifftop landscape. There the hills have been quarried back to form a second, artificial, stepped cliff upon the clifftops. The scale of the work is staggering. It is immediately apparent that only something special and highly prized could justify moving this amount of rock.

Britain's medieval economy was heavily reliant on wool and woollen garment production. Alum was used as a dye fixative, which was important to keep colours stable and vibrant. Unfortunately, Britain did not have naturally occurring supplies of the pure source mineral, so had to import alum from Mediterranean countries. It was eventually discovered, however, that adding alkali to aluminium sulphate could replicate the product. In the sixteenth century some people in Britain had started to try to locate shale beds rich in aluminium sulphate. Some early alum production sites were established on the south coast of England, but most of the industry was concentrated on the Cleveland and North Yorkshire coast.

In fact, credit for the introduction of alum manufacture in Britain is given to Sir Thomas Chaloner, whose family had acquired the lands of Gisborough Priory on the northern edge of the North Yorkshire Moors, near Redcar and Middlesbrough.

Chaloner had visited the alum works of the Papal States in Italy. His cousin (also Thomas Chaloner) had prospected for alum in Ireland, writing a scientific work on the subject in 1584. The cousins agreed that the vegetation growing on parts of the North Yorkshire estate was similar to that known to grow on alum-bearing deposits. It is said that Sir Thomas smuggled out some of the Pope's expert alum workers to help him start the industry in England.

Finding potentially suitable deposits was only the start of a difficult and laborious process. Tons of unsuitable rock had to be removed to get at the right shale. This was not without some side benefits, since the sandstone rubble overburden could be used for construction, and ironstone could feed into the iron industry. Some shale even contained jet, which would become especially sought after in the middle of the nineteenth century.

The exposed shale then had to be barrowed into huge heaps (or clamps) and burnt, fuelled by brushwood. These had to be tended and kept at a fairly consistent temperature, and then allowed to cool. The process took months. Mariners recalled seeing these cliffs glowing with flames at night. The calcined shale was then steeped in water-filled pits to dissolve out the salts, which produced alum liquor. The steeping process probably happened several times to get a concentrated product, which was further refined in settling tanks, before being transported to a nearby 'alum house' where it was further concentrated, crystallised and washed.

As the liquor boiled in lead-lined pans to reach a specific density, a very necessary ingredient was added: human urine. Vast quantities of the stuff were collected from the locality and from places such as Newcastle, Sunderland, Hull and London to be shipped into local harbours such as Staithes. If you have to convey such a cargo, it is best to do so by sea, rather than bumping along the rutted highways and byways in carts. The sea gave coastal alum works the advantage of easier import of bulk raw materials such as urine and coal, and good export routes for their finished product.

The alum industry in this region began in earnest in the early seventeenth century and the final works there closed in 1871. The clifftops between Skinningrove and Staithes, and a little further down the coast at Kettleness, are not just scarred and sculpted by alum shale quarrying over this time, but also coloured by it. The areas where this industry took place contrast greatly with the verdant-topped natural colour of the cliffs. The exposed grey shale appears like a lunar landscape, devoid of vegetation, loose and crunchy underfoot. Occasionally there are heaps of reddish, calcined and burnt shale.

The remains of this historic industry, Britain's first chemical industry, combine with the scars and archaeological remains of ironstone quarrying and mining here to give this beautiful, rugged coastal landscape an additional layer of fascination and heritage. But few tourists who visit the charming historic port village of Staithes are aware of its industrial past and the noxious substances it once handled.

Coalmining is another industry that we tend not to associate with the seaside, and yet it has had a profound effect on the British coast. The coal industry is most closely identified with the extensive coalfields of South Wales, central Scotland and the industrial Midlands and north of England, though significant coalmining also took place in areas as diverse as Somerset, the Forest of Dean and Kent. The early name for coal, 'sea-coal', may derive from the coal washed up on beaches, having eroded out of coal seams in cliffs. Another interpretation is that many people associated coal with the sea because it was delivered to them by boat. However, sea-coal was a term widely applied to the coal mined many miles inland.

Whatever the origin of the name, coalmines became a significant feature of the coasts of Wales, Scotland, north-east England and Cumbria as the industry mushroomed during the later nineteenth century. The adaptation and development of ports to handle coal happened not only in these regions, but wherever coal was needed, which was everywhere.

The huge, sprawling extent of coalmining infrastructure, the sheer griminess of the substance, and the huge impact of the industry on the coast is becoming harder for us to envisage as clear-up operations and nature reclaim coal-contaminated beaches, dunes and cliffs. Not coming from a coal-mining region, one of my formative insights into the effect of this industry on the coastline came from an unlikely source: the classic British gangster film *Get Carter* (1971).

This is a deeply unsettling film for many reasons, but the horror and gloom of its ending is perfectly accentuated by the environment chosen for the final scenes. Michael Caine's character chases his adversary along the beach at Blackhall Colliery, near Hartlepool in north-east England. The beach is black with coal, black spoil heaps envelop the cliffs. Waves coloured grey-black by coal dust slosh to the shore under a leaden sky.

An aerial pulley system suspended from giant concrete pylons relentlessly hauls its huge iron tubs towards the final pylon, just off shore, where they tilt and disgorge black mining waste straight into the sea, then return to be filled again. Spoiler alert. Michael Caine's foe ends up being dumped from one of these tubs into the sea. Caine is then shot by a distant sniper. He collapses onto the black sand and is claimed by the funereal surf.

Today this beach is unrecognisable. Barely a trace of this once all-consuming industry remains following a multi-million pound clean-up lasting several decades. The colliery buildings have been demolished, the concrete pylons that reached out into the sea have gone, and on a bright day the stretches of golden sand and green-topped cliffs here look almost tropical.

I went to Whitehaven in Cumbria in 2024, keen to explore a historic port that I knew had a fascinating history, but a place I had only briefly visited previously. Whitehaven is a famous home casualty of the American War of Independence. John Paul Jones, father of the United States Navy, attacked the port in 1778. The town was set ablaze as his raiding party attempted to destroy ships and the harbour's defences.

Spotting walls and ruins that I thought might be old fortifications connected with this episode, I went up the hillside overlooking the harbour to take a closer look. There I found a whitewashed two-storey tower with a castellated parapet. But as I approached I recognised it as a late nineteenth-century interpretation of a fortified dwelling, and certainly not the real deal. It is the sort of building that the owners of stately homes built as gate lodges, but this windswept spot is not an obvious location for a country mansion.

It was in fact the former entrance lodge for a coalmine, the Wellington Pit, on whose site I was now walking. Nearby is a tall ornate column that rises into the sky from this prominent clifftop site. I had initially mistaken this as a memorial of some kind. The 'candlestick', as it is known locally, was actually the chimney for a mine engine boiler and later served to ventilate the underground workings.

The lodge, chimney and other buildings of the mine now demolished were designed by Sydney Smirke, a celebrated nineteenth-century architect. Smirke was also responsible for the circular reading room at the British Museum, the dome of London's Imperial War Museum, the Carlton Club in Pall Mall, the nave roof of York Minster, and a host of other prominent buildings around the country. It is clear that when the pit was sunk in 1838 it was expected to be a highly important, productive presence in the locality for a very long time. Architectural quality and appearances obviously mattered to its owner, who commissioned one of the best architects available.

Once I had got my eye in, I noticed more tell-tale traces of mining. There were deep gouges in the hillside and an inclined plane where tubs of coal were once hauled. The moles had thrown up mini spoil heaps of black, coal-dust earth. A stone's throw away was the remains of the fan house and engine house of the Dukes Pit, which also resembles a ruined medieval castle from a distance. These were just two pits of the extensive coalfields in the locality owned by the Lowther family. What remains there is a mere fragment of the mining infrastructure that once sat alongside Whitehaven harbour, but it serves as an important, physical and visible reminder of the role of the coal industry in shaping the town and coast there. The mine workings extend four miles out under the sea, flooded, hidden and forgotten.

Coalmining did not just scar the landscape, but came at a huge human cost. A modern memorial on the path back down the cliff side, in the shape of a sombre black pyramid, records the region's worst mining disaster. In May 1910, an underground explosion in Wellington Pit killed 136 men and boys. It was far from the only tragedy there. On the opposite (north) side of Whitehaven's harbour an explosion in August 1947 killed 104 miners. The appalling effect of both disasters on many families in Whitehaven and surrounding villages is hard to imagine.

The Wellington mine closed in 1933. The last Whitehaven coalmine closed in 1986. Although the end of this difficult, dangerous occupation was undoubtedly welcomed by many, it left an employment vacuum that this coastal district and many other places have struggled to fill ever since.

As I walked around Whitehaven, I could not help noticing that the town was not as vibrant as it might have been on a Saturday morning. Perhaps it was the indifferent weather that day, but there seemed to be fewer people about than such a large town should attract. There were several vacant premises in prime positions. A little food fair on the harbour was not thronging either. I noticed the tell-tale signs of various regeneration initiatives over the years: public realm works, such as repaving schemes, gazebos, sculptures, and some striking new buildings, with a scattering of plaques crediting various agencies and grant funders.

That evening, I tuned into to the regional TV news. There was a report on progress with the development of the first deep coalmine in the UK for thirty years. The proposals for this mine, at Whitehaven, had been approved in 2022, but that very day a High Court judge had ruled that the planning case was flawed and had overturned the planning decision.

Representatives of various environmental groups who had challenged the planning approval gleefully waved placards outside the Royal Courts of Justice in London. They had seen off what they perceived as the return of a greenhouse-gas generating monster. Back in Whitehaven the vox pops on the street painted a different picture. Local people, some of whom said they were descended from coalminers, and therefore might have been all too aware of the direct human cost of the industry, expressed disappointment that the 500 jobs that the new deep mine promised would not now materialise.

Piecemeal regeneration initiatives only go so far. What Whitehaven, and so many other coastal towns need, is solid employment opportunities and investment. Whitehaven and its district seems prepared to live with some of the less-than-desirable aspects of industry to get them.

NUCLEAR POWER

Later that week, I turned off the main road just a few miles south of Whitehaven and followed a side road that is curiously large, well-made and purposeful for a route that I knew must terminate near the shore. From the main road, at a distance of several miles, I had glimpsed masts, flues and large hangar-like buildings through the rain and mist. Curiosity had led me there. Now I was finally up close I could see this sprawling complex was surrounded by circuits of high-security fencing, festooned with warning signs and topped with coils of razor wire. There was a giant, shiny, egg-shaped building, and something that looked like one of those massively elevated control towers you find in the largest airports in the world. It was as suitably sinister as I could have expected.

This is Sellafield, Europe's largest nuclear establishment. It comprises the widest range of nuclear facilities to be found anywhere in the world on one single site. Sellafield, along with many other coastal sites that are now modern industrial, technological and nuclear complexes, originated in military use, in this case as a wartime Royal Ordnance Factory. The Calder Hall nuclear power station, whose construction began there in 1953, was the first in the world to provide electricity on a commercial basis to a public power grid. Its primary purpose, however, was the production of weapons-grade plutonium. In October 1957, overheating of an earlier version of a reactor there sent plumes of radioactive material across the locality, the UK and Europe.

To many people the former name of the place, Windscale, was as notorious as Chernobyl is now. But this accident did not prevent the site growing to take on more roles over the decades. Long renamed, the place now specialises in decommissioning nuclear facilities, and the storage and reprocessing of nuclear waste. Sellafield directly employs around 10,000 people. Its presence supports many more jobs, having attracted science parks, educational opportunities and service industries. Employment has uplifted the prospects and spending power of the local workforce to the benefit of a very wide range of local businesses.

Sellafield is the major economic driver for the area, and after around seventy-five years there nuclear energy is as firmly part of the social and economic character of this coast as was coalmining. People seem to have grown very used to living alongside an industry that might be shunned elsewhere.

It was Friday, and at about lunchtime in a generally quiet village nearby, I saw groups of people dressed up for a night out pouring noisily out of minicabs and into the pub. Was it a hen or stag do kicking off early? 'No,' a local told me, 'these are Sellafield people. They knock off early on a Friday, and drink here before getting on the last train to hit the nightspots in Whitehaven.' I hope the night shifts are a sober bunch.

In the tiny coastal hamlet of Sizewell in Suffolk, people have lived with the strange and somewhat forbidding presence of a nuclear power station since 1966. The construction of a second reactor between 1987 and 1995, Sizewell B, with its big white dome, added an even more surreal feature to views across the charming Suffolk coastal landscape. The massive bulk of this nuclear power station appears like a space-age building grafted clumsily onto the rural British landscape for one of those old science-fiction films. This is actually Britain's most modern nuclear power station.

It is a strange and somewhat unnerving experience to approach the Sizewell power station from a walk along the beach in front. The building defines the word 'incongruous'. What possessed the authorities to place it there amid the gentle pleasures of the Suffolk coast, with its thousands of acres of marshland bird reserves, beautiful sand and shingle beaches, grassy dunes, sandy heaths, well-tended farmland and picturesque villages? The seafront location of this nuclear plant also causes some pause for reflection, especially after having seen Dunwich, only four miles or so back along the shore: the town famously swallowed by the sea. The soft low cliffs at Thorpeness, just over a mile to the south of Sizewell, still crumble away at an alarming rate.

EDF (Électricité de France) the French state-owned company that now owns Sizewell, and in fact all of Britain's current nuclear power stations, is confident that this power station will be there for the time being. EDF has announced an intention to extend Sizewell B's life from the original expectation of 2035 to 2055. Not only that, but it has permission and a massive taxpayer-funded subsidy to build Sizewell C, which means two more reactors and a vast extension to the site.

This part of the Suffolk coast caters for those who shun the bright lights and glitz of big seaside resorts. It is busy instead with walkers and birdwatchers, swimmers, sailors, history, art and music lovers. East Suffolk is a sparsely populated, quite well-off area, close enough to London and undeveloped enough to have attracted better-off citizens looking for a homely inter-war style, family seaside holiday experience. There are lots of second homes there.

The jobs promised by Sizewell C are not nearly so welcome there as they would be in Whitehaven. Judging solely by the plethora of banners and signs that have adorned roadsides in the area for several years, many local people are very unhappy indeed with the prospect of Sizewell power station's expansion. All things considered, they think that Sizewell C represents a disaster for the area. Apart from anything else, the area faces many years of construction traffic. The small cafe that serves visitors to the beach will probably continue to thrive, however. It is called 'Sizewell Tea'.

Nuclear power stations require locations that are relatively remote, away from large centres of population. At the same time they must be accessible to the transport network and power grid, and have to be within commuting reach for a sizeable, specialist staff complement. They also require lots of cooling water. There are currently nine operational nuclear reactors, located at five main sites in Britain, with others undergoing decommissioning or construction. All but one of Britain's nuclear power stations have been built at the coast. If nuclear energy remains a key power-generating tool in the transition to 'green' energy, there is every reason to expect new nuclear power stations will follow this trend. But where on the coast will they be built? Nowhere seems quite far enough away.

Then there is the question of what to do with the various kinds of radioactive waste that continues to accumulate. The solution currently being put forward is to store it in facilities under the seabed. Two sites, one off the Cumbrian coast, and another off the Lincolnshire coast, are the current candidates. The geological properties of the seabed are a crucial factor, but so too is the shore infrastructure that will be necessary to transport and process the waste. The heavily contaminated waste will go out of sight and perhaps out of mind beneath the sea, but it will need to be safely transported to the facility and prepared for storage. New rail and road links, some kind of secure depot, and of course large tunnels will all have to be built on the coast.

It is not only nuclear energy that has the potential to affect the British coastline, but also green energy. Proposals for large scale tidal and wave energy generation, which are surely the most reliable forms of renewable energy, have consistently been scuppered by concerns about their effect on the marine environment and habitats. The construction of huge wind farms just offshore has really taken off over the last twenty years or so, but these too are not without their critics.

As previously discussed, the seabed off much of Britain's coast is quite a crowded place these days. And apart from the direct physical impacts and constraints of arrays of giant turbines on the seascape, the power they generate has to be brought onshore and distributed to where it is actually needed. Huge substations and miles of pylons, built where none had previously existed, pose threats to the coastal landscape. Campaigners in East Anglia are opposing one such scheme as vigorously as the campaigners opposed to Sizewell C.

The remnants of the intensive and extensive industry along Britain's coastline are year-by-year being cleaned up and reclaimed by nature. It is important that in transforming these places again, we do not lose sight of their industrial heritage. It is also necessary to recognise that Britain will have to continue to exploit its coastal resources and advantages, though perhaps in new ways, if it is to move forward in the modern world.

CHAPTER 7

Estuaries, Canals and Crossings

Cross Keys Bridge, Lincolnshire

Britain's coast has many inlets and estuaries. These are places
where the coastline takes a detour into the land mass, and where
the influence of the sea extends far inland. They are places

where saltwater and freshwater environments mingle, and where the best of inland resources can meet the best of coastal resources. These special characteristics have been appreciated by wildlife and human life for thousands of years. We may not think of our estuaries as part of our coastline in the same way as we think of the sandy shores and bays of the seaside. But in the same way that these inlets have channelled our coastal waters inland, so too have they channelled much of the character and culture of the coast and seas beyond. They connect inland Britain to the coast and the sea in ways that we do not always immediately appreciate. It is therefore as important to explore these often-overlooked areas of our coastline as much as any other of its elements, in order to truly understand how we are shaped by our watery margins.

From above, the Humber looks like a great, snaking rift on the map of England's east coast. It is as if some giant hands have tried to rip Yorkshire away from Lincolnshire. The otherwise wide-open mouth of the Humber Estuary is partly closed by a long, narrow, curving spit of sand, strictly speaking a long tidal island, called Spurn. Around forty miles away from its mouth, the forked tail of the wide serpentine Humber is formed by the confluence of two great rivers, the River Ouse and the River Trent. The Trent is tidal as far as Cromwell Weir, a few miles north of Newark in Nottinghamshire. This is around thirty-five miles directly inland from the nearest coast, but a very much longer journey by river. The Ouse is tidal until just four miles short of York, through which it passes. Nobody would consider York a coastal city, being also around thirty-five miles from the North Sea as the crow flies, and much further as the fish swim. Yet its history has been shaped by its connectedness to the coast.

York had been a Roman city, *Eboracum,* but after Roman rule in Britain ended, urban life there collapsed, as it did across Britain. The incoming Anglo-Saxon settlers tended to live in small scattered communities at first, but after a few centuries, towns were gradually reinvented. *Eoforwic* sprang up from the ruins of Roman York. The tidal Ouse then helped the Vikings to develop a Northern administrative and trading centre at *Eoforwic*, which they called *Jorvik.*

Jorvik was connected by river, estuary and sea to the Viking settlers' Scandinavian homelands in the same way that *Eoforwic* had been connected to the north-west European land of the Angles. Similarly, the ability to navigate and control the River Trent was one reason why the epoch-defining Viking Great Army chose to establish a massive base on its east bank at Torksey, near Lincoln, in the winter of 872/873.

Ports on estuaries benefit from the ability of tides to bring in large ships from the open sea. Sometimes, as in the case of the Ouse and Trent, rivers feeding into estuaries naturally permit some navigation from the sea to extend far inland. But inevitably there comes a point where the influence of the tide dwindles and where rivers become too shallow and narrow to permit vessels to get any further.

Given the great advantages that access to the sea brings, it is no surprise that over the centuries people have tried to enhance the natural ability of waterways to link inland towns to the coast. Huge efforts have been undertaken to mitigate the natural silting and shifting of estuarine channels and thereby keep places connected to the sea. Cutting entirely new channels has extended the reach and reliability of maritime navigation far inland.

The River Mersey is one of England's great rivers. Its name derives from the Old English for 'boundary', and it formed a frontier between the powerful ancient kingdoms of Mercia and Northumbria, long before England was united as a single kingdom. The river then came to define the boundary between the historic counties of Cheshire and Lancashire. Winding its way from Stockport, past Manchester to Liverpool and the sea, the Mersey was at times in its history capable of supporting river traffic to the lowest medieval bridging point at Warrington.

As early as 1660, however, it was proposed that the river should be improved to permit navigation from the sea into Manchester. It was not until 1724 that work started under the auspices of the Mersey and Irwell Navigation Company. Throughout the eighteenth century, meanders in the River Mersey were bypassed, and weirs and locks were constructed to keep water levels high.

The development of Manchester as Britain's premier production centre for cotton yarn and fabric depended on importing not only huge amounts of raw cotton, but also vast quantities of coal to power the mills and many other vital provisions. Manchester (which became known as 'Cottonopolis') also had to get its products out to the wider world as cheaply and efficiently as possible. Transporting bulky materials by water directly from the sea kept haulage costs down and gave Manchester a crucial international commercial edge.

The navigable Mersey competed with, but also complemented and fed other waterways being constructed to boost trade.

The Bridgewater Canal came to be seen as the first great achievement of the canal age and the inspiration for the nation-wide explosion in canal construction that is sometimes called 'canal mania'. The canal originated in the 1750s and was intended primarily to feed coal into Manchester from its mining hinterland, but was ultimately extended to the Wirral. The Trent and Mersey Canal followed hot on the heels of the Bridgewater Canal, linking with it to provide an efficient route from the north-west coast right down into the industrial Midlands. These canals thereby boosted the development of the world-famous potteries at Stoke on Trent.

The Trent and Mersey Canal connected to the navigable River Trent near Nottingham, which in turn fed into the Humber to create a great waterway loop that linked the port of Liverpool with the port of Hull. The west coast and east coast had been effectively joined in the centre of England. Something similar happened in southern England with the completion of the Kennet and Avon Canal in 1810. This linked the Severn Estuary and River Avon at Bristol with the River Thames, London and the south-east coast. By the middle of the nineteenth century, Britain had a network of waterway arteries that fed its industrial centres, and connected many of them to the sea.

The various cuts and canals that had augmented, shifted and replaced the old River Mersey were eventually themselves cut through, bypassed and superseded by an even mightier engineering feat. In 1894, after six years of construction, the largest river canal navigation in the world had been built. The Manchester Ship Canal cost the then astronomical sum of around £15 million, but this investment allowed huge ocean-going vessels to dock at Manchester, which then became Britain's third largest port. Manchester may not have been brought to the coast, but the coast, nearly forty miles away, was effectively brought to Manchester.

Maritime trade at Manchester was still going strong in the 1950s, but had dwindled by the 1980s. Much former dockland has since been redeveloped and repurposed for new uses, especially at Salford Quays, where the Media City complex is situated, which hosts BBC and ITV studios and many other facilities, businesses and attractions. Nevertheless, it is still remarkable to see the remnants of huge, coastal dock infrastructure so far inland, and strange to see the occasional seagoing vessel progressing along the canal. In fact, the construction of Manchester United's new £2 billion Old Trafford stadium will depend upon ships and barges. The prefabricated components of what will become the largest stadium in the UK will be brought in along the nearby Manchester Ship Canal.

It is perhaps an even stranger sight to see a former lightship (a floating lighthouse) moored at the West Country city of Gloucester. Few visitors who come into Gloucester after bimbling through the Cotswolds would expect to find a hint of the sea there, so far inland. However, following the brown signs adorned with an anchor to 'Gloucester Quays' around the bypass, or taking the short walk from the city centre, will reward you with much more than simply another out-of-town shopping complex.

Gloucester Docks, like Salford Quays, has seen huge redevelopment in recent decades, but it retains many of its historic buildings and much of its character. Gigantic multi-storey brick warehouses and other early industrial buildings, now converted into blocks of flats, shops and restaurants, surround a series of large, water-filled dock basins. Some former dock buildings are still derelict or covered in scaffolding awaiting repair and conversion.

Among the canal boats and other vessels now moored on the water of Gloucester Docks is *LV14 Sula*. It is painted bright red and still has its lighthouse installation. This boat did sterling work warning shipping of the Spurn Sandbank off the Humber Estuary from 1959–85. Due to be scrapped, instead it went on an odyssey to several British ports under a variety of different names and uses, before being brought to Gloucester in 2010. Its journey to the city was made possible by the Gloucester and Sharpness Canal.

There had been a quay at Gloucester since Roman times and the city was officially designated as a port for international trade by Elizabeth I. The River Severn, flowing into the Bristol Channel, however, has never been the easiest to navigate. River traffic there has to contend with notorious quirks, such as a huge tidal range and the famous Severn bore – a series of mini tsunamis that propel themselves from the estuary, past Gloucester, as far inland as Tewkesbury. These occur around 260 times in the year and most are manageable, but some are severe enough to cause flooding.

The Gloucester and Sharpness Canal was the widest and deepest canal in the world when finally completed in 1827. It provided a lock-controlled sixteen-mile bypass of the River Severn and its difficult conditions, and provided much easier access for coastal vessels right into Gloucester. The city's docks flourished from then on, accompanied by a building boom of massive grain warehouses, mills, and all the facilities a busy port required. Even though ever larger ships necessitated the development of new docks closer to the sea at Sharpness, Portishead and Avonmouth, coasters and barges continued to bring goods to and from Gloucester until the 1980s.

The gradual rescue and regeneration of the historic docks is a major triumph. Almost unbelievably, Gloucester is still able to welcome from the sea some huge, stately survivors of the great age of sail, during its periodic Tall Ships Festival.

The success in turning inland places into coastal ports enjoyed at such places as Manchester and Gloucester was not guaranteed by extraordinary engineering feats alone. History tends to remember the most long-lived and successful endeavours, but forgets that even in eras of spectacular industrial and commercial growth, there was plenty of speculation and investment that did not quite pay off.

Carlisle, like Manchester and Gloucester, was a place identified by the army and officials of the Roman Empire as a strategic spot. There a significant river crossing could be controlled, and possibilities for river navigation to the sea exploited. Carlisle maintained its military importance in medieval and early modern times as a border stronghold. But when the border feuds died out and the age of industrialisation began, the shallow and tidal River Eden was found to be an unsatisfactory inhibitor of Carlisle's growth. A plan was hatched to build a new port closer to the sea on the Solway Firth, at a lonely spot called Fishers Cross.

It was initially thought that this new facility would form

part of a highly ambitious cross-country canal scheme to link Carlisle and ports on the north-west coast with Newcastle on the north-east coast. In the event this project was not pursued, but a better connection to the sea was still considered vital to Carlisle's prosperity. Therefore a canal was built to link Carlisle to its new port at Fishers Cross, soon renamed Port Carlisle. There a sea lock and canal basin were constructed.

Completed in 1823, the canal required eight locks over its eleven and a bit miles length in order to get sizeable sea-faring vessels to wharves in Carlisle. Nevertheless, this was a cheaper, quicker and more reliable way to bring bulky cargoes to and from the city than tracks and roads. It provided Carlisle with greater connectivity to ports such as Liverpool and the wider world. The canal's opening was celebrated by thousands in the city, while country people marvelled at the sight of tall ships apparently gliding through the meadows.

Among the beneficiaries of the new canal was biscuit baron Jonathan Dodgson Carr, who set about building Britain's biggest baking business. Carr's famous biscuits were exported all over the world. Packets of Carr's Table Water Biscuits still have 'Carr's, Carlisle Cumbria 1831' printed on them, even though the product and Carlisle factory have belonged to United Biscuits since the 1970s.

The canal, though, was short-lived. It closed in 1853 and its drained bed was quickly converted into a railway line to serve the port. However, the natural channels of the Solway Firth that fed into the one-time canal port and now rail port were still prone to silting. By this time better port facilities had been developed further round the coast at Silloth. The railway therefore never quite fulfilled its promise and diminished to a horse-drawn passenger service (whose special carriages were quaintly known as a 'Dandy'), then a steam railmotor service, before complete closure in 1932.

Approaching Port Carlisle feels a bit like approaching the very edge of Britain. The narrow coast road from Burgh-by-Sands mostly bypasses small villages on the slightly higher ground, giving an impression of a largely uninhabited landscape. A cattle grid marks the beginning of a long, straight stretch of narrow road across estuarine marsh. There seems to be nowhere else to go but onward into the sea. Signs warn of tidal flooding and indicate the depth of water that might be encountered on the road. Intermittent black and white striped poles at the roadside indicate the width of the road should it become partly submerged.

This would be a nerve-wracking journey on a dark and stormy winter night, but even on the good summer day that I was there, I kept a watchful eye on the creek beds that extended right up to the edge of this barely elevated causeway. I know from my experience of Norfolk salt marshes that when seawater first starts to trickle into the creeks, it is time to get a move on!

In fact, Port Carlisle is not the end of the road, as the pretty, ancient village of Bowness on Solway is next along the route. Nevertheless, taking the coastal road gives a good impression of the vision and ambition required to build a new port, canal and railway in this remote spot.

It is apparent at first glance that there is something very different about Port Carlisle. The boom-and-bust commercial past is clearly visible in the form and fabric of this unusual village. A single, long row of neat terraced, late-Georgian houses face the Solway Firth. Two short streets lead to a back lane, which is only sparsely developed and looks out over the fields. It is evident that the layout of this place was planned on a greenfield site and was probably expected to grow on a grid plan, like the street plans of industrial and commercial towns all across Britain.

Port Carlisle is not a typical Cumbrian farming or fishing village. Away from the single main street, Port Carlisle's dwellings are not quite so well-to-do. There are smaller cottages and a terrace that looks like the conversion of warehouses or other outbuildings. There is also a communal pump and wash yard. This port settlement, in common with all others, clearly had a social hierarchy. A broad range of jobs, trades and professions would have been needed to make the place work, and function as a community.

A survey of 1847 confirms the impression given by the village's buildings. It records residents directly associated with maritime trade such as a harbour master, coastguard, ship owners and master mariners, an engineer, joiner and blacksmith. But there were also a surgeon, tailor, grocer, butcher, bootmaker, linen draper and other shopkeepers, and pub and inn keepers. These are people and amenities that you might find in any sizeable village of the time.

Port Carlisle is a quiet village now. There is no bustling centre or parade of shops. The single pub has closed. Nearly all of the houses are occupied and well looked-after, but apart from clusters of walkers passing by, there are not many people about. A little footpath alongside the Bowling Club leads to the shore of the Solway Firth, and there you can make out the overgrown remains of the canal basin. A trickle of tidal creek runs through the centre of what looks like a large, dried-up village pond. This was where sizeable sailing ships once waited their turn to be towed along the canal to Carlisle.

At the shore, the huge stone blocks that form the entrance of the sea lock can be seen. It is choked with marsh growth now, and its stone walls form the revetment for a cottage lawn. The detached whitewashed cottage and its neighbour, though much-modified in modern times, look suspiciously similar, austere and old in origin. They too were once warehouses associated with the port.

The most striking remains of the port lie just off shore. I will bet that some people who walk along the Hadrian's Wall Path that runs along the shore there mistake the massive wall of red sandstone blocks they see in front of them to be part of the celebrated Roman frontier work. In fact, the line of Hadrian's Wall in this area is marked only by earthworks now. The massive stone wall in the estuary is a nineteenth-century harbour wall that revetted an island wharf. A branch of the rail line once ran out to it. Exploring this edifice further reveals uprooted, giant granite mooring bollards that once secured large ships. There is a flight of stone steps that would have led down to smaller vessels, such as tenders.

Running out from the shore on the opposite side of the sea lock is the remnant of a jetty. Jagged, decayed timbers and rusted iron brackets mark the place where people queued to alight or embark steam packet services. It was not just goods that came by sea to Port Carlisle on their way between Carlisle, Liverpool,

Annan, Whitehaven and Belfast, but also people. Some came as day trippers, to the hotel, or the hot and cold seawater bath there. Many passed through Port Carlisle on the European migration route to America, brought by rail from Newcastle.

Port Carlisle retains much evidence of the type of port infrastructure and housing that can still be seen in many historic British seaports served by canal and rail. There, however, they are fossilised in a place that did not go on to grow. Remnants of Port Carlisle's past have become archaeological monuments, just as fascinating as the remains of Hadrian's Wall.

Despite the advantages of estuaries in enabling maritime access to inland locations, albeit sometimes only after considerable engineering effort, estuaries can also be quite difficult, dangerous and unruly places. They are obstacles to land travel: features that must be bypassed with long road detours or confronted head on with some kind of crossing; either a ford, ferry, bridge, or in modern times, a tunnel. The former two options were vulnerable to unhelpful tides and poor weather, which not only delayed journeys, but often added real jeopardy and danger to travel. Building bridges has been limited by the technology of the era and has always been difficult and expensive. Tunnelling has only been possible in the modern era.

Considerable ingenuity, effort and investment has gone into crossing estuaries, thereby shortening the journey around the coastline, but care had to be taken to ensure that this did not come at the expense of ruining river navigation. Estuaries are places of opportunity, but often also tension and competing interests.

York and Newark are important historic bridging points on

their respective rivers. Other bridges were established on the Ouse and Trent as they made their winding way to the Humber Estuary. Until 1981, however, when the Humber Bridge opened, the crossing of the estuary itself could be made only by ferry. In the eighteenth century, the journey of around six miles is stated to have taken around one and a half hours, if all went well. Sometimes it did not, leaving passengers stranded. Ferry services there are well documented in medieval times. The Romans operated ferries across the Humber Estuary, which interrupted a highly important Roman road between London, Lincoln and York, but the earliest Humber ferries date back to well before the Romans.

The remains of a handful of prehistoric Humber ferry boats have been found at various times between 1937 and 1989, appropriately at North Ferriby on the Yorkshire side of the estuary. They date from around 2000–c.1700 BC. The archaeological evidence reveals that they were sophisticated vessels over forty feet long, made of planks 'sewn' together with yew withies and caulked with moss. They were ideally suited to plying a regular trade carrying people and goods across the estuary and along the coast. They may even have been capable of sea travel.

These are not the only Bronze Age ferries and coasters to be found in Britain. A fragment of a similar boat was found at Caldicot in Gwent in 1990. This one almost certainly navigated the Severn Estuary. An astoundingly complete and well-preserved Bronze Age boat, dated to 1575–1520 BC, was excavated at Dover in 1992. Looking a bit like a massive over-smoked kipper fillet with its conserved blackened timbers laid out in a display case, the 'Dover Boat' is the now the centrepiece of Dover Museum.

This vessel, probably well over thirty-two feet long, undoubtedly cruised along the south coast and across estuaries. It may have been capable of regularly crossing the English Channel.

Prehistoric sewn-plank vessels such as these carrying people, goods and livestock, would not have been an extraordinary sight to Bronze Age people on the shore. This type of vessel was characterised by a distinctive, wide-hulled design specifically suited to those purposes. It was different to the hollowed-out tree-trunk log boats belonging to earlier periods of prehistory, and to the many Bronze Age and Iron Age log boats that were mainly designed for gentler inland rivers.

The crossing of estuaries by boat has a very long history, but crossing by foot has a heritage that extends much further back into prehistory. It was surprisingly commonplace well into the modern era. In St Mary's churchyard, in the little market town of Long Sutton in the South Holland district of Lincolnshire (at the opposite end of the county from the Humber), there is one headstone that is especially intriguing. It is similar in style to some of those around it, but the dedication inscribed on it sets this one apart.

It is a memorial to Charles Wigglesworth, late resident of the nearby village of Sutton Bridge. It records two of Mr Wigglesworth's occupations. He was a coal merchant and, for fifty-two of his eighty-five years, a guide for Sutton Wash. The latter requires some explanation, for when Charles Wigglesworth died on 23 April 1840, so too did the last practitioner of a very particular service that had been vital in this region for centuries, and perhaps for considerably more than a thousand years.

Anyone at all familiar with a map of the British Isles will

recognise what appears to be a large, square-shaped bite that has been taken out of the east coast of England between the bulge of East Anglia and southern part of Lincolnshire. This is the Wash, a wide, shallow tidal inlet formed after the last Ice Age when rising sea levels gradually encroached into a basin of low-lying land we know as the Fens. Ancient meandering rivers from the Midlands and East Anglia drained lazily into the Fens and out into the Wash. This was a place where the coastline was ambiguous and ever-changing.

Drainage and reclamation schemes, especially from the seventeenth century onwards, turned this vast coastal wetland into highly productive farmland. However, even into the nineteenth century, there were substantial areas that had not been tackled. One of these was a wide, funnel-shaped estuary that ran from the waters of the Wash proper down to the port town of Wisbech, which is now ten miles from the sea. It was known as Sutton Wash, or Cross Keys Wash.

In past centuries, many travellers attempting to reach places up and down the eastern margins of England would have taken boats that plied between the east-coast ports, or followed the generally inconvenient inland tracks and roads. There were also more direct coastal routes, but these were not without their hazards. One of many who found himself having to navigate this side of the country in a hurry was King John of England, whose kingdom in 1216 was being ripped apart by civil war.

So it was that after receiving hospitality at the port of Bishop's Lynn in Norfolk (renamed King's Lynn during the reign of Henry VIII), King John set out for the north on 12 October 1216. He probably intended to reach Lincoln Castle, which was still held by loyalists. The simple version of the events that unfolded is that the evil, incompetent King John lost his crown jewels in the Wash, and it served him right.

Imagine autumnal dark and chill starting to descend on a long, slow-moving convoy of armed men, with officials, camp followers, horses, carts and wagons tentatively making its way across a wide expanse of wet sand, mud and marsh. Sticks beat at the flanks of pack and draft animals, urging them on as they stumbled and stalled in the thick, dark slime. Night is coming, the tide will soon be turning, there are still several miles to travel, and there is no refuge out there in the middle of the estuary.

A cart suddenly lurches to one side, and comes to a stop, spilling its contents as it tilts crazily and settles into the mud. It is stuck fast. Frantic efforts are made to retrieve the scattered cargo that went overboard, and to offload the rest to other carts. The convoy backing up behind is forced to wind around the scene of the accident and leave the relative safety of the narrow track. More carts grind to a halt. A large covered wagon crashes on to its side, spilling its contents of fine cloth, rich ornaments and shattered caskets of coins into the churned-up water and mud. The situation is becoming chaotic and desperate.

Various accounts of what happened during the crossing were recorded at the time and long afterwards. The medieval chronicler Roger of Wendover, who probably wrote his account not long after the event, states that King John 'lost all his carts, wagons, baggage horses, together with his money, costly vessels, and everything which he had particular regard for'.[11] Ralph

---

11 *Flores Historiarum*, Roger of Wendover, up to c.1235.

of Coggeshall, who also wrote his chronicle near the time of the incident, though again not as a first-hand witness, wrote that King John 'lost his chapel with his relics, and some of his packhorses with divers household effects'.[12]

Wendover states: 'The land opened up in the middle of the water and caused whirlpools which sucked in everything, as well as men and horses so that no one escaped to tell the king of the misfortune. He himself escaped with his army.' Coggeshall says that 'many members of his household were submerged in the waters of the sea, and sucked into the quicksand there, because they had set out incautiously and hastily before the tide had receded.' What actually happened is still the subject of myth, debate and misinformation more than eight hundred years later.

King John's convoy almost certainly did meet with some kind of disaster. However, the mishap certainly did not happen in the Wash as we now know it. The event occurred in the funnel-shaped estuary of the River Wellstream, Sutton Wash. This was the medieval coastline, but not the coastline as it is today.

Important and valuable items, money, even famous relics, may well have been among the goods and equipment that were never recovered after the accident. There would be little point in going back to try to locate the scene of the disaster in the days following, even if the continuing urgency of conflict and King John's death did not prevent that. Much of what had been lost would be almost impossible to find after a tide or two anyway. The tale of all his treasure disappearing in the incident was probably a convenient cover story for the extreme looting that

---

12 *Chronicon Anglicanum*, Ralph of Coggeshall, up to c.1224.

took place after the king's death at Newark Castle a week later. And King John may not have been right on the spot and directly culpable at the time, though his misjudgement and orders possibly contributed to the disaster.

King John had apparently left the straggling main convoy, taking a smaller group a few miles south to the town of Wisbech, which had a castle and was a bridging point. He probably instructed the larger, slower part of the convoy to take the direct route across the estuary while he took the much longer inland route, with the intention of a rendezvous on the Lincolnshire side after concluding his business in Wisbech.

There was no bridge, road or fixed causeway across Sutton Wash. Instead travellers were led by guides along a soggy route that had to adapt to the shifting pattern of creeks, mudflats and sandbanks of the estuary. It was a journey of only five miles or so across, but one that was hazardous. The crossing had to be carefully timed, with a very good understanding of tides, weather and their influences on both river and sea throughout the seasons. It demanded a good mental map of where the traps of soft sand had developed. This knowledge would have been built up locally over many years.

I can only suppose that any local guide pressed into service on this particular occasion was severely pressured into crossing when the time was not quite right. It is easy to imagine the king or his delegated commander being extremely impatient to get to their next objective during a time of conflict and immense stress.

Coggeshall's comment about setting out incautiously and hastily suggests an impatience to progress. Even if the tide was going out, a shallow depth of water may still have hidden hazards such as creek beds, soft mud or quicksand, and also covered potentially helpful features, such as firm sand. These would have been much more visible when the tide was fully out.

It is easy to envisage wagons or packhorses getting stuck, and perhaps turning over as people struggled to move them along. The contents of sacks, boxes and barrels might have spilled out into the muddy water to be churned up further by frantic feet, hooves and the wheels of other carts and wagons. Items that fell out would be trampled further down into the soft estuarine mud and sands beneath. It is very easy to lose things in that environment. I well remember childhood toys disappearing into the sand and mud of the Wash shore, never to be seen again despite frantic, tearful searching.

The tide comes in quickly in the Wash too. Many times at low tide I have walked an absurdly long way out to find the water's edge, and then much further still to paddle only ankle deep. I always keep a nervous eye out for the first signs of the turning tide: shallow water starting to edge back across the sand, and the first trickles of channels beginning to fill behind me. Sometimes it takes a brisk walking pace to keep ahead of the tide as it races back in across the flat surface.

Once I was due to do some filming at the edge of the salt marsh around the fringe of the Wash, not far from King John's assumed route. We had arranged to be there early enough to capture the incoming tide on drone and stop-motion footage. Part of the way there I realised I had forgotten my wellies and went back for them, still believing I had plenty of time. When the tide got to a certain height, however, it just raced over the marsh, and we nearly missed the crucial shots.

It was another important lesson about this dynamic coastline, and also a lesson learned for filming. Whatever happens, make sure you arrive in time. There are far worse consequences to mistimed visits. People are frequently caught out in the Wash and have to be rescued from rapidly submerging sandbanks. Lives are still lost in what some mistake as being among the most benign stretches of British coast.

After the disastrous crossing, King John was soon laid low by the illness that killed him. Incapable of riding any further, he was transported on a litter to Newark Castle and the reckoning with his maker. This was probably not a death brought on by grief at the loss of his treasures, too many peaches and too much new cider, as Roger of Wendover reported. Nevertheless, the misfortune King John met with at this estuary crossing undoubtedly weighed very heavily on an already troubled mind.

Anybody doing some kind of digging in the area is likely to be met with the gently sarcastic greeting: 'Have you found King John's treasure yet?' As an archaeologist who has worked in the area, I know this only too well. People have periodically claimed to have found something there. But many of the hopeful searchers miss the fundamental point: the coastal landscape there has changed greatly since King John's time.

The key to narrowing down where the event happened is analysing exactly how the coastal geography has altered since the thirteenth century. A certain amount of evidence for this can be read in the landscape today. The course of former sea banks mark the ever-narrowing width of the estuary. Some modern roads follow the meandering course of older roads. The distribution of old villages, farmsteads and place-names indicates medieval coastal settlement patterns. But much evidence lies buried and hidden.

The ancient route across the marshes and sands of Sutton Wash between Norfolk and Lincolnshire was formally incorporated into the highway network during the sixteenth century in the reign of Queen Elizabeth I. Travellers paid the bailiff of the local manor to be escorted across by a guide. Even as recently as the early years of the nineteenth century, Ordnance Survey maps of the area depict this route only as an ephemeral dotted line, marked 'Wash Way'. This is the route that Charles Wigglesworth guided travellers over for much of his life.

In the middle of the nineteenth century, another large-scale reclamation scheme was implemented, draining the estuary and its surroundings to create farmland. A new, straight river cut, known as the River Nene outfall, was excavated to replace the old meandering estuarine river. The new river was confined by banks, which finally made bridging feasible. The estuary bed that medieval travellers trudged across is deeply buried beneath layers of later silt and reclaimed farmland.

All estuaries have a rich social history and physical heritage. The Solway Firth (firth is a Scottish word for sea inlet) is the estuary of the River Esk and River Eden, and forms the westernmost part of the border between Scotland and England. It was formalised as part of the boundary by King Alexander II of Scotland and King Henry III in 1237, but routes across Solway between the two countries had been established long before this. Just like Sutton Wash, crossings of the Solway Firth were not without drama. In February 1216, an army led by King Alexander crossed the estuary on its way to plunder Cumbria.

Some of his troops, apparently against his orders, looted Holme Cultram Abbey. On the way back, the Scottish army with its ill-gotten gains was overwhelmed by a tidal bore.

Nearly 2000 of Alexander's troops were said to have been drowned. Ironically, this was a Scots raid undertaken as retaliation for a raid on Scotland by King John. King Edward I of England also met with his ultimate fate at the Solway Firth. He died of dysentery in February 1307 at Burgh-by-Sands, while encamped on the shore of the estuary in preparation for the crossing on the way to yet another campaign in Scotland. The king's body was brought from the marsh encampment and laid out in the village church at Burgh-by-Sands before being taken down to Westminster Abbey for burial.

There is an elegant memorial column on a lonely patch of the marshes, which is said to mark the exact spot where the great king died. First erected in 1685, the column collapsed and had to be rebuilt just over a hundred years later. In recent times the memorial has again been repaired and rescued from sinking into the marsh. In 2007, a striking statue of a purposefully warlike Edward, sword in hand, was erected in a more solid location, a playing field in the village.

The ancient foot routes across the Solway Firth and the channels of the River Eden and River Esk were not only used for occasional military expeditions by the warring Scots and English, but by generations of traders and cattle drovers. They were known as *waths*, an old Anglo-Scandinavian word for a ford, which is most commonly heard in Cumbria and Yorkshire. Occasionally cattle still wander across the Solway Firth and people cross by foot simply for the challenge, or by accident.

A fisherman who lives in a village on the English side told me that he once caught sight of a fishing friend way out in the Firth without realising he was in trouble. Both were exponents of the regional practice of *haaf net* fishing (also an old Scandinavian term). This involves wading out into the tide balancing a large, rectangular framed net suspended from a wooden pole (or beam), a bit like a partially submerged tightrope walker. If caught out by rising tides, the default action apparently is to cling on to the marginally buoyant beam, and swim, hoping that the wind and tide takes you to shore, rather than out to sea. The next this fisherman knew about his friend's misadventure in the Solway Firth was a phone call requesting a lift home from Scotland.

Travellers crossing estuaries and fishermen working in them needed all the help they could get. It was often a matter of faith. Assisting such crossings became a duty that religious organisations took on as part of their mission and good works, following the example of St Christopher (from the Greek for 'Christ bearer'). In the estuary of the River Leven, which empties into Morecambe Bay, there is a little island, an outcrop of limestone about a mile from the shore. It is known as Chapel Island, because there in the fourteenth century the Augustinian canons of nearby Conishead Priory built a chapel that acted as a refuge for those that found themselves stranded.

Even if not left marooned, travellers who made the tricky crossing between Cartmel and Conishead may have wished to stop and offer up a prayer for their safe deliverance. Religious houses sometimes built such facilities at crossing points or on bridges as an act of charity. They and other manorial landlords were sometimes given, or acquired, the responsibility for managing the crossing places. In turn, they often required their local tenants to fulfil customary duties as guides and boatmen for their own journeys and those of their officials and other important visitors.

BUILDING BRIDGES

Historically, many settlements were established and flourished at the lowest convenient crossing point of a river, just before its estuary widened towards the sea. These were places where roads converged, where seagoing vessels could provide ready access to places along the coast or far across the oceans, and where boats might navigate the upper reaches of a good river far inland. The construction of bridges at these points allowed for a reliable and continuous flow of land traffic. The coincidence of these forms of accessibility set many villages, towns and even major cities on their path to prominence and growth.

Newcastle upon Tyne was *Pons Aelius* to the Romans. The 'Aelian Bridge' they built there took the Emperor Hadrian's own family name. Exeter (*Isca Dumnoniorum*) and Chester (*Deva Victrix*) also grew from Roman bridging points on estuaries. These places gained replacement medieval bridges after the Roman bridges finally succumbed to time and tides. The Old Dee Bridge at Chester, which was rebuilt in 1387 from an earlier medieval bridge, is still in use. The Old Exe Bridge at Exeter, which was first built around 1190, also still exists, though it is now marooned in a park alongside the river.

Bristol owes its existence and its name to a bridge. The Old English name for the port city, *Brycg stowe* (meeting place by the bridge), indicates that there was a bridge there at least a thousand years ago. The first stone bridge across the tidal River Avon at Bristol was built in 1247. The bridge and adjacent port helped Bristol to thrive and it became the third largest town (after London and York) in medieval England.

Medieval times saw the construction of a huge number of bridges where none had previously existed. At Glasgow, for example, there was a bridge in place by the 1280s, at what was then the lowest feasible crossing point of the River Clyde. Glasgow then developed from a small rural settlement to become Scotland's largest seaport and most populous city. Edinburgh, with the port of Leith, on the south bank of the Firth of Forth, is an exception to the general rule. It thrived despite not benefiting from a bridge crossing. Not until 1890 was the famous Forth (rail) Bridge completed at Queensferry, several miles to the west of the city.

Stirling, nearly forty miles upstream from Edinburgh, was the lowest crossing point of the River Forth in medieval times. This explains the strategic importance of Stirling, why it was the sometime capital of Scotland, and why this city figures so prominently in Scottish and English history. The present Stirling Old Bridge dates to the fifteenth century at the earliest, but this stone version is the replacement of a succession of earlier medieval timber-built bridges built at or near the same spot.

At one of these Stirling bridges in 1297, the army of mighty King Edward I, 'Hammer of the Scots', was soundly hammered by a Scottish force led by Andrew Moray and William Wallace. In the Battle of Stirling scene in the film *Braveheart*, the absence of Stirling Bridge, which was the focus of the battle and decisive to the outcome, is notable. It is another thing the film got completely wrong, along with the dodgy accents. The scene was actually shot in Ireland, on a hill.

London is the prime example of a settlement propelled to prominence through its position at the lowest bridging point of a river. The construction of the first bridge across the Thames by the Romans set this previously unremarkable prehistoric place on a path to becoming one of the world's great capital cities. *Londinium* was not an Iron Age tribal capital, unlike several other places that became important towns in Roman Britain.

However, there were geographical advantages. A relatively firm patch of land on the south side of the Thames valley projected from low-lying, stream-crossed and island-studded mire, towards a firm higher spot on the north side of the river. Roman engineers selected this location to build their bridge. Importantly, this was a place where seagoing vessels could come in on the tide and draw up right alongside the bridge and the growing settlement. River-going vessels could navigate upstream into the country to the west.

Looking out from the city banks of the Thames today it is difficult to envisage how the Roman construction crews went about the task of bridging this forbidding, deep, fast-flowing tidal river. In Roman times, however, the Thames and its surrounding marshy flood plain was a shallower but broader obstacle than it is today. The river has since been tightly constrained between hard embankments. The Thames has narrowed as generations of Londoners reclaimed land and built wharves and revetments further out into the flow. It has deepened with dredging so that ever larger vessels could be brought up to the city.

Tantalising fragmentary evidence of London's Roman bridge was found in 1981. It comprised a square of driven timber posts filled in with rubble to create a foundation pad (caisson) for a huge pier (supporting leg of a bridge). The piers of this bridge would have been formed of huge timber posts or perhaps cut stone blocks. The lowest courses of its piers probably would have been shaped into angles (cutwaters) that met the flow of water in order to deflect its flow and ease pressure on the bridge piers.

The bridge may originally have had a largely timber superstructure and deck. This seems to have been the preferred Roman bridge construction method initially, followed by more use of stone in later Roman times. The Roman London bridge was built at a spot near the present-day London Bridge and the site of the famous medieval London Bridge. That is the one seen in old illustrations bedecked with a jumble of multi-storey buildings, and not the 1830s version that was sold and rebuilt in Arizona.

Bridges have to fulfil their primary purposes, but many also have to satisfy aesthetic aspirations. They can become icons, attributed meanings well beyond their architectural and historical identities. They can reflect or even define the character of places. Tower Bridge has become a symbol of London, recognisable across the globe. It is stately, substantial and exudes grand medieval architectural tradition. But those tall cathedral-like towers of Cornish granite and Portland Stone draw attention away from the fact that Tower Bridge is basically a steel suspension bridge, albeit one with a very important additional ability.

At the time of its inception in the 1880s, large seagoing vessels with masts and funnels still expected to dock as far upstream as London Bridge. The planned new bridge was not allowed to impede this river traffic, and over fifty designs were submitted to solve this problem. Eventually a bascule (French for see-saw or rocker) bridge arrangement was favoured. The central span of Tower Bridge's road deck is formed of two parts that meet in the centre of the river. Each part, weighing around 1,200 tons, can be tilted using hydraulic power to let shipping pass beneath.

It is an outstanding technical achievement, but not entirely without problems. On the day I wrote these words the bascules of Tower Bridge got stuck in awkward 'up' positions after opening to let a large barge through. The bridge was of course totally closed to road and foot traffic while the problem was fixed.

Back in Lincolnshire, once the former Sutton Wash had been drained and the Nene Outfall had been built in the middle of the nineteenth century, building a bridge became possible and necessary. But the task was also to ensure that ships could still reach the now well inland port of Wisbech. This problem was tackled by what reads like a substantial extract from the *Who's Who* of all-time greatest British engineers.

First up were John Rennie (the Younger) and Thomas Telford, who produced a cast iron and timber bridge. Completed in 1831, it had a deck that split into two bascules that opened upwards to let ships through, like Tower Bridge in London. Rennie and Telford's bridge did not last long. It was found to be inconvenient to operate, so Robert Stephenson, another giant of engineering, was brought in to design a replacement. This was a swing bridge, which pivoted aside to allow shipping to pass. Built in 1850, it lasted longer than its predecessor.

The present Cross Keys Bridge, which replaced Stephenson's bridge, opened to both road and rail traffic in 1897. It is also a swing bridge and pivots on a pier just off centre of the river to let ships pass. Its distinctive central span of curved bowstring-braced girder trusses is surmounted by a hexagonal watch office or control room.

Cross Keys Bridge finally provided a safe and reliable route across this formerly difficult estuarine terrain, while still allowing coastal vessels to reach far inland. It also became an important local landmark. In 1943, the flat local landscape was used to hone skills in the very low flying that would be necessary to get the Dambusters across lowland Europe to their targets. The specially adapted Lancaster bombers had to fly low to avoid radar coverage, and then at precisely 60 feet over water drop their special bouncing bombs on the German dams.

These mighty four-engined aircraft, belonging to the specially formed 617 Squadron, flew under electricity cables and then had to put on roaring power and pull up sharply to get over Cross Keys Bridge. Wing Commander Guy Gibson, the leader of the squadron, knew the area well having once been stationed at RAF Sutton Bridge, a somewhat desolate pre-war aerodrome on reclaimed land that specialised in aerial gunnery training.

There are reports that RAF 'Top Gun' fighter pilots stationed there were seen to fly under the Cross Keys Bridge, which does not seem at all credible when you look at the narrow gap between water and deck, even at low tide. A memorial to all nationalities who served at the aerodrome is situated near the bridge. It is surmounted by a bent propeller blade, but thankfully this was not plucked from the bridge superstructure or the riverbed beneath.

Cross Keys Bridge still carries increasingly busy A17 road traffic between the A1 Great North Road at Newark in Nottinghamshire, through the Lincolnshire Fens, and on to Norfolk. It is a route that greatly shortens the journey around the Wash. But river traffic has not been forgotten. Operators of both commercial shipping and leisure craft can apply to have Cross Keys Bridge opened, as long as they do so more than 24 hours in advance.

An Act of Parliament, the Lynn and Sutton Bridge Railway Act 1861, which is still in force, makes it unlawful for the bridge to delay or detain shipping on the River Nene. The forty-five minutes or so it takes to swing the bridge open to get a large ship through, then close again, often creates long traffic queues. Periods where one or another of the carriageways has to be closed for maintenance also cause long tailbacks and much aggravation at this choke point.

The bridge's hydraulic system is reaching the end of its life now, but rather than overhaul it, Lincolnshire County Council has decided to replace it with electric motors. This is estimated to cost well over £1 million more than a thorough overhaul of the existing hydraulics, but that is considered a good investment to improve the lifespan and resilience of this crucial bridge. The failure and loss of this bridge and crossing route, it was concluded, would have severe regional and even national consequences, not least because of the economic and food security importance of the Lincolnshire and Norfolk agricultural industries.

There is a now a smart new memorial tablet to Charles Wigglesworth, the Sutton Wash guide, that replicates the wording of his original headstone so that the record of his role will not fade away. It is important to remember a time before there was a Sutton bridge, when travellers faced inconvenience and danger in making crossings that we easily take for granted today. Cross Keys Bridge has been designated a grade II* listed building. This places it in the top 8 per cent of all listed buildings nationally in terms of architectural and historical significance. In fact it places Cross Keys Bridge among much more famous bridges, such as Westminster Bridge adjacent to the Houses of Parliament in London. For the time being Cross Keys Bridge is still very much needed, and it still swings.

Tower Bridge, Cross Keys Bridge and the Humber Bridge managed to meet the twin requirements of providing a convenient crossing for land traffic, while still permitting coastal vessels access to ports. The building of bridges to connect places that were formerly completely separated usually ushers in new dynamics and encourages them to thrive. We should not take them for granted as we cross. However snarled in traffic our journeys across estuaries might be today, they are still very much easier than in times past when inconvenience and delay could easily turn into tragedy.

Part of the fascination of estuaries is that they are bountiful places of opportunity on the one hand, but obstructive and treacherous on the other. These ambiguous, marginal places are so often forgotten about, but they are crucial features of Britain's coastline and criss-crossed with traces of human history. Stories of everyone from kings to farmers are steeped in the ebb and flow of their tides.

CHAPTER 8

LOSS AND GAIN

The Marrams at Hemsby, Norfolk

Britain's coastline is continually changing. Some of these changes
are subtle and barely perceptible over many years. A little bit
more sand and shingle can build up gradually in one place or
another without anyone much noticing. A minor rock fall from
a cliff can occur without much altering its appearance. Over
decades or hundreds of years, however, the cumulative effect of
gradual deposition and erosion can be profound. The ways the
coastline shifts can also be sudden, extensive, and life-altering.

The consequences of the sea nibbling away part of the coast or
suddenly inundating the land, or silt choking a former channel,
can be much more far-reaching than their immediate impact

might suggest, however severe that appears at first. Erosion, flooding and reclamation, loss and gain on the coastline, have always been about more than simple economics. They are highly emotive and political subjects, and ones with implications that reach far inland.

The disappearance of the Suffolk town of Dunwich beneath the waves has inspired folk tales and speculation, but the facts of this dramatic loss are well documented and researched by historians and archaeologists. The evidence is also plain to see. Dunwich is a fascinating place to explore, and somewhere I have returned to again and again.

On the short walk up the lane from Dunwich's large beach car park back towards the village, there is a footpath sign almost buried in hedgerow that is easy to miss. The path winds through a wooded area, but periodic glimpses of the sea, and the sounds of the beach, which seem very close, soon indicate that this has become a clifftop walk. After a few minutes, just off the footpath in a tiny clearing, there is a single gravestone. It is right on the edge of the cliff.

This is the last visible grave marker in the graveyard of the last of the Dunwich churches to topple over the cliff and into the sea. A series of etchings, paintings and old photographs show the Church of All Saints seeming to edge ever closer to the cliff. Its long nave was gradually nibbled away until only the tower remained as a landmark. That too finally toppled over the cliff in 1919, leaving only a sliver of masonry, a tower buttress, perched precariously on the cliff edge. This was dismantled and rescued before it had joined the rest of the church in the surf at the foot of the cliff.

Dunwich is often rather inaccurately and sensationally described as a sunken city or 'Britain's Atlantis'. However, the town was not instantly swamped by the sea to lie intact on the seabed, but instead was gradually eaten away. Debris from the stone buildings that collapsed onto the shore and were then submerged beneath the ever-encroaching sea has been mapped on the seabed by archaeological surveys. Artefacts from everyday medieval life are periodically recovered from the sea by fishing boats and divers. Some of these are on display in the excellent little village museum. This may not be Britain's Atlantis, but the gradual, alarming disappearance of Dunwich is one of the most spectacular and infamous examples of coastal erosion in the British Isles.

Dunwich was a far from insignificant and obscure place. The Domesday Survey records that just before the Norman Conquest, when towns were very rare indeed, Dunwich was already thriving. Dunwich grew in importance under the Normans and, by the standards of the day, had become a substantial port town by the middle of the thirteenth century. It had several thousand inhabitants. Its large fleet of ships (around eighty in number according to one medieval survey) traded internationally and participated in military campaigns. King John, for example, hired thirty Dunwich ships in 1211 for his campaign in Ireland.

The church of All Saints was a massive church with Norman origins. It was in fact one of the largest in a county known for its huge 'wool churches', splendid, lofty churches built on the proceeds of woollen cloth manufacture and trading. The intact and pristine church of St Edmund's at nearby Southwold (still happily in the middle of the town and not under imminent threat of being washed away) gives some idea of the scale and grandeur of the lost All Saints. There were several churches and chapels, two friaries and a small Benedictine monastery in Dunwich, along with other religious and secular institutions that were common in the larger medieval towns.

Not far from the cliff edge is a large meadow enclosed by a wall. This was the site of the Franciscan friary. The ruins of the medieval refectory stand in the middle of the field. Impressive gateways stand on the other side of the field, overlooking the main lane into Dunwich. The foundations of the vast friary church and other buildings lie hidden beneath the turf. It was Henry VIII's dissolution of the monasteries rather than the sea that did for this place. The sea, however, had destroyed the Franciscan's first friary at Dunwich, so a new friary was built on land much further from the shore, just outside the town's landward, western ramparts.

At least it was further from the sea in 1290 when the new site was acquired. The current proximity of the cliff to the friary indicates how total the loss of the town of Dunwich has been. What was once right at the back of the town is now right on the shore. Nothing of what was once enclosed by the medieval town's ramparts survives above ground, or above sea. The coastline at this point has been eaten back about a mile from the shore the Norman's knew, almost a thousand years ago. Dunwich is now only a small village, mostly comprising cottages built in the last two hundred years, well away from the sea.

Walking down the lane from the Franciscan priory back towards the village gives a clue as to why coastal erosion has been especially severe at Dunwich. Sand erodes from the verges where the tyres of visitors' vehicles catch the grass as they pull over to make room for each other. 'We live on a big sandcastle,' a resident once told me. Happily, changes in the formation of sandbanks offshore seem to have slowed the erosion for now. Today the cliff face at Dunwich is well colonised by shrubs, rather than a raw scar. On my last visit I could see none of the graveyard bones that were once commonly found, scattered at its base.

A few miles south along the coast the thriving, fashionable ancient port town of Aldeburgh fared better than Dunwich. Nevertheless, the position of the town's early sixteenth century Moot Hall gives an impression of the extent of historic coastal erosion there. It was formerly in the central market place, but is now at the seafront.

Elizabethan maps confirm that around half the medieval town has been eaten by the sea.

Aldeburgh townsfolk must have looked towards Dunwich and thought, 'there but for the grace of God go we', but in practical terms there was very little indeed that they could do to prevent a similar fate. They had to let nature take its course and try to re-plan accordingly. Aldeburgh's sea front is now protected by a low concrete sea wall. It is doing its job for now, but for how much longer?

Dramatic coastal erosion is not a thing of the past, but very much an issue of the present and for the future. In 2023 a climate campaign and advisory group called One Home Climate Solutions sought to highlight one of the effects of climate change by assessing the value of the coastal homes at direct risk from coastal erosion in England. It used data from the Environment Agency's National Coastal Risk Mapping to identify well over 2000 homes in twenty-one villages and hamlets that are probably not going to survive into the next century.

The places they identified ranged from Chuck Bank in Northumberland and Coulderton in Cumbria, to Fairlight Cove in East Sussex and Marazion East in Cornwall. The most at-risk places, however, are along the east and south coasts of England: the East Riding of Yorkshire, East Anglia, Essex, Kent and the Channel coast.

The value of the homes predicted to be lost was estimated to be just under £600 million. Though generating news headlines and comment, even this figure does not represent the true character and magnitude of the potential loss. Observation of creeping erosion and perceptions of vulnerability also affect confidence and investment in these places. It is becoming extremely difficult to get insurance in neighbourhoods perceived as under threat from flooding and attrition by the sea.

In several places around Britain the immediate, direct risks of seaside living are all too apparent. The Marrams at Hemsby in Norfolk is a community of chalet-style bungalows perched on a low cliff overlooking the North Sea. The problem is that the cliff is really just a large sand dune, the last row of what was once a dune belt that has been relentlessly eaten away by the waves.

The coastline there has been pushed back by around a thousand feet since the 1970s, and the pace of erosion seems to be increasing. Eighteen homes were lost there between 2013 and 2018. Five more had to be evacuated and demolished in December 2023 as they teetered on the edge of the cliff. Another

30 feet of cliff face disappeared in 2024 alone. In December 2024, a tidal surge destroyed the concrete ramp that gave access to the beach, leaving a forty feet drop to the shore. This not only prevented locals and tourists from visiting this popular beach, but also prevented the launch of the Hemsby Lifeboat.

The community there feels abandoned by the authorities, who they say have failed to provide appropriate sea defences, unlike those provided in other places not far away, or offer any other meaningful help. They do what they can to help themselves. Access to the beach was quickly restored using a digger to drag sand into place. In March 2023 a former soldier, Lance Martin, on finding that Great Yarmouth Borough Council was due to demolish his bungalow home, now a mere three feet from the cliff edge, used two diggers to drag it a few feet further back inland.

Mr Martin told reporters that when he moved to the area, he was well aware of the prospect of losing his home eventually. But when he bought his house for £95,000 in 2017, it was 130 feet from the cliff edge. Erosion was averaging around three feet per year then. He thought he would get around forty years of use from his home on its original spot, rather than the six years it turned out to be. Mr Martin's house-moving efforts have been in vain. His home and several others were demolished just before Christmas 2025, as the alarmingly unstable cliff edge approached their walls. Existing residents and new purchasers are very conscious that their tenure near the seafront is time limited. Storm surges and complex dynamics offshore, however, make erosion rates very difficult to predict. Climate change seems to be causing more severe and frequent 'exceptional' weather events.

Other Hemsby homeowners with sufficient means have quietly moved away. Save Hemsby's Coastline, a local campaign group, worries that in the absence of sufficient defences and mitigation, the village and resort, which generates tens of millions of pounds to the economy, will simply dwindle away. Homeowners on the Suffolk coast are planning and fighting in other ways.

One of the reasons that I love to return and re-explore what I think are familiar stretches of coast is that it is impossible to take in everything in just one or two visits. I am usually reacquainted with something that has been half-forgotten and discover something I had not noticed before. On my most recent visit to Thorpeness, I wandered along the beach below the crumbling silt and sand cliff, looking for the remains of a Second World War 'pillbox' fortification that I had seen there a few years previously. I could not find a trace of it. It must have been completely washed away. Instead I noticed, protruding from the top of the cliff, a tangled mass of rusty scaffold poles that I had not seen before. These are probably the remnants of wartime beach scaffold defences. When dismantled at the end of the Second World War, they were perhaps dumped in some hollow well away from the shore, only to be exposed by the erosion of the cliff decades later.

I was tempted to have a closer look to test my assumption, but I kept well back. In 2017, a man in his fifties was buried there by a sudden collapse of the cliff. Emergency services fought in vain to dig him out and save his life. An elderly lady narrowly escaped the same fate with minor injuries.

Thorpeness is a characterful, distinctive seaside village, quite unlike anywhere else along Britain's long coastline. It is not an opportunistic, ad hoc development of miscellaneous prefab bungalows and beach huts intermittently grafted on to an old village inland, but a carefully and purposefully designed resort for the Edwardian well-to-do. There are some elegant bungalows facing the beach at Thorpeness, but most of the houses are far more substantial than those you might expect to find in most beachside villages. Many are mansions.

Faced with much faster receding cliffs than predicted when her house was purchased in 2009, Lucy Ansbro reportedly spent £500,000 piling massive rocks under the cliff to protect it. This must have seemed like money well spent as she watched the cliff edging ever closer to her neighbour's mansion, the Red House. Built in the 1920s in grand neo-Georgian style, this elegant home had to be demolished in 2022 before falling into the sea. It was once worth £2 million. Lucy Ansbro's own home finally succumbed to the wrecking ball and waves in January 2026, along with several others.

The East Yorkshire coast suffers similar issues to those faced in Suffolk. There the Environment Agency calculates that ongoing erosion will account for more than 1000 properties in the next thirty years. It claims that without planned preventative measures the number could in fact be five times greater.

Over the centuries dozens of villages, hamlets and farms mentioned in the Domesday Survey and in later medieval documents have been swept away as the coast between Spurn Head on the Humber Estuary and Flamborough Head (around forty miles to the north) edged ever further inland. The soft glacial silts along the coast there are said to be eroding faster than anywhere else in Europe. Erosion and sea-level rise look like they will eventually take places now on the edge such as the present village of Kilnsea, just as they took Old Kilnsea.

Home and business owners today, confronting the unmitigated, uncompensated, uninsured loss of their property to the sea, find no comfort in the knowledge that this kind of thing has been happening for a very long time indeed. In fact, they might be inclined to wonder why the modern world, with all its resources and technological and engineering advances, cannot come up with a solution. Attempting to slow the pace of climate change and rising sea level by reducing carbon emissions, however worthy, will not work quickly enough for many facing coastal erosion right now.

I once heard the comedian Paul Merton remark, on a panel show, that the main purpose of seaside towns was to stop Britain fraying at the edges. In comedy there is much truth. The largest investment in sea defences tends to be where property and population is at its most concentrated and where the economic stakes are highest. Take a stroll along the promenade of most notable seaside towns and you will find stone or concrete sea walls, piles of imported rocks, and a series of wooden groynes (barriers projecting from the shore). Many places now periodically replenish their eroding sand or shingle beaches with material dredged from nearby.

Now look at the same view in one of the books of old photographs and postcards that you will almost certainly find in the local bookshops and newsagents. The seafront scene around a hundred years ago or more will look quite different. There is likely to be a much more ramshackle dividing line between shore and town. In fact, many seaside promenades were created with the dual purpose of creating a seafront public space and a robust sea defence. It is hindsight and bitter experience that has often led to investment in sea defences, rather than foresight.

On the night of Saturday 31 January 1953 a massive storm, combined with a high spring tide, drove the North Sea onto the land along the east coast of Britain, Belgium and the Netherlands. In Holland, the catastrophic event is known as the *Watersnoodramp* (flood disaster). This kind of event had occurred throughout history in these places. There were plenty of references to similar occurrences in medieval and early modern records, so lack of precedents was no excuse for failing to plan for it again.

However, interest and investment in sea defences had waned during the depression, in wartime and in the post-war austerity years. Meanwhile, beachfront settlements of huts, prefabs (prefabricated homes introduced as temporary housing after the war), chalets and bungalows had been allowed to spring up in many vulnerable places. It was these places that were hardest hit when tempest and tide combined to overwhelm the shoreline from Scotland to the south coast of England.

The widespread flooding and destruction began in Scotland, where sixteen people lost their lives. The disaster became ever more severe as the surging water was pushed into the shallower part of the North Sea and lower-lying coastline further south. Mablethorpe and Sutton-on-Sea, on the Lincolnshire coast, were particular badly hit. Forty-two people lost their lives. At Felixstowe in Suffolk, forty-one people died. They were mostly residents of a prefab estate in an area known as 'West End' near the port.

Thirty-seven people died at Jaywick, the inter-war, low-cost property development and self-build community in Essex. Fifty-nine people lost their lives on Canvey Island, on the Thames Estuary, where a sprawling resort and settlement had developed on former coastal grazing land. They perished not only by drowning, but through hypothermia while perched on rooftops waiting to be rescued. Around 13,000 people were evacuated from Canvey Island, virtually the whole population. Overall, just over 300 people were killed in Britain, and around 1,800 in the Netherlands. It was the most disastrous North Sea flood of the twentieth century.

Many stories of hardship and heroism emerged from those few hours of trauma. At Hunstanton on the Norfolk coast young American serviceman Reis Leming rescued twenty-seven people from the freezing waters, despite the fact that he couldn't swim. His colleague, Staff Sergeant Freeman A. Kilpatrick, rescued another eighteen. Both were awarded George Medals, the highest non-military award for bravery, and an extremely rare honour for American citizens. Kilpatrick and his family were among the community of Americans who preferred to live in civilian homes at the coast rather than on the nearby airbase. Sixteen Americans were among the thirty-one that died in the flood at Hunstanton, On that single night the town had lost nearly twice as many people as soldier sons killed during the whole of the Second World War.

There were many more casualties on the few miles of coast between Hunstanton and the port town of King's Lynn. Memorials in Snettisham village and just off the beach at Heacham recall the catastrophe, those who lost their lives, and those that strove to save others. It was there that my late father-in-law and fellow National Servicemen were hastily trucked in to fill sandbags and temporarily repair breaches in the sea banks. The sea defences at Heacham and Hunstanton were subsequently beefed up with heightened earth banks and permanent, concrete sea walls. As I child, I remember having to clamber up and down rusty iron ladders to access the beach from the iron sheet-piled concrete sea wall built after 1953.

Those defences were themselves overwhelmed in January 1978, when a severe storm surge produced even higher water levels than those experienced in 1953. That storm swept away our family caravan, along with hundreds of others theoretically protected behind the iron and concrete sea wall, and smashed it to pieces. Hunstanton also lost its pier that night. The pier had opened in 1870 and was once considered one of the finest on the east coast. The small fragment that survived the 1978 storm, the head of the pier offshore, was subsequently demolished. The pier has never been replaced.

The central section of the extraordinarily long pier at Herne Bay in Kent was also smashed away by the storm that same night. The ruinous head of the pier now sits isolated in the sea, a long way from the shore. The Victorian pier at Skegness in Lincolnshire was similarly damaged, but later repaired. Cleethorpes' Victorian pier a few miles up the Lincolnshire coast stood firm, but a party of around 150 elderly and disabled people enjoying an end-of-pier show were stranded as the structure was bashed by the waves.

There is now a new sea wall from Heacham to the cliffs at Hunstanton. It is higher and more robust than its predecessor. Along most of its length it steps down to the beach, so families can sit on it like stadium terraced seating, and watch the sea even when the tide is well in. At dusk people assemble to watch the unique sight at an east-coast resort of the sun setting on the sea. The 2.5 mile-long, wide promenade that is integral to the sea wall is also very popular with walkers, joggers, cyclists and ambling ice-cream eaters.

The sea defences there will hopefully be sufficient for many years to come, but even now it is sobering that flood warnings are issued periodically. The promenade is occasionally washed over by seawater, and the debris of high tides and storms piles against the highest part of the wall.

Such sea-defence infrastructure is expensive to construct and maintain. Following another east-coast tidal surge in 2013, the under-protected Suffolk coastal town of Lowestoft eventually got one mile of new flood defences. However, the next phase of the protection works, a tidal barrier similar in principle to London's Thames Barrier was suspended due to a £124 million 'funding gap'. The tidal barrier at Ipswich in the same county was completed in 2019 at a cost of nearly £70 million. This huge floodgate rotates upwards from the bed of the River Orwell to protect the port town from tidal surges. The cost-benefit analysis considered that more than 1,600 homes and at least 400 businesses would be better protected.

Even in well-populated towns, tough financial decisions have to be made about what to protect. Unfortunately, seaside chalet communities, small villages and farmland, however treasured and productive, are seldom going to be at the top of the priority list for massive public expenditure on the construction and maintenance of sea defences.

The twenty-one communities identified by One Home as being at particularly urgent, direct risk from coastal erosion are a small fraction of the 1.8 million homes and properties in England that the Environment Agency calculates are at risk from coastal erosion and sea flooding overall. Of the £5.2 billion the agency expects to spend on its nationwide 'flood and coastal erosion capital investment programme' between 2021 and 2027, £1.3 billion has been earmarked for coastal schemes. Some of this will not be for defences as such.

COASTAL REALIGNMENT

In addressing potential threats to life and property on the coast, the concept of 'coastal realignment' or 'managed retreat' (which sounds like a euphemism for running away) has found much favour in recent years. This essentially means giving up trying to protect vulnerable parts of the coastline, and letting the sea break through, albeit with some 'soft engineering' management. This might involve deliberately breaching old flood protection banks, rather than maintaining and augmenting them, and building some new flood mitigation measures further inland, where it is hoped that they will be much less tested by the tides.

The advantages of this approach to managing coastal erosion are that it can be vastly cheaper than maintaining existing lines of defence, even with compensation payments to landowners, and it offers the opportunity to extend or create new wildlife habitats. Affected communities, however, are often dismayed that productive land, in many cases painstakingly reclaimed from coastal marsh centuries ago, is simply given up in this way. And it can feel as if the sea is being invited to get too close to their homes.

At Alnmouth in Northumberland, some coastal agricultural land won from the sea after the Second World War, when the country was short of food, is now being allowed to return to tidal mudflats. The natural and man-made defences of the shore are being deliberately breached to create a habitat that will be attractive to wading birds. The direct cost of the work is a modest £38,000. Nature will do the rest over a period of time.

Somewhat ironically, perhaps, this scheme is being funded through the 'Farming in Protected Landscapes Programme' managed by the government's Department of the Environment, Food and Rural Affairs (DEFRA). Even more ironically, it was at this location that a major facility to vastly improve agricultural productivity was established in the nineteenth century.

Before the artificial fertilisers were available, guano – seabird poo rich in nitrogen, phosphate and potassium – was imported all the way from Peru. Northumberland's grain growing belt, vital to feed a growing industrial society, depended on the stuff. So it was there at Buston Links, at a discreet distance south of Alnmouth, that barns were pressed into service as storage sheds for the precious but extremely smelly substance. One of those barns still stands, now without its roof, amid the land that will become salt marsh.

Rambling across the salt marsh that already exists there alongside the farmland reminds me of how much I love this type of coastal landscape, and how much we miss if we simply head for the beaches, coves and cliffs when visiting the seaside.

I love the mix of sand, winding muddy creeks, spongy carpets of salt-loving vegetation, and the colourful seasonal dustings of delicate marsh flowers. The haunting whistles of curlews and lapwings, the plaintive cry of gulls and chirruping of summer birds, all add to the special atmosphere of these places.

I appreciate that salt marsh is not everybody's idea of a beautiful or productive landscape, but there is no argument about its valuable biodiversity, nor its role in absorbing some of the eroding effects of the tides. Nevertheless, I worry about the loss of agricultural land. The 'managed retreat' at Alnmouth is relatively small scale, and will not make a huge difference to agricultural productivity. Elsewhere, however, schemes such as these are much more extensive.

The 'managed realignment' project at Medmerry on the West Sussex coast was claimed to be the largest of its kind in Europe when completed in 2013. The shingle bank that protected the coastline there was periodically breached by storms, which flooded property and necessitated millions of pounds of expenditure in addressing damage. After several years of deliberation, the decision was taken to breach the shingle bank and allow the sea into 183 hectares (452 acres) of low-lying land.

Approximately four miles of new earth sea banks were built, effectively placing the new coastline over one mile inland. Other works were required, such as beefing-up flood defences around the margins of the area to protect neighbouring properties, caravan parks and a sewage works. The scheme cost £28 million. Online you can find stop-motion footage of the breach being made, with tracked excavators nibbling away at the former sea defences. The sea seems to push impatiently at the diminishing shingle bank, urging the excavators on, until it finally bursts through to claim its new territory.

The new area of intertidal habitat is now managed as a reserve by the Royal Society for the Protection of Birds. From above, the little nubbin of headland known as Selsey Bill that sticks out into the English Channel looks even more exposed. The little seaside town of Selsey is said to be safer as a result of the Medmerry coastal realignment, but bracketed by this new wetland, Pagham Harbour and the open sea, its Old English name 'seal island' seems fitting once more.

The Medmerry scheme is no longer exceptional. The coastal realignment at the Steart Marshes on the Severn Estuary in Somerset ('interestingly' close to the Hinkley Point nuclear power station) quickly followed as the UK's largest scheme of this type.

At Hurst Spit on the Hampshire coast, the initial public consultation on the proposal to allow the sea defences to be gradually 'rolled back' (i.e., overwhelmed) by the waves has thrown light on the consequent loss of the important salt-marsh habitat that already exists there. The Environment Agency has said that this could be compensated by creating salt marsh elsewhere. Consultees are also concerned that Hurst Castle would become inaccessible

Sometimes human intervention, rather than lack of it, is held responsible for accelerating or prompting coastal erosion, rather than preventing it. There are cases where the construction of coastal defences and other coastal infrastructure is said to have caused unforeseen problems elsewhere, despite (presumably) the thorough modelling of possible hydrological side effects.

The construction of groynes and walls to slow erosion in one spot on the shore, for example, is sometimes blamed for causing erosion or silting elsewhere. Tidal barriers and sluices built at the coastal outfall of a river are designed to prevent flooding upstream. Other engineering works at the mouth of a river can have consequences inland.

The long-awaited third crossing of the River Yare at Great Yarmouth on the Norfolk coast was greeted with widespread enthusiasm. The new bridge is intended to ease traffic and provide better access to the town's enterprise zone and port. It is a bascule bridge, with a road deck in two parts that join in the centre and rise to permit shipping to pass to and fro. A public vote was held to choose the name of the bridge. The most popular of the official options was 'Herring Bridge'.

Construction of the bridge was not without some hitches and delays, caused among other things by the discovery of an unexploded Second World War bomb and the 'potential burrow' of a vole. However, even before the £120 million bridge finally opened to road traffic in 2024, it caused controversy.

The bridge's abutments (the structures at each end of a bridge that anchor it to the banks and support its weight) have narrowed the width of River Yare at this point by about a third. Residents upstream in the low-lying Broads, claimed that this restriction in the flow of the river near its coastal outfall was causing water to back up and flood their homes during times of high rainfall. There was talk of bringing collective legal action against Norfolk County Council, which commissioned the bridge. Residents of the Broads know all about the region's historic relationship with water and the sea.

The Broads (often referred to as the Norfolk Broads though they also extend into Suffolk) is a large area of former estuary, coastal marsh, tidal rivers and their floodplains. The area is now a National Park. The wide stretches of waterway and open-water meres that give the area its name are familiar to thousands of holidaymakers. They come to experience the gentle delights of cruising around on the water under sail or motor, learning how not crash into each other, and to enjoy its special natural environment.

This is Britain's largest protected wetland, but it is not a product of nature alone. Many of the waterways are rivers that were widened for navigation and drainage or newly cut for that purpose. The open bodies of water large and small are workings from which peat and clay were extracted from medieval times onwards. They flooded when digging ceased and drainage and flood defences were not maintained.

Several factors are probably at play to cause the recent episodes of exceptional flooding in this low-lying coastal landscape, but fingers have been pointed at the Herring Bridge. Latterly, high river levels have prevented leisure boats from going under bridges in the Broads, and to and from the boatyards that maintain them. The effect on the tourism industry could be massive if the situation does not improve.

One of the most striking cases of coastal erosion that was brought on or accelerated by misjudged human intervention is the destruction of Hallsands in Devon. This old fishing village developed and existed quite happily at the foot of a cliff overlooking a beach. In the 1890s, however, dredging for sand and gravel began offshore. These raw materials were needed for a construction campaign at the Navy's dockyards at Keyham, part of the extensive naval centre at Plymouth, a few miles around the Devon coast.

In response to local concerns about the possible effects of dredging on the shore, the Board of Trade set up an inquiry. This concluded that there was little risk to the village of around forty houses, 150 residents, an old chapel and a pub. However, by the beginning of the twentieth century, the beach at Hallsands had begun to subside. Further protests brought a new inquiry, which recommended that dredging should cease. But it was too late. By then the village was especially vulnerable to natural disaster. In 1917, storms destroyed what remained of Hallsands' beach defences and within a year only one house was habitable. There is no beach there at all now.

Hallsands' woes were not over. Houses on the clifftop had remained unaffected by what was going on below. However, a landslide in 2012 required the evacuation of more houses. Even the viewing platform that was built on the cliff so that curious visitors could see the unreachable remains of the old village is no longer accessible. Storms in 2016 removed beach sand nearby, revealing an ancient peat bed and the remains of prehistoric woodland beneath. This is an area of coast where natural fluctuations in sea currents and levels has caused the formation of beaches and their redeposition over many centuries. There is little doubt, however, that human interference made a naturally dynamic situation even more unhelpfully dynamic.

Hallsands is an example of material being removed from one place at the coast promoting erosion in another. Similarly, bad outcomes have arisen from people adding material to the coastal environment. At the other end and other side of the country, at Chester and the Wirral, misguided attempts to improve navigation and halt silting of the River Dee Estuary have had profound consequences for the history and character of the settlement, trade and the economy.

Chester was a very important place in Roman times. A huge fort was built there, and a large civilian settlement then developed. Walking around the excavated remains of the Roman amphitheatre, just outside the city walls, gives some idea of the significance and magnitude of the place. This venue could probably seat upwards of 8000 people. Chester Football Club's average home attendance in the 2023/24 season was a little over 2000. Just saying. Apart from obviously enjoying Roman entertainment and lifestyle, the Roman authorities and the people of Chester were acutely aware of the natural advantages of the place.

This was the lowest feasible bridging point on the River Dee at the time and a significant port. Roman navy and trading ships could moor right under the city walls. Chester's ability to supply the northern military bases by sea, its commercial potential and the obvious investment Rome put into the place, has led to theories that Chester was earmarked to be a capital of the province of Britain. It was also potentially intended to serve as the springboard for the Roman conquest of Ireland, which never came.

Flying over Chester for the first time in 2017 and looking down on the River Dee gave me some hint of why the city is no longer a major port. The larger boats plying the river there were churning up a muddy wake. The Dee is a silty, shallow river and this, compounded by sediments washing into the estuary from the Irish Sea, has caused problems in maintaining Chester's access to the coast. After the Roman period, silting increased and an island formed near the city walls where once ships had moored. This became known as the Roodee, 'the island of the cross', a hybrid name of Old English and Norse. Chester Racecourse now occupies the former estuarine and island site.

Chester went on to flourish as a port after the Norman Conquest, but silting remained a problem throughout the medieval period and the city continued to decline as a port in the early modern era. Increasingly, places further out on the Wirral, such as Neston, Parkgate and Hoylake, became the preferred anchorages for larger ships. In the 1730s, a new cut was made to the sea, around five miles away, in an attempt to improve the situation and attract the larger sea-going ships back to Chester. This is the artificial straight course of the River Dee we can see today.

Unfortunately for the ports on the English side of the estuary, the new channel of the River Dee was cut too close to the Welsh shore of the estuary. Without the flushing effect of the main river channel, the English side silted up even more. Finally, in an attempt to halt accelerated erosion on the Welsh side, cord-grass, *spartina anglica*, was introduced in the 1920s. This too had unforeseen consequences for the English side.

I had first encountered the village of Parkgate from the air, when flying over the Dee Estuary. I wondered then why the place appeared to have the white-painted, sea-facing buildings and promenade so typical of many seaside towns, and yet was separated from the sea by a vast expanse of grassy marsh.

A few years later I took a boat trip, intending to get as close to Parkgate as possible. We had to start the trip in a different country, Connah's Quay in Wales, and we got no closer than about two miles to the shore at Parkgate. Even then, we checked the depth of water nervously as we went and nearly ran aground several times, despite deliberately using a small, shallow-draft boat.

Later that day, having given up on boats and driven to Parkgate, my views from a distance were confirmed. This place did indeed have the appearance and character of a seaside town. There were ice-cream parlours and cafes, elegant sea-facing villas, a sea wall and people strolling about 'taking the sea air'. But the sea itself was nowhere to be seen. When a guest at the fictional, comically chaotic seaside hotel, Fawlty Towers, complained that their room did not have a sea view, an exasperated Basil Fawlty remonstrated: 'You can see the sea, it's over there between the land and the sky!' At Parkgate, there is no sea between the land and the sky, only green marsh.

To be fair, especially high tides do occasionally overwhelm the marsh and lap against the sea wall. On rare occasions they have even overtopped it and caused flooding in the village. To have far too much sea seems very unfair in a place that usually lacks it completely. Nevertheless, it is very hard now to imagine ocean-going ships anchored just off Parkgate, their tenders busily going back and forth to the shore carrying passengers and goods. It is equally difficult to imagine bathers on the sandy beaches that once existed there. Parkgate effectively lost its seashore as a consequence of the 1920s experiment in 'natural' erosion control on the Welsh side. Cord-grass colonised the

English side of the estuary far too successfully, trapping silt, creating extensive marsh and cutting off Parkgate from the sea.

In addition to natural and accidental silting, the Wirral and the Dee Estuary have been subject to a lot of deliberate, engineered land reclamation. This in itself often has the knock-on effect of altering natural drainage patterns in ways that promote erosion or silting, or both, depending on the local environments affected. The steady silting of the River Dee side of the Wirral and the inability of larger ships to reach Chester and the other moorings and anchorages benefited the Mersey side of the Wirral, especially Liverpool, which developed as one of the world's premier ports from the eighteenth century onwards.

RECLAMATION

At many other places around the coast, people have taken the opportunity to grab valuable land from the sea by building banks, drainage channels and sluices, and pushing the tides back from otherwise intermittently flooded coastal marsh. Reclaimed coastal land, whether supporting grazing cattle and sheep or a mix of crops, is often superficially similar to the higher, old farmland around it, but it is nevertheless distinctive.

It will be generally flat, of course, and often divided into regular, rectangular parcels of land by drainage ditches. Long, straight or slightly meandering rivers or main drainage channels may run thought it. There are likely to be large, long earth banks, which may be straight or meandering to contain a river, drainage channel, or some former tide line. This is the type of landscape that characterises the Fenland region of eastern England, which is broadly defined as the low-lying area between Lincoln in the north, Cambridge in the south, Peterborough in the west and the Wash to the east.

In the Fenland region, the contrast between reclaimed land and the landscapes of surrounding regions, or even the scattered former islands of higher land within Fenland, is especially notable from the air. From above, the winding courses of former natural rivers that were straightened and bypassed by artificial channels can be seen as soil marks in cultivated fields. Their slightly raised silt banks, grazed by ploughing, contrast with the surrounding black peat soil of the former marsh. In old Fen dialect these extinct watercourses are known variously as 'roddons' (or 'rodhams'), 'old slades', 'old runs' and 'old ways'.

They can also be traced as different ripening patterns in crops, especially cereal crops. The cereal plants on the silt banks, which are generally drier and a bit less nutritious than the surrounding soil, will be a little more stunted and ripen quicker than the plants on the black soil. In effect, each cereal plant acts like a pixel on a computer monitor and displays what is going on beneath the topsoil. Under the right conditions, the 'display resolution' of the crop marks that indicate buried features can be stunning. Archaeologists have made great use of aerial photography and this phenomenon for more than a century. Buried built archaeological features, such as roads, ditches, pits and building foundations are also spectacularly reflected by soil marks and crop marks.

During flights along the Norfolk and Lincolnshire coast, active salt marsh creeks, with their distinctive tree branch or root-like pattern, are easy to find. Remnants of the same features can be seen in adjacent partially reclaimed pasture as slight depressions that still occasionally hold water. Turning away from the coast, I can trace their long extinct, buried ancestors, right back to my home airfield thirty miles inland.

I not only see roddons as soil marks and crop marks, but I can also feel them in the seat of my pants if I get my landings slightly wrong. Part of one former creek system lies under our airfield and causes slight undulations in the grass runways. Motorists who drive too fast along the Fenland roads will also experience a moment of weightlessness and then bump to earth as the road surface dips and rises over the buried beds and banks of these old watercourses.

In many places in the Fens, traces of Roman settlements that once clustered along watercourses are visible. More than twenty miles inland, these channels were once sufficiently brackish to serve Roman salt production sites. In places now ten miles from the sea, the mounded silt waste from medieval salt production sites (salterns) can also be seen. It is astonishing to observe the ghostly remains of a buried coastal landscape as it reveals itself from beneath well-drained, well-cultivated farmland so far from the present-day coastline. Flights over this landscape are flights through time, from today's coast to the coastal marsh of up to 5000 years ago. They are flights back to different coastlines.

The transformation of this vast inland and coastal wetland, up to 1,500 square miles in extent, into some of the most productive farmland you will find anywhere in the world, is an epic story. From around 10,000 years ago, rising sea levels caused by melting ice sheets began to penetrate this low-lying landscape adjoining the coast. Streams and rivers flowing in from slightly higher, adjacent inland regions backed-up and produced a morass of pools and swamps in this basin-like region. The area of Fenland closest to the sea and primarily influenced by seawater incursions is known as the 'silt fens'. Its soils are sandy-coloured.

In contrast, the 'black fens' or 'peat fens' are closest to the inland fringes of the Fenland region. This is where freshwater marsh developed and we find the preserved organic plant matter, peat, which generates a rich, black soil. However, at various times over several thousand years the incursions from the sea have either extended to overwhelm the freshwater marshes, or receded to be overwhelmed by their growth.

The gradual accumulation of water-borne sediments and organic marsh matter has produced a soggy layer-cake of deposits from which the environmental history of the region and the story of shifting coastal influence can be read. The deep soils of Fenland are rich in such things as preserved plant matter, timber, fragile fish bones, mollusc shells, insect remains and fossil pollen. They also hold exceptionally well-preserved evidence of human activity.

The Roman Empire understood the potential of this diverse and resource-rich wetland environment. Contrary to received wisdom, the Romans were not responsible for comprehensively draining the Fens. Nevertheless, the Roman authorities grasped the opportunities presented by a natural period of slightly less wet conditions.

They developed settlements, farms and salt production sites

on any scrap of land just high and dry enough to permit them. They dug ditches and colonised the exposed, raised silt courses of dried-up prehistoric rivers. Natural water meadows provided valuable grazing land for flocks of sheep and herds of cattle. Roman engineers built local tracks and roads, and a twenty-four mile causeway right across the Fens. They also built canals. The Emperor Hadrian himself, known to have an interest in wetland reclamation, may have taken a direct hand in guiding the exploitation of Fenland.

The first substantial banks to constrain the tides and coax rivers to their outfalls were built before the Norman Conquest, well over a thousand years ago. The monasteries of the region, which had succeeded the island refuges (or is that colonies?) of the early saints realised that very valuable new land could be won there. They were major landowners and prime movers in 'assarting'– draining land for grazing and growing crops through embanking and ditching, straightening meandering watercourses and building sluices. They built causeways, bridges and farms (granges), established farming communities, and increased the sparse population of the region.

The works that were carried out over several hundred years throughout the medieval period were largely piecemeal, not part of some grander plan to drain the whole Fenland region. There were continual disputes about the effects of one set of works on the rights and works of others. There were disagreements about exactly who was responsible for maintaining and repairing what. There were also disastrous episodes of flooding as the sea broke through the defences.

Medieval records recall terrible tempests, sudden 'extraordinary inundations' of the sea, the 'outrageousness of the sea', the 'violence of the tides', and their effect on the property and communities in this precarious, reclaimed land. During these events thousands of acres of crops were ruined, and towns and villages were swamped. Livestock and people drowned. The medieval chronicler Matthew Paris wrote of a great destructive storm in 1236 when ports lost all their ships and the sea swamped the land for two days without retreating with the tides. Afterwards '. . . were seen the buried corpses of drowned people lying in hollows made by the sea . . .' and particularly in Wisbech and its neighbourhood, 'an infinity' of people perished.

Official state documents describe commissions and inquiries to look into the problems of managing this landscape, and specifically note the inability of communities to pay their taxes as a result of these misfortunes. Nevertheless, the land was too valuable to give up, and so each disaster was followed by patching up and raising the banks, ploughing the fields and starting again. Here again we see this sense of resilience, a characteristic strongly associated with coastal communities and all those who have to live with the vagaries of the sea.

I saw physical evidence of the persistence of the medieval people during the first ever substantive archaeological excavation in the historic core of Wisbech in 1996. Like most urban archaeological excavations, this one was prompted by the clearance and proposed redevelopment of an existing property. At that time I was managing fieldwork projects for an archaeological unit. This involved tendering for commercial work commissioned by developers who had to comply, often very reluctantly, with planning conditions requiring archaeological investigations. I was particularly excited to secure this job, since I knew of Wisbech's largely unappreciated history, its battles with the sea, and the great archaeological potential of the place.

The historic pattern of urban land use, especially on marginal land, is to keep trying to raise ground levels, rather than digging down to find a solid geological base to build up from. That means building on top of existing foundations, rather than removing them, and dumping whatever material was to hand, including rubbish. Archaeology thrives on old rubbish. It can provide an amazing document of past communities' activities, consumption patterns, trading partners, economic and social hierarchies, health, cultural influences and fashions. It tells us about everyday life in a way that nothing else can.

Our excavation site was within what we believed to have been part of Wisbech's large central marketplace, north of the castle. This was the 'New Market', which was probably laid out as part of the Norman replanning of the town.

The excavation area available to us was very small, and as always we had too little time, but the results exceeded expectations and more than rewarded the effort. Digging ever deeper in trenches that had to be shored up by sheet piles, the small team revealed an extraordinarily well-preserved sequence through the medieval and early modern history of the town. Inevitably, people passing by called out to ask if we had found King John's treasure yet. Instead the excavation revealed that at least twelve buildings had stood on this site prior to those mapped in 1830. Each of them had been destroyed or damaged, dismantled and built again following episodes of flooding.

The relative severity of the flooding episodes was indicated by bands of silt of varying thickness that had been laid down within and around the structures. The buildings contained all sorts of informative items that had been lost by their occupants: a coin and purse mount here, a brooch and buckle there, bone needles, stone spindle whorls, a jet seal matrix. But I was particularly intrigued by a large pot, left upright, which contained a complete smaller jug, a small copper bell, a copper barrel lock and a nail. It appeared that the large pot had been used as a cistern of cooling water for the metalworking evidently going on there in a late medieval phase of occupation, before this too was interrupted by another flood.

Butchery practice and diet were indicated by an abundance of sheep or goat bones, but there were also cattle, pig and horse bones, along with those of geese and chicken. Cat, mouse and shrew remains contributed to a picture of earthy domesticity. Duck, heron and kittiwake bones hinted at wildfowling in the surrounding fen and coastal marsh landscape. There was also a wide range of bones from common fish such as eel, pike, carp, perch, dab, sole, cod, herring, salmon, skate, and the slightly more exotic thornback ray. Those bones were an indication of the dietary variety that living next to coast and fen can bring.

To my frustration, we only managed to excavate down to thirteenth-century levels, broadly the time of the disastrous flood recounted by Matthew Paris, before we ran out of time, money and space. We know that Wisbech had been a significant place for at least two hundred years prior to that. Preservation was getting better and better, the deeper the team excavated, and I would love to have reached the earliest activity on the site. Perhaps there will be another chance in years to come.

Similar archaeological stories have been revealed at other medieval east-coast port towns such as Spalding, Boston, King's Lynn and Great Yarmouth. At Wisbech, however, we had shown for the first time that exceptional archaeological riches lie beneath this often overlooked, historic port town. And we had shown that the medieval accounts did not exaggerate the periodic hazards of life there, on the edge.

It was not until the early seventeenth century, with the monasteries long dissolved and dispossessed of their land, that the Crown, major landowners, aristocratic investors and engineers could envisage and begin to carry out the comprehensive reclamation of the entire Fenland region. It was not going to be an easy or quick task. Firstly, there was little money available to finance these schemes. Investment had to come from outside the region. Those who risked only their money in such schemes were known as 'Adventurers'. 'Undertakers' were those who risked their own funds and their reputations by actually contracting to carry out (or undertake) the works. The return for these investments was gaining ownership of productive, profitable farmland.

Fenland people, who were used to treating the Fens as a huge commons from which they could eke out a living by harvesting its rich and varied resources, fought back against the drainage and private enclosure of the area. A whole way of life was under existential threat. They rioted, broke banks and sluices, and filled in newly dug ditches. Armed guards were called in to protect the works. The Civil War in the middle of the seventeenth century stopped progress altogether, and much of the drainage work already undertaken was undone. A shortage of labour, partly caused by lack of regular pay, necessitated the mobilisation of Scottish and Dutch prisoners of war. A community of French-speaking refugee Huguenots were settled in one area of Fenland specifically to help facilitate its reclamation and cultivation.

From the outset there were arguments against carrying out the drainage work and exactly how it could be done. Some said it was against God and nature, and only possible with witchcraft. Dutch expertise was brought in. One prominent Dutch engineer, the appropriately named Jan Barents Westerdyke, was among those who promoted the idea of improving the flow of the existing rivers to the sea, primarily by deepening them. Another, Cornelius Vermuyden, favoured the excavation of direct new drainage channels to shorten the journey of river water to the sea.

Vermuyden's scheme eventually won, and it is the ruthlessly straight watercourses with their accompanying earthwork banks that now characterise the Fenland region. On 25 March 1653 it was agreed that the whole of the Bedford Level, the southern half of Fenland, could be considered fully drained. A thanksgiving service was held in Ely Cathedral. This, however, was far from the end of the story.

The idea of quickly flushing the region's water out to sea via straight channels was a sound one. However, it was not fully appreciated that the gradients across the Fens to the sea, which were already very small, would become even more marginal as time went on. As the peat soil inland dried out, shrank and literally blew away, the land surface gradually lowered, requiring windmills to pump water up into the main drainage channels.

The flow of the channels was insufficient to scour away the sand and silt brought in by the tides at the channel outfalls. Sluice gates that could be closed against the tides, periodic de-silting and re-engineering of the outfalls were all required to prevent water backing up in the drainage system and spilling out onto the newly won farmland. If high water levels in the channels (perhaps caused by heavy rain or melting snow inland) met high tides and unhelpful onshore winds at the coast, the drainage system could suddenly collapse and widespread flooding would occur.

At the beginning of the nineteenth century there were still large areas of the Fenland region that had not been drained. There were also plans to push reclamation right out into the middle of the Wash, where the troublesome outfalls of the main rivers, the Witham, Welland, Nene and Ouse would be combined into one main outfall. The ambition was to win at least another 150,000 acres of land from the sea and thereby create an entirely new English county. It would be named Victoria.

This grand scheme was never carried out, but during the nineteenth century thousands of acres of land were reclaimed by embanking and pushing the coastline further out into the Wash. The new farmland was shared between Lincolnshire and Norfolk. Some of the new farmland around the Nene outfall and the old Sutton Wash was named 'Wingland' after Tycho Wing IV, the so-called 'King of the Fens'. Tycho Wing IV was from a family line of stewards and surveyors to the major Fenland landowners, the Dukes of Bedford. He jointly masterminded the outfall and reclamation work there.

In truth, the drainage of Fenland, this massive area of coastal wetland, was always going to be an ongoing, or indeed a never-ending project. Wind pumps were replaced by beam-engine steam pumps, then diesel pumps, then electric pumps. New cuts and outfalls have been made, banks have been greatly raised. Various agencies and authorities have to manage the complex dynamics of the region. Special taxes (drainage rates) are levied on agricultural properties in each drainage district in order to help maintain the system.

In 1947, catastrophic flooding highlighted the ongoing vulnerability of the region and the need never to neglect maintenance and improvement. For weeks, huge areas of Fenland reverted several hundred years back to their wetland past. There are some people today who would be perfectly happy to see the whole Fenland region, or at least a large part of it, permanently given up to swamp and sea. It would be an enormous ecological opportunity, they argue. Wetlands are among the most diverse, precious and threatened natural landscapes on the planet. But the cost to Britain's economy and food security would be immense and unsustainable.

The drainage and continuing maintenance of Fenland is the foremost example of the reclamation of coastal wetland in the UK. The drainage schemes undertaken before the Victorian period in particular, when the work relied totally on labour with spades and barrows, is an unparalleled feat of pre-industrial British civil engineering. All around the coast however, similar smaller schemes have been carried out. Vermuyden himself masterminded a reclamation scheme at Hatfield Chase, on the Isle of Axholme, at the west end of the Humber. He also had an earlier hand in reclaiming land at Canvey Island in Essex and later acquired several thousand acres in the Somerset Levels.

Romney Marsh, at around 100 square miles in extent, is the largest coastal wetland on the south coast of England. Its history is typically dynamic for such places. A series of storm surges reshaped this landscape. The storm in 1287, for example, resulted in the former port of New Romney becoming landlocked while the port of Old Winchelsea was entirely lost beneath the waves. A brand new Winchelsea was laid out on a grid pattern, wisely on higher land. Reclamation of Romney Marsh began in the medieval period by constructing sea banks and ditches to take in portions of salt marsh. A dedicated local marsh corporation was founded in 1462 to coordinate and oversee this work.

Much of the area is now fertile arable land and pasture. The latter has been strongly associated with sheep rearing for hundreds of years. The area is famous for the Romney or Romney Marsh breed. Romney Marsh has required the same sort of ongoing management and periodic re-engineering that the other reclaimed coastal wetland landscapes have required over the centuries.

Reclamation and maintenance work that once took months or years to carry out manually in these places can now be managed in a matter of hours and days with the huge mechanical excavators and the other tools now at society's disposal. Huge coastal reclamation projects are still being planned and carried out around the world, in places such as Hong Kong, Indonesia, Nigeria (where an entire new city is being built on reclaimed land), and just across the North Sea in Holland. In Britain, however, only relatively modest projects to grab more land from the sea, such as those associated with port infrastructure at Lerwick and Dover, are being carried forward.

Society now has the resources and technology to shape the British coastline in ways that people in the past could only dream of, but for the time being has chosen mainly to allow the land to retreat. 'Managed retreat' or 'coastal realignment' schemes are more complex and more far-reaching than they might at first appear. All the consequences will only be known after a long period of time, when nature has had a chance to interact with the new man-made coastal engineering works. However, many more schemes of this sort, large and small, have already been carried out or are at the planning stage around Britain's coastline, and we can expect many more to come.

Vermuyden, Wing, Rennie, Stephenson, the communities of the Fens and Somerset Levels, and all the others that grappled with enterprising and ambitious coastal reclamation schemes, would no doubt be amazed at today's loss of appetite for pushing the coastline back and creating new territory.

CHAPTER 9

FIGHTING ON THE BEACHES

Martello Tower, Slaughden, Suffolk

*I would observe that there has never been a period in all
these long centuries of which we boast when an absolute
guarantee against invasion, still less against serious
raids, could have been given to our people. In the days
of Napoleon the same wind which would have carried
his transports across the Channel might have driven
away the blockading fleet. There was always the chance,
and it is that chance which has excited and befooled
the imaginations of many Continental tyrants . . . we
shall defend our Island, whatever the cost may be, we
shall fight on the beaches, we shall fight on the landing
grounds, we shall fight in the fields and in the streets, we
shall fight in the hills; we shall never surrender . . .*

Sir Winston Churchill, speech to the
House of Commons, 4 June 1940

It is sometimes claimed, mistakenly, that England has not been successfully invaded since William the Conqueror landed on the beach at Pevensey in 1066 and then set about subduing the country. A later successful invasion and takeover by another William tends to be forgotten. William and Mary of Orange landed with their army at Brixham on the Devon coast in November 1688 and were proclaimed King William III and Queen Mary II in February 1689. The couple had been invited to intervene by an influential faction who wanted to deal with the generally disliked king in possession, James II.

The reason this is not usually acknowledged as a foreign invasion is that it was more like a civil war or family feud, given the political machinations, and since Mary was the daughter of King James II and William was his nephew. William and Mary's expeditionary force did not need to storm England's coastal defences or do battle with James's wavering navy and army. James fled to France and any minimal resistance quickly melted away. In Catholic Ireland, which was still loyal to James, the invasion and battles fought by William's forces are viewed very differently. They echo down the years in dramatic and highly politicised ways.

Invasion and submission to a force from overseas was something that England never endured again, but throughout history foreign powers did not stop thinking about it, planning it, and occasionally trying. The defence of the coastline played a very important part in fending off invasion and preventing these islands succumbing to the will of others. Building coastal fortifications has been a major political and economic issue for British monarchs and governments throughout history.

When we think about invasion attempts, we perhaps tend to forget those that happened as a result of disagreements a little closer to home. British history is punctuated with outbreaks of fighting between the individual countries that occupy these islands. Land campaigns across the borders characterise these conflicts, but the coastline has also played a vital role in this kind of warfare.

Scotland launched several invasions of England, perhaps the most audacious of which led to the progress of the Jacobite army as far as Derby in 1745.[13] Estuary crossings and coastal raids figured prominently in the wars between England and Scotland from medieval times through to the eighteenth century. Throughout this time the navies of both nations played roles in transporting troops and supplies. The ships of the two nations also occasionally clashed directly, and respective monarchs certainly prepared for naval warfare.

James IV of Scotland and Henry VIII of England typify the particular antagonism between the rival nations. The two monarchs engaged in a warship arms race. James commissioned *Michael* (or 'Great Michael'), which was probably the largest warship then afloat when completed in 1512. It was very much bigger than Henry VIII's celebrated *Mary Rose*, which had been completed two years earlier. Henry, in reply, commissioned an even larger warship, *Henry Grace a Dieu* (or 'Great Harry').

Henry VIII is credited with building up a proper Royal Navy, rather than relying chiefly on requisitioned merchant ships for campaigns and emergencies, or capturing enemy ships, as many medieval kings had tended to do. The construction of many new ships requires plenty of raw materials such as timber and iron, lots of skilled labour and good shipyards, all of which have impacts on the landscape and social effects well inland.

---

13 Although the full-scale invasion of the Wembley pitch in 1977 comes a close second. Scotland had beaten England 2–1 and the Wembley goalposts did not survive the celebrations of jubilant Scottish fans!

The wars between Scotland and England left a physical legacy in the coastal and estuarine landscapes of the north and south. The castles at Edinburgh, Carlisle, and the fortified border town of Berwick-upon-Tweed testify to the hundreds of years of border strife. In Wales too, mighty medieval coastal and estuarine castles (such as those at Conwy, Caernarfon, Beaumaris, Harlech, Pembroke, Newport and Cardiff) graphically show how important seafaring and ports were considered to be in the conquest and control of that country. King Edward I, who was responsible for many of the finest castles in Wales, relied on his fleet to support invasions and conquest of Wales in the 1270s and 1280s, and then to supply his castles and quell rebellion.

Thankfully (almost) all home national conflict ultimately subsided with annexation and union. However, leaving internal 'family' feuding aside, all of the British nations have been subject to serious threats from overseas, some close calls, and instances of foreign forces actually landing on British shores. Many of these episodes have been all but forgotten as inconvenient contradictions of the 'invulnerable since 1066' boast. They have nevertheless left a striking physical legacy on the British coastline.

The first line of defence has long been the natural moat that surrounds the British Isles and the presence of a navy, but that could not be relied upon to discourage and repel invaders on its own. Fortifying Britain's coastline has been an urgent necessity, a long-term precaution and significant deterrent throughout recorded history. The Romans appointed a special commander, 'The Count of the Saxon Shore', to stem the increasing seaborne attacks on Britain from non-Roman Northwest Europe.

In the third century, a chain of distinctive coastal 'Saxon Shore' forts (which also probably functioned as depots and trading settlements) was built around the south and east coast of England, from the Solent to the Wash. Roman forts and signal stations were also built along the north-west and north-east coasts to offer protection at the northern margins of the Roman province. Burgh Castle in Norfolk is an excellent example of a Saxon Shore fort. A short walk from the village of the same name will bring you face to face with an astoundingly complete and impressively large and lofty circuit of Roman walls and towers.

This was a serious fortification. Its flint walls, striped with levelling bands of red tile, still amply convey the engineering prowess and determination of the Roman administration and the severity of the threat. This fort, probably known to the Romans as *Gariannonum*, was built to control a North Sea estuary, at which the rivers Waveney, Yare and Bure met. The mouth of the estuary was subsequently diverted and narrowed by the growth of Great Yarmouth, but you can get a good impression of its former extent, and the strategic importance of this site, by looking out over the adjacent Breydon Water and the Halvergate Marshes of the Norfolk Broads.

Pevensey Castle (*Anderida*), near Eastbourne on the East Sussex coast, was built in an equally strategic location, but has become landlocked a mile from the current shore by coastal reclamation. Its walls failed to protect a Romano-British community still trying to resist Saxon invasion at the end of the fifth century, decades after Rome had withdrawn its protection of Britain. The *Anglo-Saxon Chronicle* records: 'Aelle and Cissa besieged Andredescester and slew all the inhabitants – there was not even one Briton left there.' This part of Britain soon became the land of the South Saxons: Sussex.

William the Conqueror probably refortified the abandoned Roman fort after landing at Pevensey in 1066. It was later permanently remodelled and augmented to become a medieval castle. Portchester Castle (probably *Portus Adurni* to the Romans), the Saxon Shore fort that guarded Portsmouth Harbour, was similarly adapted to become a medieval castle. Many ancient coastal fortifications regained great strategic value in the following centuries as similar threats by different foes appeared.

Entirely new castles were also built at or near the coast throughout the medieval period. They projected power and protected vulnerable areas, and made good use of the sea to ensure the flow of supplies to garrisons, but these were not part of a coordinated national coastal defence campaign. Imposing and effective castles such as Dunnottar in Aberdeenshire, Dunstanburgh and Bamburgh in Northumberland, Orford in Suffolk, Hadleigh Castle near Southend in Essex, Rochester in Kent, and even Dover Castle, were built at separate times by different people in the medieval period, for varying (often regionally specific) reasons.

CASTLES ON THE SAND

It was not until the reign of Henry VIII that what could be considered the first comprehensive national coastal defence policy was implemented. This was prompted by an alliance between the French and Spanish kings and the Pope. Their collusion opened the way for a Holy War against (largely) Protestant Britain, an invasion and the imposition of Catholic superstate control. Henry not only commanded new fortifications to be constructed on the English coast and the coast of South Wales, but he also took a direct hand in designing them. The document ordering the work was known as the 'Device by the King'.

The most radical of the new forts, intended to defy cannonball barrages, were squat, thick-walled and based on interlocking and concentric circles. Others, borrowed from continental designs, had sharp-angled, spearhead-shaped bastions, again to deflect cannonballs. Simple, smaller, thick-walled blockhouses sufficed where more elaborate designs were not justified. They all looked very different to the lofty medieval castles that preceded them.

Many of these robust structures survive to this day. Walmer Castle in Kent, a building in which both the Duke of Wellington and W.H. Smith (of the high-street shop family) also once lived and died, eventually went on to house the Queen Mother. Surrounded by magnificent gardens, Walmer Castle's moat became a delightful, lush lawn with colourful shrub borders. Its former gun ports were enlarged into glazed windows so that the castle's occupants could gaze out over its luxurious grounds in comfort. Walmer Castle is now furnished like many stately homes and country houses, albeit a very quirky one with a maze of strangely proportioned rooms and curving walls.

The transformation of one of Henry VIII's 'Device Forts' into a luxury home for the great and good, rather than being left to ruin, was a result of it becoming the base for the Lord Wardens of the Cinque Ports. This was a role that was once vital to the development and defence of the principle south-coast ports of Sandwich, Dover, Hythe, New Romney and Hastings, but it became a ceremonial appointment in modern times. Walmer Castle is now managed by English Heritage and is open to the public. Even better, it is possible to book a short stay there and have the grounds to yourself in the evenings, which my family and I have enjoyed a couple of times. You do not get the Queen Mother's state apartments, but the Garden Cottage is more than ample.

At Deal, an easy walk or cycle ride away from Walmer Castle along a beach path, a sister fort can also be visited. Deal Castle, also now managed by English Heritage, is in a more original, austere, warlike form. It provides a contrasting insight into the much less genteel lives of castle captains and their garrisons.

Another of the many Device Forts, 'Henrican' forts or blockhouses that can still be visited is Southsea Castle near Portsmouth. Southsea Castle is prominent in a remarkable painting of the Battle of the Solent in 1545. The painting is titled *The Encampment of the English Forces near Portsmouth* and dates to the time of the battle, or only a few years later. The original painting was lost in a fire, but thankfully it had been faithfully copied in the 1770s.

In the foreground of the painting, the walled port town of Portsmouth is shown, along with the grassy expanse of Southsea Common. The greensward is crowded with troops and colourful tents. Southsea Castle, bristling with cannon, occupies the midpoint. Just beyond in the Solent, the English and French fleets converge, exchanging the first shots. The *Mary Rose* is shown as already sunk. Rescue boats head for survivors in the water and clinging to the crow's nests.

In the background, to the right, the Gosport side of the harbour can be seen, with another fort on the headland. At the top of the painting in the background, buildings on the coastline of the Isle of Wight burn after a failed French attempt to capture the island. It is a busy and dramatic picture. In illustrating a full-blown French invasion attempt, the painting also provides a glimpse of the character of this stretch of south coast in an era when such illustrations of coastal scenes are few and far between.

Henry himself watched from Southsea Castle as the English and French fleets clashed, and saw his favourite warship, *Mary Rose*, sink in front of him. Southsea Castle had been completed only a year earlier, and Henry must have considered the huge cost of his coastal fortification programme money well spent. He was now confronting a massive French invasion fleet, many times larger than the later and more famous Spanish Armada. Southsea Castle was not put directly to the test on this occasion, but the French did try to capture Sandown Castle, a Device Fort still under construction on the Isle of Wight. They failed. The French force also landed at Seaford on the East Sussex coast, where again they were driven back.

Catholic Europe, especially Spain, continued to pose the main threat to the realm of Henry's daughter, Elizabeth. Everybody knows about the defeat of the Spanish Armada, a huge invasion force sent against England in 1588. It was thwarted through a combination of British skill, pluck and British weather, with divine intervention, according to some, thrown in for good measure. A commemorative medal struck afterwards is inscribed: *Flavit* [Jehovah] *et dissipati sunt 1588,* which translates as, 'God blew and they were scattered 1588.'

Less well known are the more successful smaller raids made against Britain by Spain. In 1595, for example, a Spanish force landed in Cornwall, attacking and burning Mousehole, Newlyn, Paul and Penzance. If you wander the back streets of Mousehole, you can find the only building said to have survived the Spanish bombardment, pillage and fire. A plaque on the wall records the death of Squire Jenkyn Keigwin while defending his home against the raiders.

Without getting too politically controversial, it is a fact that Britain, at one time or another, has had serious quarrels with many European countries, and has needed to defend itself against them. Feuds with the French have been de rigueur throughout most of British history, except for Scotland, which traditionally and frequently has allied itself with France against England.

These encounters have left a strong folk memory on both sides of the Channel, which feeds into much humour today, and perhaps a bit of lingering mistrust and suspicion. By contrast, remnant animosity for the Dutch seems to have completely dwindled away over time. Nevertheless, over a period of more than 150 years, from the mid-seventeenth century to the early nineteenth century, the British and Dutch fought intermittently but bitterly for control of the seas at home and away.

The humiliating Dutch raid on the Royal Navy's Medway dockyards and other east-coast ports in 1667 caused mass panic and even threatened King Charles II's grip on the crown. Coastal defence immediately came under increased scrutiny, and Charles spent the rest of his reign building and beefing-up fortifications, particularly around the key ports.

Tilbury Fort on the Essex bank of the Thames is an excellent example of the result. Henry VIII built the first small artillery fort there as part of his chain of coastal defences. Henry's fort was augmented in Queen Elizabeth's reign, and it was not far from there that she gave her famous rallying speech to the troops getting ready to fight the Armada. However, it was not until after the events of 1667 that construction began on a massive new Tilbury Fort.

Ironically it was designed by a Dutchman, Sir Bernard de Gomme, who had served as a military engineer in Britain since the beginning of the Civil War. It took nearly fifteen years from 1670 onwards to complete de Gomme's elaborate fort in this marshy, desolate spot. Based on a pentagon, the stout ramparts formed by brick-lined earth banks had angled bastions at their corners, and were surrounded by concentric wide moats on the landward side. Narrow wooden bridges that incorporated drawbridge sections controlled access.

Tilbury Fort went on to play many military roles in war and peace. In 1916, anti-aircraft guns mounted on its venerable ramparts even brought down a Zeppelin. The old fort was finally vacated by the army in 1950 having been a very effective deterrent to raids on London for nearly four hundred years. Nobody was able to repeat what the Dutch had done in 1667. In fact, the only fatalities suffered by the Tilbury garrison are reported to have occurred in 1776 when a cricket match on the parade ground went badly wrong. A fight started between teams from Kent and Essex, guns were grabbed from the guardhouse, and two members of the garrison and one player were killed.

Throughout the eighteenth and early nineteenth centuries, many old coastal forts were adapted and upgraded to modern artillery standards, but entirely new designs were also introduced. Martello towers were a key element of coastal defence in the Napoleonic Wars. The unusual name 'Martello' derives from a mispronunciation and typo.

The Royal Navy was very impressed by the resistance to its bombardment offered by a defensive tower at Mortella Point, while attempting to capture Corsica in 1794. So before the tower was destroyed during the British withdrawal from the island in 1796, it was sketched so that its design could be scrutinised and copied at home. The British engineers decided to name their new type of artillery tower after the structure that had given them so much trouble at Corsica, but they got the name slightly wrong.

Like Henry VIII's forts, the near circular, ovoid shape of British Martello towers was designed to ensure that the enemy's cannon and musket shot struck mainly glancing blows. However, Martello towers were far simpler and smaller than Henry's forts. They looked rather like a sandcastle made by a plain round, plastic bucket. Typically, a traversing cannon was placed on their roof, and this was protected by a substantial parapet. Narrow gun loops allowed muskets to fire at attackers from within the thick walls of the tower. Each tower was intended to house a garrison of one officer and twenty-four soldiers.

Between 1804–12, a chain of 103 Martello towers was constructed from Seaford in Sussex around the south and east coast of England. They were situated within cannon shot of each other, and were expected to offer stiff resistance to Napoleon's invasion forces. Martello towers were also built on the coasts of Scotland, Wales, Ireland, Jersey and Guernsey, and in British colonies around the world. More than forty English Martello towers have survived demolition and destruction by the sea. Some have been converted to residences and holiday homes, like Henry VIII's Walmer Castle, though on a far more humble scale.

My wife and I once stayed in the Martello tower at Aldeburgh on the Suffolk coast for a short winter break. This one is the most northerly and last to be built in the chain. The building campaign was finished with a flourish, as Aldeburgh's is the largest Martello tower, and the only one with a quatrefoil plan (effectively four intersecting towers). The Landmark Trust rescued this tower from dereliction in 1971, and it is now part of its wonderful portfolio of quirky, atmospheric and picturesque historic buildings that have been adapted for holiday lets.

The views from the rooftop gun platform across the sea and coastal landscape are stunning at any time of year, but after a chilly hour or so scanning the wide horizons and imagining French ships looming into view, we retired to the quarters below. As darkness fell, the wind lashed sea spray around the walls of what was briefly our very own Martello tower.

I settled down to read out the comments in the visitors' book, which is usually good fun in these places. However, somebody had concluded the (largely favourable) review of their stay with the question: '. . . but why is there a human femur in the basement?' I quickly went down with a torch to look, but found only rubble in the partially flooded floor below. If a human femur ever was there, it could not have been the severed leg of a French attacker or British defender, since Napoleon did not attack this area, though his and other forces did land elsewhere on the British coast.

Infamously, one French (and partly Irish) force of around

1,400 troops successfully landed at Fishguard in Wales in 1797. The invading soldiers split into ill-tempered factions, which variously looted farms and villages and got drunk, or took up defensive positions and pondered their next objective, which was to capture the port of Bristol. The campaign descended into complete chaos.

A woman named Jemima Nicholas is said to have played a key role in foiling the would-be invasion. It is claimed that she encouraged her female neighbours to put on their traditional Welsh dress of red cloaks and tall black hats in a successful ruse to convince the French that there were more 'redcoat' British soldiers in the area than there were. Jemima is credited with capturing twelve French soldiers herself, armed only with a pitchfork.

Warfare became increasingly global during the eighteenth century. Fights with competing powers raged in colonies and on the seas. American ships attacked British ships just off the British coast during the American War of Independence, and in the 1770s American raiding parties actually went ashore in some places, terrorising coastal communities.

Even in times of relative peace, there were threats to coastal communities from far across the sea. From the early sixteenth century into the nineteenth century, North African corsairs – 'Barbary pirates' – together with some European renegades, were encouraged by the Ottoman Empire and its Muslim states to plunder the shipping of Christian countries and capture their crews. They ranged around the Mediterranean, along the Atlantic coast of Europe, around Britain and as far as Iceland.

Not content to attack ships, they also went ashore to raid coastal communities and cart off more captives. The people they caught were destined to be sold in the slave markets of North Africa, which had been a centre of Black African enslavement for centuries before Europeans began the transatlantic slave trade in West Africa. A variety of fates awaited the unfortunate British, French, Italian and Spanish citizens captured, sold and bought by magnates in Algeria, Morocco, Tunisia and Libya. Enslaved sailors might be sent to the oared galleys and sailing ships. Many others were sent to labour on vast, often entirely pointless, building projects. Women captives almost inevitably faced sexual slavery.

Estimates of the number of European Christians taken into slavery by North African Muslims over a period of around three hundred years from the 1500s onwards range from hundreds of thousands, to well over one million. Perhaps more than two million Europeans of all origins suffered this fate, but the exact number is not known with any certainty. In the British Isles, the south-west coast of England and coast of Ireland were particularly harassed. In one incident in 1625, around sixty people were taken from the Mount's Bay area in Cornwall, which had also suffered from Spanish raids a few decades earlier.

The navy seemed to be unable to stop the free-ranging pirate ships. In 1627, Barbary pirates even captured Lundy Island in the Bristol Channel and occupied it for several years, under the Ottoman flag. At times the raids became so frequent and disconcerting that fishermen and traders refused to set out from their ports.

There were other economic and social consequences. Customs revenue included an additional 'Algerian Duty', which had to be paid by merchants, to raise funds to deal with the problem. Substantial amounts of money were collected from coastal communities in order to try to relieve the suffering of British captives and to pay huge ransoms where possible. However, coastal communities and the captives felt that the protection provided by their government was woefully inadequate. How this experience fed into the civil unrest of the seventeenth and eighteenth centuries, and British attitudes towards the enslavement of others, is difficult to assess. It must have at least contributed to the general distrust of authority and acceptance of rugged independence that characterised many coastal communities.

Along with expeditions to purchase the release of slaves, Britain occasionally sent warships to bombard places on the Barbary Coast and 'negotiate' in a different way to paying ransoms. Even the young nation of America, many of whose citizens were also captured and enslaved by Barbary pirates, sent warships to fight on the North African coast in the early 1800s. Barbary piracy was eventually stopped with the French conquest of Algiers in 1830, Scandinavian naval expeditions to Morocco in 1843 and a final French bombardment of the Moroccan port of Sale in 1851.

It was the French, a persistent old enemy, who prompted the next huge coastal-defence building programme around Britain's coast. In 1860 a Royal Commission on the Defence of the United Kingdom drew attention to the growing power of the French navy. Lord Palmerston, the Prime Minister, backed a plan to build a chain of new coastal fortifications in strategic areas around the coast, particularly to protect naval bases. In fact forts were already being built, but this modest start then turned into the most extensive and most expensive campaign of fortification construction ever undertaken in peacetime.

By the time the building of these new giant forts was brought to a close, the potential threat from the French had passed and they were immediately redundant. The forts were soon lampooned as costly ornamentations resulting from a daft idea. They were widely known as 'Palmerston Follies'. Again, some of these fortifications, though very outdated, were adapted to find some military uses during the two world wars of the twentieth century. Subsequently a few have found surprising new uses in the modern world, not just as museums and tourist attractions, but holiday lets, hotels, and even sports centres.

Cliffe Fort on the Hoo Peninsular, overlooking the Thames, was completed in 1870. It was paired with Coalhouse Fort, built at the same time, on the opposite bank of the river. These two forts were designed to provide a complete curtain of firepower that no enemy ships could pass through, however strongly iron-clad. Cliffe Fort is now marooned and crumbling within an aggregates site and not accessible to the public. I was once given permission to visit under the supervision of an experienced guide. Gaining access to the interior of the fort required a mechanical digger to excavate sand and gravel away from an entrance that had been deliberately blocked to prevent 'urban explorers' and others getting in.

This really is a very dangerous place now. I could not believe the sight that greeted me after I had scrambled through the narrow gap between sand and masonry. The interior, a huge courtyard, is completely flooded. Trees and shrubs have taken hold everywhere. Looking across the interior swamp to the fort's vegetation-encrusted inner walls was like a film version of explorers coming across an ancient temple in the jungles of South America. Using alpine walking sticks, we tentatively groped our way around the edge of the swamp made even more treacherous by hidden rubble, iron fittings, and other debris dislodged by deliberate dismantling and natural decay.

Up on the gun floor, the huge casemates gave a good impression of the size of the guns that were once housed there. All the guns have long gone, but another intriguing feature remains on the shore. This is the launch ramp for a Brennan Torpedo. Considered to be the world's first truly successful 'guided missile', this torpedo could be manually steered by wires towards a moving ship. It was never fired in anger at Cliffe Fort, but one fired from there did manage to hit and sink a ship, totally accidentally, during a trial. This at least proved the concept of this Victorian coastal defence innovation, albeit in a highly embarrassing and expensive way. Thankfully, no lives were lost.

EXPLOSIVES

Empty stretches of the coast have been used for gunnery practice as long as guns have been around. Local militia and regular army firing ranges nestling in the dunes were not problematic before the age of mass tourism and the popularisation of long coastal rambles. Other preparations for war presented far greater dangers to coastal communities and have left much more impact on the coastal landscape.

On the Hoo Peninsula not far from Cliffe Fort is a vast, intriguing complex of earthwork mounds, revetments, enclosures, ruined concrete buildings and other structures. You can get some impression of this mysterious place from the coastal path that runs along the sea bank bordering the site, but flying over it (or looking on Google Earth and similar sources) reveals much more of its pattern. The regimented layout of this huge complex is superimposed on the earlier landscape of crooked ditches that drained former coastal marshland. The widespread use of earthworks and the generous spacing between the various buildings and structures of the complex is significant.

This is the former Cliffe Explosive Works. It was established around 1890, first to store and distribute gunpowder, and then to manufacture explosives. During the First World War it was taken into government control and massively expanded in order to feed the insatiable demand for cordite. The manufacturing process involved mixing nitroglycerine, guncotton and other materials, before drying the result. The cordite would then be shipped out to various 'filling factories' to be placed into ammunition and explosive charges of various kinds. Needless to say, this remote spot was chosen to lessen the impact of accidents. And accidents did occur.

On 4 February 1904, four workers were killed by an explosion during the 'fuming' of nitroglycerine, a highly volatile substance. There were at least twenty-one fatalities and thirty-eight injuries severe enough to be reported at this site between 1904 and its closure in 1921. It only took some foreign contaminant to fall into the mix at the wrong stage of the process, or for an unguarded spark to occur, for instant and non-survivable explosions to happen. The separation of buildings and liberal use of earth banks prevented one explosion turning into many. The little village of Cliffe tragically witnessed the loss and burial of several villagers employed at the Works, but was far enough away to avoid serious damage.

Stretching for around nine miles on the north side of the Solway Firth and River Esk, from Eastriggs in Scotland to Longtown in Cumbria, is a similar complex to that at Cliffe, but even more vast. This was His Majesty's Factory Gretna, built in 1915 in response to the 'shell crisis'. Britain's shortage of suitable ammunition was threatening to hand Germany victory by default and became a political scandal. Gretna, like Cliffe, specialised in cordite. It was the largest such facility by a long way, producing more cordite than all the other British factories put together.

In the wartime peak workforce of more than 16,000, the 'Gretna Girls', women workers, outnumbered the men two to one. Barrack towns of wooden huts had to be built to accommodate this huge new coastal population, which arrived from all over Britain. The village of Eastriggs, previously just a farm and scattering of cottages, was effectively created for this purpose. A new town at Gretna was planned and rapidly built in red brick in a socially enlightened way. It not only included plenty of green space between houses and hostels, but amenities such as churches, a dance hall, cinema, library, school and hospital.

Arthur Conan-Doyle, in his role as a war correspondent, visited HM Factory Gretna and saw how the Gretna Girls handled the cordite mixture, actually kneading it with their hands. He called it the 'devil's porridge'. The feminist writer Rebecca West likened it to honey cake. It was, however, a far more unpleasant substance than either of those things. Gretna Girls gradually turned yellow through exposure to sulphur and came to be nicknamed 'canaries'. Gum problems and tooth loss were among the other medium-term health issues. Instantaneous vaporisation by explosion was among the short-term health issues.

Nevertheless, jobs at Gretna were taken voluntarily by the civilian workforce and offered pay levels and opportunities not previously open to women. There was a female fire brigade and female police force. There was good accommodation, amenities and companionship of kinds hitherto unavailable to most of those who arrived to work there.

An impressive number of eminent physicians and scientists gained formative professional experience at HM Factory Gretna, including the Australian chemist who went on to invent Vegemite, which is devil's porridge to some and honey cake to others. I make no comment about the inspiration for this Australian staple. Cordite production ceased rapidly at Gretna after the armistice, but the site went on to be used for munitions storage in the Second World War. The Devil's Porridge Museum at Eastriggs tells the story of this fascinating place.

Lydd in Kent lends its name to 'lyddite', an explosive developed there and widely used in the Boer War and First World War. The coastal marshes and shingle there also hosted major military camps and artillery ranges from the late nineteenth century onwards. Formative aerial reconnaissance units came there too, using large kites to lift brave human artillery observers hundreds of feet into the air. Balloons and man-lifting kites were succeeded by airships and aircraft in the First World War, and a new form of warfare was born.

Aerial warfare allowed Britain's enemies to avoid its vigilant navy and hop over the watery moat and coastal defences that hitherto had protected the home islands. Impotence in the face of this new kind of threat was graphically illustrated by the onset of German airship raids and then Gotha bomber raids. In the winter of 1914, German battleships managed to get close enough to the British coast to lob shells into Great Yarmouth, Scarborough, Hartlepool and Whitby, causing significant damage and casualties. This type of attack, though causing outrage, was treated as a wake-up call and something that could be countered. The aerial raids, however, produced a panic out of all proportion to their initial impact.

On Christmas Eve 1914, a Mr Terson of Dover was out picking sprouts when his vegetable patch was instantly transformed into a smouldering crater. German aircraft had just dropped the first aerial bomb to land on British soil. Mr Terson and his neighbour, who was up a tree cutting holly, escaped serious injury. Damage was limited to some broken windows and the loss of vegetables for a Christmas dinner, but this raid foreshadowed a new and terrifying threat. Zeppelins[14] had first appeared off the south and east coasts in the autumn of 1914, but the German authorities had been reluctant to

---

14 Zeppelin is a name now commonly used for all German airships, but in fact it derives from the name of the premier airship manufacturing company, Luftschiffbau Zeppelin. Schutte-Lanz airships also played a prominent role in the air war over Britain.

sanction aerial bombing that might kill civilians. Early in 1915, however, the Kaiser lifted the ban.

On the night of 19 January 1915, aerial warfare started in earnest. A small fleet of Zeppelins set out to attack London and the Humber ports, but due to bad weather two of the airships found themselves meandering around the Norfolk coast in the darkness, where their crews spotted the flickering lights of coastal towns and villages below. The first bombs fell on the little fishing and resort town of Sheringham, a place with no value as a military or industrial target. A couple and their sleeping baby had a narrow escape when a bomb smashed through the roof of their house but failed to explode.

Along the Norfolk coast people were amazed at the novel spectacle of these aerial behemoths passing overhead and, without realising the dangers, came out to gaze in awe. At times the airships were flying so low that the spectators on the ground could see the faces of their crews. A few more bombs were scattered along the Norfolk coast, mostly without injury. At Great Yarmouth, however, a cobbler named Samuel Smith was killed by a bomb blast when he went outside to take a look at what was going on. Martha Taylor, an elderly spinster, was also killed. There were further injuries and fatalities at King's Lynn that same night. These unfortunate people were the first ever casualties of aerial bombing in Britain.

The authorities had to act swiftly to counter this new method of warfare. Home defence aerodromes and landing grounds with some rudimentary facilities were quickly established along the south and east coasts. A series of aerial patrols were set up between them. Many of these early aerodromes were short-lived and have disappeared without trace, but some went on to have important roles in other conflicts.

RAF Marham in Norfolk, for example, established in 1916 to defend against Zeppelins, is still very much active in the defence of Britain. During the First World War, attempting to intercept high-flying airships and bombers at night with the primitive aircraft then available for home defence was fraught with danger, and almost impossible to achieve. Other counter-measures had to be developed.

On the highest ground on the Hoo Peninsula in Kent, at a place called Lodge Hill, is a mini fortified barracks with an early pillbox, ammunition store and two circular gun emplacements. The purposeful but humble, derelict appearance of the red brick and concrete structures today belies their significance. This was the first purpose-built, permanent anti-aircraft battery in Britain, and undoubtedly one of the first in the world. Anticipating possible airship raids on the complex of military depots in the area, temporary anti-aircraft guns had been placed in this spot as early as 1912. By April 1914 quick-firing guns had been mounted there and at nearby Beacon Hill, and the rest of the permanent infrastructure was under construction.

During the First World War, observation posts, searchlights and anti-aircraft guns were sited in many places around the coast, particularly where vital military and industrial infra-structure had to be protected, Often the ramparts of ancient fortifications were adapted and reused for this purpose, extending military roles which began with Roman ballista bolts, medieval arrows and Tudor cannonballs into the era of modern warfare. However, the experience of defending against early aerial raiders led to the realisation that the human eye and ear were simply not capable of giving sufficient warning of an attack.

The inter-war period, therefore, saw the development of new defensive technology. Strange structures sprang up around the coast. At various places on the coasts of Kent, West Sussex, Yorkshire, and Tyne and Wear you can still see so-called 'listening ears'. These large concrete, dish-like structures set upright, are more properly called 'acoustic mirrors' and were designed to detect approaching enemy aircraft long before they could be seen or heard by human spotters. The concrete 'ear' directed the very faint sound of distant engines towards a microphone placed in front, so it could be amplified and heard by operators. In the 1920s and 1930s, before radar technology had been developed and deployed, acoustic mirrors were an ingenious but somewhat desperate attempt to gain some slightly advanced warning of impending air raids.

Over the Thames Estuary I once had another of those 'flight back through time' experiences that surpass even the privilege of seeing the historic landscape from above. A gaggle of historic aircraft, including two Spitfires and a Hurricane, sped past at the same height on a reciprocal heading a few hundred yards off to starboard. Among the formation I could also see the distinctive colouring and shape of a Messerschmitt Bf 109, the Luftwaffe's ubiquitous and formidable Second World War fighter.[15]

The formation of aircraft was undoubtedly cruising at a leisurely speed between summer airshow appearances. Their

---

15 Actually, to be pedantically accurate, I recognised it as a Hispano Buchon, which were Spanish-built versions of the German Bf 109 fitted with British Rolls-Royce Merlin engines.

engines were definitely not on wartime combat 'boost' settings. Nevertheless, with a closing speed of perhaps 400 mph, the formation was gone in an instant. A 'listening ear' would not have given much warning of the approach of the new types of combat aircraft being produced in Germany during the late 1930s, such as the Bf 109 and the latest bombers. Britain's coastal early-warning system had to develop very quickly indeed to face the crisis presented by the early years of the Second World War. In fact, the problem was being tackled before war broke out at secret locations on the Suffolk coast.

Bawdsey Manor is an elegant seaside mansion set in lush grounds overlooking the Suffolk shore and mouth of the River Deben. It dates to the 1890s and was built as a huge second home for Cuthbert Quilter, a stockbroker and MP. A plaque on the building commemorates the achievement of Robert Watson-Watt, his assistant Arnold Wilkins and their team, who in 1936 and 1937 developed the world's first operational air-defence radar station there.

It all started when the Air Ministry wanted to investigate the possibility of bringing down enemy aircraft with some kind of 'death ray'. This was not feasible, but it was discovered that shooting a beam of microwave energy, or radio waves, at an aircraft would result in reflected beams that could be measured to gauge its distance, direction, size and movements. At the outbreak of war, Bawdsey was considered far too vulnerable as a research station, so the team was moved to Scotland. However, all three operational versions of the early-warning radar (Coast Defence, Chain Home and Chain Home Low) were installed at Bawdsey, which made it additionally unique in the chain of radar stations that kept watch from the British coast throughout the war.

A restored Radar Transmitter Block building is now a museum that captures the story of radar, its role in winning the war, and the people who worked at Bawdsey, many of whom were not able to discuss their work at the time or for many years after. 'Bawsdey Stories' records the experience of women such as Hilda Pearson, a secretary from Newcastle, who joined the Women's Auxiliary Air Force and found herself called to the secretive world of Bawsdey as a Radar Operator in 1943. Billeted in Bawdsey Manor itself, she worked in shifts around the clock with her colleagues in a windowless, security-sealed bunker plotting and interpreting the blips on radar screens. Nevertheless, Hilda loved the work. Among the other novelties of the experience, she recalled that it was the first time she had ever worn trousers.

Only a few of the huge, electricity pylon-like Chain Home radar transmitter masts that once stood all around Britain's coast still survive. There are examples at Stenigot in Lincolnshire, and in Kent at Dunkirk near Faversham and Swingate near Dover. To see the most complete one, however, you will have to travel a little inland to Great Baddow near Chelmsford, where the Marconi company re-erected it after the war to aid their research. This and the ones mentioned above have been designated as grade II listed buildings because of their historical importance and rarity. Radar was crucial in guiding fighters to their interceptions, but it was impossible to prevent or break up all bombing raids.

Coastal and estuarine cities, towns and villages suffered from being readily identifiable targets, and opportunities for lost and harassed returning bombers to dump their bomb loads before they went home, just as they had in the First World War. Places such as Plymouth, Exeter, Portsmouth, Southampton, Liverpool, Glasgow, Aberdeen, Belfast, Bristol and Cardiff were hit harder and more frequently than inland cities and towns. Peterhead, north of Aberdeen, is said to be second only to London in the number of raids it received.

Hull was Britain's most bomb-damaged town. Around 95 per cent of its housing was affected and around half its population was made homeless. Dover had the double misfortune of being both bombed by aircraft and shelled by massive German guns on the French coast. Later in the war, when Germany ceased to be able to mount mass air raids on Britain, 'tip and run' raids by fast, low-flying fighter bombers caused nuisance and damage even to non-strategic coastal towns and villages.

The pretty little Suffolk village of Orford with its medieval castle and church, though surrounded by various military and top-secret sites, was itself a totally insignificant and unjustifiable target. Nevertheless, a memorial and communal grave in the churchyard records the deaths of thirteen villagers who were killed by a lone bomber on 22 October 1942. Most were civilian young people and children. Two were servicemen on home leave.

Countering threats from the air was crucial, but Britain also had to stop German boots from coming ashore. The responsibility for home defence following the fall of France was entrusted, briefly, to the wonderfully named General William Edmund Ironside. The plan he outlined to the War Cabinet in June 1940 was one of 'defence in depth', whereby layers of static defences and mobile counter-attacking forces would attempt to halt the German invasion that was fully expected to come.

In practice, Ironside had very little to work with. Much equipment and weaponry had been left in France, the defeated expeditionary force was in tatters, and the Local Defence Volunteers (later renamed Home Guard) were barely trained. Ironside's first line of defence was the so-called 'coastal crust'. Beaches were seeded with mines, festooned with barbed wire, covered in scaffolding and iron-girder obstacles, and declared out of bounds to locals and holiday makers.

People in coastal villages and towns were evacuated as the armed forces moved in and artillery batteries, observation posts, strong points, anti-tank ditches, flame-throwers, concrete forts, infantry trenches and various other anti-invasion measures were hastily constructed. It was not only the south and east coasts that had to be protected, but the entire coastline. Defence measures such as these extended right up along the coast of Scotland.

It might seem pessimistic in the extreme to have built anti-invasion obstacles so far from the Channel coast, where the full impact of a Nazi invasion was expected to be concentrated. However, just as in the era of the Vikings, northern Britain would have been vulnerable to raids from occupied Northwest Europe. There were important coastal military assets such as ports, airfields and radar stations to protect. Happily, Hitler delayed and then missed entirely the opportunity to invade Britain. The effectiveness or otherwise of the coastal defences was never really tested, except as a serious factor in German invasion planning.

My mother remembers being taken to the seaside as a child,

after the ban on public visits to the beaches had been lifted. But it was less of a picturesque seaside scene and treat than she might have anticipated. She was led down a narrow path between cordoned off minefields to sit on a patch of sand surrounded by coils of barbed wire and arrays of beach scaffolding. The great beach clean-up operation of all this defensive infrastructure started late in the war when the threat of invasion had receded. It went on long after the war had ended. All along Britain's coast, army engineers and civilian contractors were employed to clear the beaches and fields of anti-invasion defences. But they were not always quite as thorough as they might have been.

Concrete 'pillbox' forts (so-called because they looked a bit like old-fashioned containers for medicinal pills) and concrete, coastal gun emplacements designed to withstand explosive shells often proved too difficult to demolish. Where structures such as these were not obstructing anything by their mere physical presence, they were often just left alone. Anti-tank blocks, great concrete cubes, pyramids and cylinders that had been placed in vulnerable locations to hinder the enemy's mobile units, were often left in place or pushed slightly aside if they inconveniently narrowed a road or access to a beach.

A long run of anti-tank cubes can still be seen on the beach at Alnmouth in Northumberland, north of the entrance to the little haven of the River Aln. There is another set further north along the coast within sight of the ancient fortress of Bamburgh Castle. Some of these have acquired comical graffiti. They have been painted as dice and Rubik's Cubes, which somewhat detracts from the appreciation of their historic purpose!

Nature has taken its toll on coastal fortifications. In many places they have succumbed to erosion, breaking up and tumbling into the sea; concrete, brick and steel slowly yielding to the crash of waves and salt water. Scrub and tree growth is burying and breaking up many other remnants of this era. However, much still remains to be explored.

OCCUPATION

We tend to forget that in the Second World War not all British islands were successfully defended against German occupation. The Channel Islands, a short hop from the coast of France, were given up without a shot being fired in June 1940 as Hitler's victorious armies swept across Europe. The Channel Islands had been deemed strategically unimportant by the British Government and had been 'de-militarised'. British troops were evacuated, along with many civilians, and there were no anti-invasion measures in place. Nobody told the Germans, however, who bombed lorries carrying tomatoes for export at St Peter's Port on Guernsey thinking they were an army convoy.

Guernsey was later visited by a single Luftwaffe reconnaissance pilot, Hauptmann Liebe-Pieteritz, who landed on the island's deserted aerodrome and reported the strange situation back to his superiors. A handful of Luftwaffe personnel were then flown in to take possession of Guernsey, while the German army's invasion force was still preparing for an amphibious operation and a hard fight. Jersey was also lightly bombed, again with civilian casualties, but it too was taken without further bloodshed in similar fashion.

The response to the expected German invasion and occupation of the Channel Islands during the Second World War is in stark contrast to the huge efforts made to defend them during earlier periods of history. Jersey, for example, bristles with fortifications dating from medieval times, the Tudor period, and the eighteenth and nineteenth centuries. France presented the usual threat over this span of several centuries of coastal defensive construction, and the island's defences were largely successful. Despite several French attempts to grab Jersey, it persisted under British protection until those fateful days in June 1940.

Once in German hands, Hitler was determined to ensure the Channel Islands remained part of his one-thousand-year Third Reich. There was also much propaganda value in capturing British soil. The posed photographs of German officers being given directions by British bobbies, German troops milling about in English-style shops and tearooms, and parading down British streets, no doubt went down very well indeed with the German public and Germany's allies. However, there was little military value in occupying the Channel Islands, and certainly nothing to justify what happened in the next few years.

Hitler obsessively set about integrating the Channel Islands within his so-called 'Atlantic Wall'. This was a chain of coastal defences over 1,600 miles long that ran from Scandinavia down the west coast of Europe. In the Channel Islands, the defences were almost ridiculously robust. Nowhere along the entire length of the main Atlantic Wall were there more fortifications per square mile than in the Channel Islands. The German gun emplacements, bunkers, concrete anti-tank walls and ditches, observation posts, beach obstacles, minefields, tangles of barbed wire and radar stations made mainland Britain's 'coastal crust' defences look decidedly flaky.

Expecting heavy casualties from aerial attack and British attempts to liberate the islands, the Germans even built a vast underground hospital complex on Jersey, which though never completed, still comprises around a mile of tunnels. This is now a museum called 'Jersey War Tunnels', and is an impressive example of one of several wartime structures now filled with exhibits and artefacts that tell the grim story of German occupation. All this infrastructure was built under the auspices of Organisation Todt, the civil and military engineering agency of Nazi Germany. Thousands of captured soldiers and civilians from across Europe were brought to the Channel Islands as forced labour to undertake the construction works.

The Germans, like the British, were not above a bit of improvisation and economy in constructing defences. Captured old French tank turrets and field guns were set in concrete emplacements. They also used existing buildings and inventive camouflage to mislead reconnaissance and would-be attackers. On a visit to Gorey in Jersey, I noted that a house near the end of a row of buildings on the harbour side had a strange narrow, elongated ground-floor window, facing the harbour entrance. I recognised this as the embrasure for a rifle or machine-gun emplacement, similar to those of British pillboxes. The owner allowed me inside, and it soon became apparent that this was not really a house at all, but a concrete bunker. A metal ladder led from what was now a storeroom on the ground floor to a hatch above.

The first floor was also lined with concrete. Its large, single central window was originally an embrasure for an anti-tank gun. It was rumoured that there were hidden passages connecting many of the elegant and innocent-looking houses, shops and restaurants on this side of the harbour. German troops could have flitted from one building to its neighbour on the row without being exposed to attackers' gunfire. Sure enough, back on the ground floor of this property and the adjacent house, I saw blocked doorways that once connected them.

At the end of the war in 1945 when Jersey had finally been liberated, almost a year after D-Day and the Allies' return to France, the former German occupiers were made to help with the clean-up operation. Much ammunition and weaponry was simply pushed into the trenches and fox holes they had once sat in, or tipped over the cliffs into the sea. The Jersey authorities are well-used to dealing with finds of unexploded ordnance.

Periodic controlled explosions to destroy Second World War mines, bombs, artillery shells and other ordnance are still quite common around the coastline of mainland Britain. Lingering wartime hazards around the coast can be serious.

During the Cold War, a mighty explosion was something that the authorities certainly made provision for at Orford Ness on the Suffolk coast. Orford Ness, the huge, sometime expanding, sometime eroding expanse of shingle, was identified as a suitably remote spot for secret experimentation with aerial warfare. Purchased by the War Department in 1913, an aerodrome was built there on drained marshland. It was protected from flooding by an earth bank known as the 'Chinese Wall', because (almost unbelievably) it was constructed by the Chinese Voluntary Labour Corps.

Research on aerial bombing, gunnery, parachutes, camouflage, and a host of other things took place there during the First World War and inter-war period. Robert Watson-Watt and his team also went there to experiment with radar and the place continued to host vitally important secret work in the post-war years. We probably still only know part of what went on there. Today Orford Ness is in the care of the National Trust, and the public are allowed to visit this extraordinary and evocative place. From rare plants, grey seals, migrating and nesting birds to giant brown hares and rare spiders, the wildlife is as special as you might expect in the distinctive environment of Europe's largest vegetated shingle spit.

What sets my spine tingling each time I visit, however, are the mysterious structures and rusting debris scattered across the flat landscape. The excitement of visiting Orford Ness is heightened by having to book a short ride in a small open ferry boat to get there. As I approach the little landing stage, I get the strong feeling that I am about to get a privileged peep into a mini-world that was closely guarded and totally out of bounds for most of the twentieth century.

The most striking structures that can be seen from a distance are nicknamed 'pagodas'. Up close, although you are not allowed too close because of safety concerns, these two buildings are recognisable as huge concrete bunkers with flat concrete roofs supported on concrete pillars. Shingle has been deliberately piled on to their roofs and mounded up around them. But why the peculiar design?

From 1956, this part of Orford Ness became the Atomic Weapons Research Establishment. The task there was to help develop Britain's nuclear deterrent by testing various atomic weapons' resilience by subjecting them to the sort of environments and stresses they would encounter during operations. This meant heating them, freezing them, whirling them around, bashing them, and dropping them from a great height to see what happened. The pagodas' unusual roofs were designed to collapse into the building to contain whatever had exploded within.

The other test laboratory buildings, without pagoda roofs, were similarly half-buried in shingle to help contain mishaps. 'Blue Danube' atom bombs, Britain's first nuclear weapons, were dropped on Orford Ness in trials by a 'V' bomber, adding to the craters produced by dropping much less potent weapons from earlier generations of aeroplanes. The bombs were filled with an inert material for these trials. Nobody really knows whether any armed nuclear weapons were ever examined there.

In addition to taking in the eye-opening displays in various intact and intriguing old research buildings, visitors are free to wander on trails around Orford Ness to take in the unique beauty and atmosphere of the place. Though again, visitors are asked not to stray from paths and to leave suspicious-looking scraps of metal well alone; unexploded bombs are still encountered there. Away from the National Trust-managed part of the site, and inaccessible to the public, is a huge grey block of a building that looks every inch a Bond villain lair. It was built in the 1960s for an American experimental radar that could see over the horizon, codenamed 'Cobra Mist'. It used a gigantic, fan-shaped array of antennas that once spanned out across the shingle. Although Cobra Mist offered the prospect of being able to detect anything in the air across Europe to the USSR, it suffered from interference and false readings, so was eventually abandoned. The sinister-looking building and a few scattered antennas were then used as a radio transmitting station. The BBC World Service, former pirate Radio Caroline and Dutch radio stations (Holland really is not very far away) have used the facility.

Measures taken to protect Britain from invasion have left an extraordinary, varied and evocative heritage around the coastline. It may seem perverse to the builders of formidable fortifications of the past that a considerable number of these places have found new, non-military uses. But it is entirely fitting that having played their part in protecting a way of life and the freedom to enjoy it, they now play important roles in the peace that has followed.

It is certainly vital to retain and conserve as many examples as possible to act as physical reminders of a nation's and people's struggles to defend themselves. Many old coastal forts now play an important part in the tourist economy. People enjoy ice creams, cold lagers, holidays, festivals and even weddings where big guns once frantically pounded at the enemy. The legacy of war and defence, and the modern need to remain prepared, is still very much part of the fabric of the British coastline.

CHAPTER 10

THE SEASIDE

Cromer Pier, Norfolk

Jane Austen, *Persuasion*, 1818

The varied and abundant resources of the coast have been appreciated since prehistoric times. The ability of those early communities not only to subsist but to thrive there is evident. The archaeology of prehistory, however, is short on evidence of their appreciation of other qualities of the coastal landscape, such as its beauty. Nor does it cast much light on opportunities for leisure and fun. Fragmentary early written history is also not a very representative source of information about everyday joyous aspects of human life at the coast.

Surely even the pious St Cuthbert, though enduring all sorts of privations and trials on his Farne Island, must have had some moments of pure bliss? Did he occasionally look at sunshine glinting on the sea, go for a paddle in the shallows and say to himself, 'Ah, this is the life!' Perhaps this was one reason why he was so reluctant to be elected as a bishop and called away from the island.

To many people of past societies, the sea was full of malicious dangers and mysterious creatures. But those who lived at the coast would have recognised some of its benign and pleasant characteristics too, and perhaps found some time to indulge in an occasional bit of seaside frivolity. It is a mistake to think that life in the distant past was unrelentingly 'solitary, poor, nasty, brutish and short'.[16] It was not all fighting, subsistence and suffering. Every society in recorded history seems to have made some time for fun, and there are ample opportunities for that at the coast.

However, we will never know who it was that first saw the sea lapping against a sandy beach and thought to themselves, that looks nice, I will go for a stroll and a paddle, just for the joy of it. The hominid group who left their footprints at Happisburgh in Norfolk around 900,000 years ago is usually assumed to have been venturing into the estuary shore on a hunter-gathering expedition, perhaps fishing or searching for shellfish, or journeying to or from home. What if this family of human ancestors was merely larking about, paddling on a sunny day, untroubled by predators and with tummies already full?

The origins of visiting the seaside for pleasure or wellbeing are obscure. However, during the sixteenth and seventeenth centuries the health benefits of visiting the coast and immersion in salt water were expounded by a handful of advocates and

---

16 As philosopher Thomas Hobbes considered it might have often been in his 1651 book *Leviathan*.

physicians. The supposed healing properties of the spring waters of inland spas such as Bath, Buxton, Harrogate and Malvern were already well known when Mrs Thomasin Farrer noted mineral-rich water trickling from the cliffs at Scarborough, probably in 1626.

A few decades later, Dr Robert Wittie's books not only advocated drinking pints of Scarborough's spa water, but also the complementary therapies of walks on the beach and bathing in the sea. Thereafter, increasing numbers of 'health tourists' came to sample both spa and sea, providing Scarborough with the claim of being Britain's first seaside resort. Places such as Margate and Brighton quickly followed as notable sea-bathing centres and resorts.

In the eighteenth and early nineteenth centuries, ports such as Liverpool, Southampton, Portsmouth, Plymouth, Swansea, Dover and Harwich also offered seawater bathing facilities right alongside the infrastructure of trade and industry. This seems odd to us now, but these were relatively accessible places, served by shipping routes and coaching roads, and they already had lodgings for visitors. Glorious, secluded beaches were not initially sought after, as they are now, but it did not take long before resort development started to spring up in some spots that had little or no existing settlement.

Throughout the eighteenth and early nineteenth centuries, many formerly remote coastal hamlets and villages began to develop the kind of accommodation and facilities that visitors came to expect. A hotel with seawater bathing facilities might be the first new building to be constructed. Bathing machines, covered wagons pulled by a horse, would also offer some privacy to those wishing to take a dip – it would not do to be seen in a state of partial undress.

The bathing machines would be towed from the beach into a sufficient depth of sea, where their occupant would emerge to enjoy or endure the seawater. Local people became attendants to assist people into the sea, 'bathers' for men and 'dippers' for women. Their immersion treatment could be quite brutal, the bathers and dippers repeatedly forcing their clients underwater to make sure they got the full benefit.

For a growing sea-bathing resort, attracting the fashionable nobility and even more impressively, royalty, was a massive marketing coup and ticket to success. King George III, famously in need of health care, went to Weymouth in 1789 to convalesce. He became a regular summer visitor to the town over the next sixteen years and occupied a house already owned by his brother as a summer residence. Gloucester House (or Gloucester Lodge) is still there on the Esplanade, in altered form, having been later converted to a hotel and now flats.

Weymouth became increasingly famous as a fashionable place to visit and be seen, with the cream of high society tagging on to the royal coat-tails. When these sorts of people descended on an up-and-coming seaside resort, they wanted much more than a bracing dip in the sea. Bathing did not take up much of the day, so opportunities for socialising were sought. In addition to suitably luxurious hotels, elegant holiday houses and apartments, venues for dances, theatre and concerts were soon built by entrepreneurs and investors.

Outdoors, untidy shorelines and beachfront roads were re-engineered with sea walls and paved to form promenades and esplanades. Gardens and parks were also created as places where gentlefolk could take in the sea air, stroll, congregate with their peers, and perhaps even form the special relationships to further their dynasties.

The increasing popularity of holidays at the British seaside was not only due to doctors promoting health benefits and the additional opportunities for socialising, but was also influenced by another factor. The traditional 'Grand Tours' of the cultural sights of Europe enjoyed by members of British high society were curtailed by wars throughout the later eighteenth and early nineteenth centuries. Grand Tours in any case were out of the reach of all but a select few and were already becoming less fashionable as the eighteenth century progressed.

Nevertheless, the earliest seaside resorts were formed to cater for the leisured classes, and by definition were exclusive. Only those who did not have to work in the fields and factories for a living had the means to travel by coach (at a time when this was time-consuming and expensive), could pay for temporary accommodation and have somebody to take care of matters at home, and afford to holiday at the seaside. That began to change with the extension of the railway network in the second half of the nineteenth century. The expansion of steam packet routes, and the construction and promotion of railway branch lines specifically designed to serve resort towns, provided hitherto unknown speed, convenience and affordability for trips to the coast.

The introduction of statutory Bank Holidays in 1871 also helped. The amount of time that Victorian families could spend on holiday at the seaside was still inextricably linked to class, profession and wealth. Nevertheless, by the beginning of the twentieth century most of the labouring classes could look forward to at least a day trip or two to their nearest seaside resort. Works outings and trips organised by churches and chapels took millions to the seaside who would not or could not travel independently.

Certain seaside resorts became known for catering to particular sorts of visitors from different inland areas, depending on their rail connections and how the resorts were promoted. Workers from Lancashire mill towns tended to favour Blackpool. Morecambe, not far away, drew Scots and people from Yorkshire. Well-to-do Quaker families from North Yorkshire were particularly attracted to Seaton Carew near Hartlepool.

Most workers could not contemplate taking a whole unpaid week off work for a holiday, though some employers had holiday schemes and were prepared to negotiate time off. Paid leave from work was finally promoted by statute in 1938, though it took some years for this to develop into a universal right to that benefit. The Victorian era, the inter-war years, and the immediate post-war period were characterised by an almost incredible growth in both the number of seaside resorts and their rapid expansion. Many areas of the British coast were transformed. The seaside day trip or holiday became part of most people's life experience and was firmly cemented in the collective national consciousness and shared culture.

Music, literature and, above all, art played significant roles in introducing land-locked British citizens to the natural splendour of their coast, and in promoting tourism and visits to its built attractions and resorts. Before radio, film and TV, describing the coast for those who had perhaps never seen much of it was in the hands of a few travelling writers, but above all artists. During the eighteenth century, views of ports and formative seaside resorts were published by various engravers and printmakers, and these did much to bring these places to wider public notice.

Samuel and Nathaniel Buck, for example, produced a series of townscapes in England and Wales called *Cities, Seaports and Capital Towns*. From 1724 and over the next twenty years or so they travelled extensively, drawing as they went. Painters such as J.M.W. Turner (1775–1851) found much inspiration at the coast, and helped to create a strong tradition of seaside artistic endeavour that has been popular ever since. The Turner Contemporary art gallery, which opened in a purpose-built facility near Margate's Harbour Arm in 2011, commemorates his association with that seaside town.

A sense of seaside fun, rather than serious artistic commitment, was behind a peculiarly British coastal pop-art phenomenon: the saucy seaside postcard. Producing postcards of seaside resorts and coastal scenes became an industry after 1894 when the Royal Mail permitted this kind of post to be sent, and as day trips and holidays at the coast became more possible for the masses. The seaside postcard was probably one of the cheapest and most effective promotional tools ever invented, unless it rained all week and the 'wish you were here message' was more like 'wish we weren't here'.

For many years postcard subject matter was fairly edifying, portraying scenes from the resort, such as its genteel attractions, notable buildings, pretty local landscapes, donkey rides, and so on. In the 1930s, however, cartoon cards with a humorous message or scenario started to become popular. Slapstick, innuendo, double entendres, voyeurism and other obviously lewd themes were played out by caricatures of a cross-section of British society in generic seaside settings.

It may seem strange that some of this coarse humour, which would not have been acceptable in any other everyday media of the time, flourished in a family-orientated seaside setting. Perhaps it was something to do with leaving the constraints and standards of regular life behind when on holiday, and pushing the boundaries in pursuit of fun. In fact, not all of the saucy postcard material was tolerated. A leading exponent of this art form, Donald McGill, was actually tried and found guilty in 1954 under the Victorian era Obscene Publications Act. At this time Censorship Boards of local worthies were set up to check and veto the unacceptably risqué output of postcard publishers.

This kind of seaside art has dwindled today as fashions and sensibilities have changed, but you will still find these postcards at the seaside. Their particular visual style and the gentler aspects of humour are reflected in the colourful fun caricature art of Beryl Cook and others. The saucy seaside postcard is defiantly as much a part of British seaside heritage as donkey rides and Punch and Judy shows. It reflects the other side of British reserve and manners: the cheeky, bawdy, irreverent humour that Brits can indulge in when encouraged to let their hair down.

Railway posters were another enormously popular and influential art form that did much to glamourise and popularise trips to the seaside. The classic examples were produced by the main railway companies from the early twentieth century to tempt travellers on to their networks. Some of them were akin to the cartoon-like postcards, such as John Hassall's famous ruddy-cheeked, rotund fisherman skipping along the sand with the caption: 'Skegness is *so* bracing.' Produced in 1908 for the Great Northern Railway, this image and slogan was adopted by the town of Skegness, and has been reproduced with variations many times over. There is even a statue of the fictional character in the resort.

The railway posters held in greatest esteem by collectors, however, are those that depict seaside scenes in Art Deco and Art Nouveau-inspired styles. They convey the resorts' most scenic and characteristic features, always with vivid colours, and blue seas under blue skies. Originals are highly collectable and reproductions are still very popular on souvenirs such as tea towels and fridge magnets. People love to take home an idealised memory of the coast.

Artists and appreciative audiences of their work are inspired by the fact that seaside towns and villages look different to those inland. It is not only the adjacent presence of sand, shingle, cliffs and an expanse of sea, but something distinctive in their own form and character. In a seaside town you will see buildings and structures that are not quite the same as those of inland towns.

Historic inland urban development generally emphasised main roads and market places, parks and garden squares, sometimes river frontages, as the most desirable locations. As seaside resorts grew, there was instead jockeying for the premier position right at the sea front. Developers vied to make sure their buildings and their principle rooms had good views out over the sea. This often led to long, continuously built-up seafront terraces where few or no buildings had previously existed.

Merchants, ship owners and sea captains' houses sometimes incorporated sea views so they could keep an eye on comings and goings. Historically, however, most people in coastal communities were content to build and occupy houses that were end on to the sea, or faced inwardly to the streets running from the shore, so that they were sheltered from the harsh coastal environment. A sea view generally was not desirable if all your working day was spent at sea or on the shore. Cosiness was more of a priority.

The old winding, narrow streets, inns and cottages of a fishing town or trading port were often left more or less intact as it grew into a seaside resort. Grids of streets were built out from the old core of a place. These were often comfortably wide for carriages and extended outwards into the surrounding fields, onto clifftops, or down slopes and cliff sides. Places that were not previously favoured for building.

A quick glance at a map of a seaside town to find a few crooked streets among the uniformity quickly tells you where the centre of the old settlement is and where the oldest buildings will be found, even if it is not labelled 'Old Town'. Tenby in Pembrokeshire, for example, is a medieval walled port town onto which was grafted a Georgian and Victorian resort. Terraces of colourful elegant villas, town houses, guest houses and hotels with sea-facing views outside the medieval walls, contrast greatly with the narrow streets and tightly packed cottages and shops within. Tenby, with its layers of history, is a fascinating and beautiful place; an exceptional treat to explore. It also has the benefit of superb beaches.

Seaside architecture is distinctive and often quirky. Many seaside building types borrow heavily from existing inland styles, but they tend to do so with a seaside twist. Other buildings and structures are more or less unique to the seaside. The hotels, guest houses, lodging houses and villas that sprang up during the huge growth of seaside resorts from the late eighteenth century through to the early twentieth century take much from their inland urban cousins, particularly the grandest and most 'polite' examples. Architects looked to the elegant terraces, crescents and squares of town houses in Georgian cities and spa towns and hotels in Victorian cities for inspiration.

The general idea was to convey a sense of respectability and luxury, something that set them apart from humdrum everyday life. The basic forms of these buildings may not differ much between inland towns and coastal places, but decoration and finishing touches are often more extravagant. A lot more external render tended to be used on seaside buildings. This helped to mitigate the weathering effects of the harsh seaside environment on masonry. It also disguised many buildings that were quite hastily and cheaply built to tap into a growing market. Painting buildings white, cream, or various pastel colours, gave a fresh, clean and cheerful appearance to them.

Ornate shelters, gazebos, pavilions and bandstands on promenades and in seafront gardens offered respite from sun and rain. These features of the Victorian seaside were not so different to the facilities found in many inland town parks, though their ornate ironwork and woodwork often featured nautical themes.

There is one structure, however, that particularly came to define a gentle stroll and fun at the seaside: the pleasure pier.

PLEASURE PIERS AND AMUSEMENTS

Breakwaters, jetties, harbour walls and piers have practical functions to support fishing, industry and trade. The origin of the seaside pleasure pier is to be found in holidaymakers simply walking out onto these functional structures to get a bracing, closer (though mainly dry) feel for the sea, and novel views back over harbours and seafronts. Jane Austen visited the up-and-coming Dorset resort of Lyme Regis in 1804. She bathed in the sea, danced in the assembly rooms and walked along the Cobb, a stone-built harbour wall and pier that originated in medieval times. The Cobb featured in her novel *Persuasion*.

If Jane Austen had gone on holiday to Margate a few years later, she would have paid a penny to walk along that town's new stone harbour pier, or Harbour Arm. John Rennie, the prolific civil engineer associated with many notable marine and inland building projects and innovations, included a raised promenade on the structure for casual visitors. Completed in 1815, it was a pragmatic approach to keeping visiting pedestrians away from the serious maritime business at the pier, while also giving them a good vantage point. Rennie's pier is still there, and you will not have to pay to walk along it.

The varying origins, intentions and uses of many of the early harbour pier and jetty structures means that it is arguable which of them can take the title of the first ever seaside pier. However, the Promenade Pier at Ryde on the Isle of Wight, completed in 1814, is usually considered to be the first of the classic seaside piers. It was a wooden pile construction with a plank deck. It is still there, and you can promenade along it, though it has been greatly extended and modified as the access to the ferry terminal, and augmented with adjoining tramway and railway piers.

During the nineteenth century, private investors and corporations increasingly realised that if they had to build a jetty to allow passenger boats to pick up and disgorge their customers, they could also build features to attract other visitors to stroll out and watch the comings and goings. The increasing use of cast iron pile construction allowed for longer, more robust and attraction-laden piers to be built in the Victorian period.

A kind of seaside pier mania or pier arms race developed with resorts vying to have the most magnificent pleasure piers festooned with booths and kiosks, amusements, fairground rides, cafes, restaurants and theatres. Many had miniature railways to convey those who could not or did not want to walk the increasing distances of their full length. Few seaside resorts that considered themselves worthy of a place among the most popular felt they could do without a pier.

Blackpool has no less than three piers, all originally designed with particular clientele in mind. The North Pier, the oldest, opened in 1863 and was financed by the Blackpool Pier Company. A fee to promenade along it was supposed to encourage only the 'better', wealthier sort of visitor. A rival company built the second pier (later known as Central Pier) a year later, to offer less exclusive, livelier entertainments. Finally, yet another company raised funds to build and open the South

Pier in 1893, which was supposed to be more upmarket than the other two were by then.

In 1894 a London-based company swooped in to build Blackpool Tower, intended as a replica Eiffel Tower, and a novel alternative to yet more piers. The company wisely had a former Blackpool mayor, John Bickerstaffe, as its chairman. He soon had to bail out the company, but his gambled investment paid off handsomely. The new attraction soon made a profit and financed the acquisition and construction of other Blackpool attractions.

Around one hundred pleasure piers were built at the British seaside. Many had a tough time after the glory days were over. Storms, fires, being rammed by ships, and deliberate demolitions for wartime anti-invasion measures all took their toll. Around fifty piers remain today, though some of these national treasures are vulnerable or at considerable risk. A National Piers Society was founded by Sir John Betjeman and others in 1979 to promote appreciation of these wonderful seaside structures and campaign for their care and rescue.

The longest seaside pier in Britain, in fact the longest in the world, is at Southend-on-Sea. Originating in 1899 as the replacement of an earlier wooden pier, and subsequently modified and extended, it reaches an awesome 1.34 miles out into the Thames Estuary. It is a very good pier, but length is not everything. There are many delightful piers around the coast. Among those that I have visited, Cromer Pier stands out as a classic. Built in 1901, it is long enough to get that all important feel of the sea and views along the coast. It has amusements, gift shops, a cafe, bar, and one of only a few remaining end-of-pier theatres. It is not quite at the end, though. An RNLI lifeboat station is situated at the very end of the pier.

Southwold Pier in Suffolk is another favourite. Like Cromer Pier, Southwold has suffered the full range of calamities that can befall a pier since its construction in 1900. It was even damaged by a stray sea mine during the Second World War. Rebuilt in 1948, yet more damage followed until the pier was finally reduced to a stump. Happily, it was rebuilt again in the early 2000s. Its T-shaped end was added in 2002, allowing the world's last seagoing paddle steamer and other heritage passenger boats to visit once more.

Southwold Pier is Britain's only twenty-first-century pier. I cannot accept Redcar's 'vertical pier' (or Redcar Beacon) built in 2013, because it is in fact a tower. Despite being modern, Southwold Pier has all the traditional pier features: a promenade deck for a bracing walk, lovely views out to sea, along the coast and back towards the beautiful old town of Southwold with its brightly coloured beach huts. It has places to eat and drink and buy things you do not really need. It also has the quirkiest amusement arcade games you will find anywhere on earth.

Built by engineer and cartoonist Tim Hunkin in 2001 the 'Under the Pier Show' (which is actually on the pier, not below it) features custom-built, coin-operated games in the style of seaside slot machines, but with a tongue-in-cheek, satirical twist. Only on Southwold Pier can you play 'Whack a Banker', 'Mobility Masterclass' (a Zimmer frame simulator that involves crossing a motorway), 'The Housing Ladder' (buy the house or die trying) and 'Rent a Dog' (a dog-walking simulator). Or how about testing your nerve by placing your hand in a dog's mouth for as long as possible? In case you are wondering, it dribbles warm 'saliva' on you, and gives your hand a good nip if you leave it there too long.

Tim Hunkin and colleague Will Jackson also made the eccentric water clock that greets visitors to Southwold Pier. It features a figure in an overflowing bathtub and two characters that pee on the half-hour.

Amusements come in many forms, some of which are more physically challenging than arcade games. Travelling fairs with serious commercial purposes, but also with stalls of food, entertainment and games to play, have been a feature of British life since medieval times. Communities in market towns and villages would keenly await their traditional fair days, a chance to escape the daily grind and opportunities for fun. As early as the seventeenth century, simple swings had become one of the first 'rides' on offer at fairs. These developed into swing boats operated by punters pulling on ropes to get ever larger thrills.

Carousels were also originally rotated by hand until steam engines started to be used to propel these and other rides in the second half of the nineteenth century. By this time fixed fairground rides had been installed at some inland parks and pleasure gardens and at some seaside resorts. Now people did not have to wait for the fun to arrive in their town or village, they could go to the seaside to experience these novelties. Slides of various kinds have long been a feature of amusement parks. The idea seems to have originated in the ice slides created for amusement in Russian cities, which then progressed to wheeled cars that ran in grooves. There were examples in Britain in the first decades of the nineteenth century. Ferris wheels began to appear in the 1890s, helter-skelters not long afterwards.

Switchback railways, the forerunner of rollercoasters, were built in Britain very soon after their introduction in America in 1884. These were undulating tracks built on a wooden superstructure. Punters entered the cars at the top of the track and gravity did the rest. Rollercoasters and big dippers allowed more dramatic undulations, tight bends and speed as the cars were held in place on the tracks and cranked to ever greater heights under power.

The development of amusements and fairground rides at seaside resorts may seem like a frivolous footnote in British history. It is anything but. When tens of thousands of workers were given their annual summer holidays and a chance to work off their own steam after labouring in steam-powered mills of the north, where did they go? What did they do? To put it as kindly as possible, the weather in Britain, especially in the north, cannot be relied upon to provide endless days of summer sun for strolls, bathing and sitting on the sand. Even if the weather is fine, not all resorts around the coast can boast a huge array of natural attractions to keep families entertained.

There is only so much dancing, cream tea consumption and beer drinking that can be done before the lure of traditional indoor venues wanes. Anybody who has taken their young children on holiday knows how quickly and disastrously their boredom can manifest itself. But very few children are bored at a funfair. Blackpool's Pleasure Beach has an ancestry in encampments and booths brought to the South Beach sands by Romany Gypsies. The installation of more and more seafront amusements and rides by local businessmen from the last decades of the nineteenth century onwards was absolutely fundamental to the resort's spectacular popularity and success.

In 1911, Blackpool's Central Railway Station, with its fourteen platforms (the same as London Paddington today) was reputedly the busiest in the world. Blackpool, increasingly, was not about sedate seaside pleasures, it was about crowds, excitement and fun.

At Blackpool Pleasure Beach you can still ride on one of the oldest fairground rides in the world: Sir Hiram Maxim's Captive Flying Machine was built in 1904. Its missile-shaped cars suspended on wires 'fly' around a central drive shaft. Sir Hiram was the inventor of the machine gun and the ride was an adaptation of a test rig he had designed to assess the lift properties of various types of aeroplane wing. The ride's original cars were actually submarine-shaped, rather than aeroplane-shaped. The present versions reflect the 1950s fascination with space and rocketry. This ride, like early wooden scenic railways (or switchbacks or rollercoasters) at Margate's Dreamland (built in 1920) and Great Yarmouth (1932), is now a listed building.

Seaside amusement park operators could not rely on their earliest innovations and rest on their heritage-ride laurels, but have had to compete with other attractions home and away to draw visitors and their cash. Increasingly huge, fast, scream-generating rides have been built. As part of almost continual development and modernisation of Blackpool's Pleasure Beach over more than 130 years, Europe's first fully looping rollercoaster, 'Revolution', was built there in 1979. A new gyro swing ride, the tallest of its kind in the UK, is due to open in 2026. I have never ridden on the former, and will not be queuing up for the latter either. Others have also preferred to skip the more adrenaline-fuelled, nausea-inducing seaside diversions and instead sought healthier invigorating activities.

Private bathhouses and cold plunge pools were built by the nobility in the grounds of their country houses during the eighteenth century to promote good health. The design for two sea baths featured surprisingly prominently on the plan drawn up for the Duke of Montagu's 'Montagu Town' in the eighteenth century. The Duke's Bath Cottage, a little thatched building of 1760 that can be seen near the tidal Beaulieu river today, is quite different to the grandiose, neo-classical building depicted on the earlier plan, but presumably fulfilled the same function.

The convenience and pleasure of bathing in the sea are of course dependent on tides and weather, and a decent beach. Some places had muddy foreshores that did not lend themselves to bathing machines. Therefore, many of the early seaside resorts offered alternative seawater bathing facilities. Bathhouses built near the shore provided indoor baths in warm seawater, regardless of the elements.

Swimming, rather than just bathing in seawater, became increasingly popular throughout the nineteenth century. Victorian Acts of Parliament encouraged local authorities to build public swimming baths. The seaside had the natural advantage of being able to create swimming pools on the shore that could fill with the tide, and retain water for bathers when the tide went out. Any seaside resort worth its salt had seawater or freshwater outdoor pools at the seafront.

Sadly, most seaside open-air swimming pools closed and were filled in for new developments in recent decades as a seemingly less hardy public shifted to warmer indoor pools and other activities. Nevertheless, the seawater-fed Tinside Lido, built in 1935, is still open for business during the summer months on Plymouth's waterfront. The Jubilee Pool at Penzance, which opened in the same year, is also still loved by devotees of seawater bathing. It was restored after storm damage in 2014, rather than being left to decay. It even has a geothermal pool, which opened in 2020. At Hunstanton some consideration has been given to constructing a new 'marine lake' or open-air swimming pool near the site of an old seafront lido. The 1920s open air pool, named 'The Blue Lagoon', closed in 1967 and was succeeded by an indoor pool and leisure centre. Renewed interest in the benefits of outdoor swimming may yet prompt a resurgence of open-air pools at other coastal resorts.

BEACH HUTS AND HOLIDAY CAMPS

At some point one of the operators of a seaside bathing machine must have given the horse that pulled it a day off, and asked their customers to walk a few extra yards into the sea instead. Having a private place to change was important to most Victorian and Edwardian bathers, but as swimming increased in popularity most folk would have felt much less self-conscious about being seen walking down the beach into the sea in their bathing costumes.

Simple wooden huts or even canvas tents above the reach of the tide provided sufficient privacy for those who did not wish to squirm around under coats and blankets to change. And if old bathing machines were no longer being towed down to the water and new fixed wooden huts were being built, why not give people the opportunity to rent them for a day, season or own them outright? Then they could come and go as they pleased, shelter from the sun or rain, brew up a cup of tea and have a picnic.

Rows of beach huts have become a much-loved and usually colourful feature of many seaside resorts. It is not known for certain where the first purpose-built beach huts as we now recognise them were built, but a photograph of Felixstowe's seafront in 1895 shows a classic line of beach huts beneath the cliffs. No similar earlier images have yet come to light as far as I know, so this Suffolk resort has a pretty good claim.

Beach Hut number 2359 at Bournemouth, built in 1909, is reputed to be Britain's oldest surviving example. Sadly, however, it was reported in January 2025 that this hut and twenty-eight others in the row were going to be demolished to make way for repairs to the pier. The Borough Council defended its decision by saying that the huts were too run down to restore. It added that the blue plaque that adorns the hut is intended to commemorate the *site* of the first municipal beach hut. However, the wording of the plaque, which was installed by the Borough Council in 2011, implies that this is in fact the original.

It is a claim that also seems to be backed by the Bournemouth Beach Hut Association, though structures like this are perhaps similar to a trusty old broom that is totally original, except for the replacement of its brush, handle and all of its other parts over the years. This beach hut may have had a charmed life, though, as at the time of writing it has just survived a fire that destroyed its neighbours.

In many places beach huts have been built and operated by municipal authorities. These facilities can be quite uniform in appearance, having conformed to a single design and management regime. Some seaside resorts have lines of council-built concrete huts or changing cubicles, and these can be arranged in tiers or storeys as part of larger seafront developments.

Elsewhere huts are highly individual. Different owners use the available footprint creatively and come up with a wide range of variations on the basic theme, often incorporating small verandas or elevating them on stilts. Their huts are often decorated and furnished with extraordinary care. People can become almost fanatical about their beach huts, even though, let's face it, they are not really anything other than garden sheds by the sea. Beach huts generally have no electricity supply, no running water, no heating, no toilet and local regulations usually prohibit overnight stays.

But for beach huts, as for house prices, location is paramount. Huts in the most sought-after seaside spots can sell for ridiculous prices. A beach hut at Mudeford Sandbank, near Christchurch harbour in Dorset, reportedly sold for £485,000 in 2024. Prices of well over £100,000 are not unusual in many resorts. In March 2025 the average price of a house in the UK was around £270,000, though of course homes in nice beachfront locations tend to be worth very much more.

Not everybody who wanted a family holiday at the seaside was content to join excursions by train and bus, compete for rooms at hotels or run the gauntlet of guest-house chatelaines.

Victorian and Edwardian people who aspired to more than a day in a beach hut looked for other opportunities for days by the sea. Inter-war working families who could not afford to build their own holiday chalet or did not wish to do so, and were not attracted by soggy tents or caravans, found another option rapidly developing around the coastline. It was also to become a British institution.

Billy Butlin, or Sir William Heygate Edmund Colborne Butlin MBE to give him his full title, was raised in fairgrounds. Born in South Africa, where his mismatched parents emigrated, his mother brought him back to England when the couple split up. She was from a showman dynasty and the young William travelled the country with the family fairground, learning the tricks of the trade. Clearly very ambitious, he bought his own stalls, and by 1927 had made enough money to set up a small amusement park in Skegness, followed by a zoo.

In remarkably few years during the 1930s, Billy Butlin had tapped into the growing seaside holiday market and created a small empire of amusement parks and zoos at several places around the English coast and on the Isle of Man. To ensure a year-round income he had winter fairs at Olympia in London, in Edinburgh and Glasgow, and along the way acquired an exclusive license to sell dodgem cars across Europe. He opened the first Butlin's holiday camp at Ingoldmells near Skegness in 1936, and got the hugely famous aviator Amy Johnson to do the honours. A second Butlin's camp soon opened at Clacton-on-Sea in Essex, but the completion of more camps was interrupted by the Second World War.

The holiday camp was not an original idea of Billy Butlin.

Tented holiday camps were already very well established. The first of these is generally considered to be Cunningham's Young Men's Holiday Camp on the Isle of Man, which opened in 1894. Some of the tented seaside camps that followed in the twentieth century began offering a few wooden huts alongside the canvas facilities.

In 1920, Herbert Potter established a camp comprising wooden hut accommodation at Hemsby in Norfolk. 'Pa' Potter came from a very poor background, but struck it lucky by winning £500 in a national newspaper competition. Inspired by his annual holiday in the tented camp at Caister near Great Yarmouth, he set about investing his winnings in his own version of a holiday camp. Potters Resorts is the only one of the original holiday camp companies still operating as a family business, with resorts in Norfolk and Essex.

Captain Harry Warner opened a holiday camp at Hayling Island in 1932, establishing Warner's holiday parks. Fred Pontin opened the first camp in his holiday resort empire in 1946. In addition to commercial holiday camps, many religious, educational and charitable institutions established their own holiday retreats at the coast. For example, in the late nineteenth century a convalescent home specifically for Derbyshire miners was founded at Skegness. In 1939 The Derbyshire Miners' Welfare Holiday Centre was opened in its grounds. It could accommodate around a thousand holidaymakers per week in its wooden chalets. Meals and entertainment were available in a large hall, and over the following decades the amenities developed to include replacement brick-built chalets, outdoor and indoor swimming pools, an amusement arcade and supermarket.

In 1949 the Derbyshire miners opened a similar facility in Rhyl, North Wales. Both camps closed down with the decline of the coal industry in the 1980s and 1990s, but by then generations of Midlands mining families had forged loving bonds with the seaside. At Rhyl street names such as Chatsworth Road, Buxton Court and Haddon Close recall the connection between Derbyshire and this Welsh seaside town.

Despite the variety of communal holiday accommodation at the seaside it is Butlin's camps that became as synonymous with the British holiday camp as Hoover became with the vacuum cleaner. Entertainment, activities and the famous 'Redcoat' role to welcome guests and get them participating in the fun were soon vital ingredients to the all-inclusive Butlin's holiday camp package. Butlin's camps, like those of his competitors, were requisitioned to act as military barracks, but reopening after the war was followed by expansion around the coast.

Fashions change, however. The business expanded into other types of hospitality and was sold in 1972. Nevertheless, three Butlin's holiday camps, much modernised (and now called 'resorts' not camps) still welcolme holidaymakers at Skegness, Minehead and Bognor Regis. At Ingoldmells, Skegness, you can see one of the original 1936 chalets. The last to survive, it is now a listed building and after a spell as a gardener's hut is now presented in its original, sparsely furnished single-room form. Its simple timber-framed, asbestos panel design conveys the speed and economy of construction that Sir Billy adopted in building his camps. This spartan chalet is no longer available to rent for a holiday!

Holiday camps have become part of Britain's cultural

heritage. Though memories of knobbly knees competitions, bathing beauty pageants, wheelbarrow races and boozy singalongs in the clubhouse may be fading, they have left an enduring legacy. Millions of Britons have been to holiday camps, and those that have not are nevertheless familiar with them through TV and film comedies (most famously *Hi-de-Hi!*) and archive footage. The careers of many successful and beloved comedians, singers and entertainers of all sorts were forged on the holiday camp circuit, or began as Redcoats, Bluecoats or Greencoats.

The entertainment in holiday resorts may have modernised. The sophistication and ferocity of fairground rides may have increased. The themes of the rides and the subject matter of their garish decoration change with the popular culture of the times. The music blaring out (eventually) changes with the charts. But the smell of candyfloss and frying food, the laughter and shrieks of pleasure have not.

Donkeys on the beach and Punch and Judy shows are a much rarer sight now. But the gentle pleasures of a walk along the prom, pier or seafront gardens with an ice cream, or sitting on a bench or in a shelter and watching the sea and the world go by, have not changed much. Nor has building sandcastles, burying loved ones in the sand, or paddling in the sea. A modern trip or holiday at the seaside today is not so different to a trip to the seaside a century ago. It is now as much a British tradition or custom as it is a modern leisure activity.

CHAPTER 11

A Place by the Sea

Converted boat, Norfolk

In previous chapters I have explored the attraction of the coast to early people. Prehistoric hunter-gatherers came because of the rich resources to be found there. They left the debris from making their flint tools and middens of shells from shellfish consumption. Prehistoric communities exploited coastal resources and navigated coastal waters in increasingly sophisticated ways, as finds of fish weirs and boats show. They built monuments and settlements at the coast, most of which differ little from those found inland. Though in some places there are hints that their structures responded to the coastal environment or reflected particular coastal cultures.

The famous stone-built Neolithic village on the shore at Skara Brae, Orkney, is one such place. It was occupied for around six hundred years. The houses featured home comforts such as cupboards and cots built of stone. The settlement may have been finally abandoned around 2500 BC because of climate change, erosion and sandstorms, like the one that revealed the site in 1850. Similar sites have been recently revealed elsewhere in Orkney, but there is nothing much like them in the rest of Britain, where wood was more plentiful and buildings were mostly of timber.

Iron Age promontory forts, built by cutting off a headland with a deep ditch and bank, are particularly common around the south-west coast of Britain, the Isle of Man and Ireland. These have parallels with inland hillforts, but it must have been a purposeful defensive or cultural choice by some coastal communities to build sanctuaries surrounded by the sea, rather than on the nearest hill.

A particularly distinctive kind of prehistoric dwelling is associated with the coast of northern Scotland and the islands. These are called 'brochs', and were built from around 300 BC to perhaps as late as AD 200. They are circular, dry-stone-wall structures that rose several storeys to look a bit like mini cooling towers. Stair passages were built into their wall structure, and some brochs were surrounded by small integrated settlements. They seem to have been built by elites who were keen to distinguish themselves with these tower dwellings, which enabled surveillance and control over the coast. Brochs have a single ground-floor door and no windows, so would have been good refuges if enemies went on the rampage, much like bastle houses and 'pele' towers in later Scottish and borders history.

From Roman times onwards, coastal ports and estuarine bridging points attracted settled and transient populations to the coast. Coastal trade and industry prompted the growth of some of Britain's greatest towns and cities, on the shore rather than inland, from the medieval period onwards. And since the eighteenth century, the development of seaside resorts increased the coastal population further. A significant part of the British population now lives permanently at the coast. In England just over 10 million people (18.5 per cent of the population) live in coastal communities. In Scotland, 41 per cent of people live less than 3 miles from the sea.

The pull of the coast is strong. In the modern era it has been a dream for many people to have their own place away from it all by the sea. Not just for a day in a beach hut, or a week in a tent, hotel or holiday camp, but a seaside home that they can return to again and again. Some have deliberately sought out a more independent, simpler and wholesome seaside experience away from the crowds, bright lights, amusements and novelties. The coast, always a place of opportunity, can accommodate different lifestyle choices, whether temporary or permanent. So those drawn to the seaside have come for a wide variety of reasons, and have shaped coastal communities in many different ways.

Artists seeking the particular inspiration of the coast found it ever easier to access as the railway network expanded throughout the later nineteenth century. For some, the occasional trip to the sea was not quite enough. From the Victorian period and after the First World War a clutch of renowned coastal art colonies established themselves in Cornwall, Suffolk, North Yorkshire, Northumbria and Scotland. Artists were drawn to the coast by the same special qualities of light and drama that had appealed to Turner and others, but also perhaps to enjoy the pleasures of belonging to a community of like-minded people by the sea, a little apart from modern life inland.

The Staithes Group took its name from the harbour village on the North Yorkshire coast, but is also associated with the equally picturesque nearby village of Runswick. Dozens of artists belonged to the group, which was active for around twenty years from the 1890s. They included notable artists such as Dame Laura and Harold Knight, Ernest Dale, Joseph Ridgard Bagshawe and Mark Senior. Many of the Staithes Group members seemed to be particularly interested not only in the characterful, rugged coastal and moorland landscapes, but also in representing the rugged lives of their communities. They were documenting traditional ways of life that were disappearing with the increasing industrialisation of the fishing industry and its concentration in fewer, larger fishing centres.

Though inspired by the French Impressionists, there is not too much evidence of the flowery, sunny sentimentality that seems to characterise a lot of that work. The Staithes Group dealt more in grittier northern reality, with a distinct dearth of parasols. Their clients included the new classes of urban professionals, who might wonder at the fact that people and places such as this still existed in modern Britain. Nevertheless, one person's run-down cottage, or struggles to launch a fishing boat in the surf, can look like a quaint coastal retreat and the prospect of a boating adventure to others.

There is little doubt that their work, and that of the other coastal art colonies, fed an interest among those with means in getting away from it all, escaping the smog, and going to explore the 'romance' of the coast, if only for a few days over summer. Runswick Bay was soon 'discovered' for family holidays and leisure sailing, and remains incredibly popular today.

The Newlyn School was a similar group operating in and around the Cornish fishing village at about the same time as the Staithes Group. Its members, which included the Knights who moved there from Staithes in 1907, were also interested in depicting the everyday lives of fishing folk. They provided some practical assistance by taking lodgings with local families, paying them to sit for paintings, and often taking a genuine interest in their welfare.

The St Ives School in Cornwall also originated in Victorian times, but is probably most famous for its new members' avant-garde emphasis after the Second World War. Few of its earlier members could have predicted that the little fishing town of St Ives would go on to thrive as a renowned centre for art. A branch of the Tate Gallery was opened there in 1993 in a striking new, purpose-built facility overlooking the beach, on the site of an old gasworks. The town also has a museum dedicated to sculptor Barbara Hepworth, the leading light of the post-war artistic community there.

You do not have to be an artist to appreciate and be drawn to the creative, aesthetic vision of others. Glencairn Stuart Ogilvie was the son of a successful Scottish railway engineer who had undertaken contracts in Suffolk and had purchased a coastal estate there. Glencairn inherited Sizewell Hall and a place called Thorpe in 1908. There was not much to distinguish the latter. It had been a fishing community, but had declined to a cottage or two with a marshy area along a stream just behind the shingle beach. It did not have the feel of a prized or promising coastal asset.

Ogilvie junior had not followed in his father's footsteps but had trained as a barrister, a profession he also did not pursue. He was better known as a playwright, and counted J.M. Barrie, the creator of Peter Pan, as a good friend. One day Glencairn Stuart Ogilvie apparently gazed upon the misty, flooded marsh he now owned and envisioned a picturesque lake at the centre of a holiday village, where wholesome family outdoor pursuits would be encouraged. A man of means, considerable ingenuity and imagination, he began to turn his vision into reality.

The lake, forty acres of open water, was completed in 1913 and named 'The Meare'. It was dug deliberately shallow so that children could safely row and sail with confidence. To encourage childhood curiosity and exploration, the Meare was themed around Peter Pan and other adventure stories of the time. It was peppered with islands and coves, many of which had little buildings on them or model creatures peering from them. Ogilvie was keen to ensure that his resort village had a unique, whimsical and unplanned appearance, so despite rapid construction he avoided uniform house designs.

Instead, he and the two architects he employed adopted styles that borrowed from the vernacular architecture of Suffolk and the Low Countries, and interpretations of the architecture of merry old England generally. Some buildings were direct copies of real old buildings, such as a house based on the ancient Moot Hall at nearby Aldeburgh. However, the careful finishes of Thorpeness buildings with their clay tiles, red brick, stone dressings, weatherboarding and render, black timber studs and braces, hide a secret. Much of the construction was in fact carried out with concrete blocks. These were made by a machine imported from Australia, using sand and shingle from the beach. It was the reason why Ogilvie could build so quickly and economically.

The buildings of the new village held other secrets. A huge cathedral-like, red brick gate tower with stone dressings, including battlements and arrow loops, actually houses a water tank. The village windmill nearby looks as if it has been there for centuries, but again it is not quite what it seems. The white-painted weatherboarded post mill is a genuinely old building, probably dating to the early nineteenth century, but it was not built there. It served a nearby village, and when the last miller there retired it was bought by Ogilvie, dismantled and reassembled at this spot in 1923. Rather than grind corn, it pumped water from a well into another water tower, which was subsequently converted into an extraordinary, elevated home known as the 'House in the Clouds'.

Thorpeness (by now renamed from the earlier Thorpe) was formally opened in 1913. The village houses were offered for rent to well-to-do families who could stay for as little as a week or for several weeks. They could either bring their servants with them, or draw on the services of local cooks and cleaners. Ogilvie built accommodation for these workers, a workmen's club and impressive-looking almshouses for retired estate employees.

Every time I visit Thorpeness I find some interesting feature or building that I had not appreciated before. On a recent visit, wandering a sandy back lane, I found tucked away a row of timber chalet bungalows set in tidy gardens, and realised there was something familiar about them. A resident of one these homes confirmed my suspicion that these were adapted military huts. She said that they had been brought from a local aerodrome at the end of the First World War. They are the only prefabricated and mass-produced homes in the village, and I assume that originally they accommodated servants and employees.

Facilities built for the holidaying families at Thorpeness included a country club, which was named the Kursaal, after German spa facilities. It had tennis courts and was the centre of village social life. A golf club, a boathouse to serve the Meare, a pub and a church completed the amenities.

Ogilvie could have advertised rail excursions to Thorpeness. A rail line ran just outside the village. He could have encouraged day trippers by building a promenade, public parks and gardens, amusements and entertainment venues. But this was not his vision for Thorpeness. Instead he wanted a sporty, outdoor, family-orientated retreat where children could have character-forming mini adventures, within limits, and grow to become the next generation of decent, healthy, patriotic adults.

In the 1970s, Ogilvie family death duties resulted in the sale of Thorpeness houses and plots of land to different private buyers. By this time long leases had already been purchased on some properties. This fragmentation of ownership might have meant unrestricted development, the loss of Thorpeness's unique character and precisely the sort of thing that Ogilvie was trying to avoid. However, the village is remarkably little changed today. There are not any mini-supermarkets, fast-food chains, slot machines or video games. All the buildings and amenities Ogilvie built are still enjoyed.

In striving to reinforce social ideals by creating a harmonious built environment, Ogilvie's Thorpeness is similar in philosophy to Ebenezer Howard's Garden City movement. The latter produced Letchworth Garden City and Welwyn Garden City at about the same time as Thorpeness was being built, and has produced many derivatives since. A key feature in this approach to development is that it is controlled by a masterplan, a firm set of design principles, and steered by a guiding individual or corporate hand.

Elsewhere around the British coast a more anarchic approach to creating seaside holiday villages was underway.

South of the seaside town of Cleethorpes in North East Lincolnshire there is a distinctive coastal settlement called Humberston Fitties. Marginal coastal land there was used for holiday camping in Edwardian times, and during the First World War wooden barrack huts were built alongside the dunes for soldiers guarding the coast and Humber. At the war's end these billets came to be occupied by civilians.

By the time of the formation of the Humberston Fitties Campers' Association in 1925, the seasonal tents and former army huts were being joined by a motley array of caravans, converted buses, trams and railway carriages. Plots were leased by the landowner so that people who otherwise would never get the chance to own a place by the sea could build their own holiday bungalows or chalets, as cost effectively as possible.

By the 1950s, the Fitties had a few hundred individually built holiday homes, alongside the makeshift vehicle conversions. This was an extremely popular holiday destination for working families on a budget and at the height of the season accommodated thousands. The local council long ago cleared the old converted vehicle accommodation, and although some of the original chalets have been totally replaced by modern constructions, or re-clad or extended almost beyond recognition, a surprising number survive in near original form. They provide a show site of the range of inexpensive building materials available in the first half of the twentieth century. A wide variety of individual approaches have been taken to achieve the same basic format: a neat little single-storey home just about big enough for a couple or small family. Many chalets are rendered and painted cream or in cheerful colours, which in some cases probably hides concrete or asbestos panel construction. Nearly all seem to be very well cared for and most sit in tidy little gardens enclosed by picket fences. Humberston Fitties was designated as a conservation area in 1996 in recognition of its special architectural and historic character. It shares this status with many, very much older, historic villages and with Thorpeness, though Humberston Fitties is a markedly different kind of place.

Some people began to view their chalets as full time residences, but this was not exactly a place suited to permanent occupation. It was vulnerable to flooding and lacked amenities, other than those available to holidaymakers in the summer season. Flood defences, roads and sewage works were built in the post-war years, but it was not until 1999 that the three hundred or so early chalets and bungalows were connected to mains electricity. In recent years, after occupants failed in a bid to buy their village, the ambiguous residential status of the site has been tested in tussles with a new landowner which has reinforced rules against year-round occupation.

Many other self-built, pop-up communities grew up around the British coast. Their varied and often eccentric architecture reflect both ad hoc individual opportunism, communal enterprise and patterns of periodic commercial investment over the last century or so. My family's regular seaside haunt on the Norfolk coast is situated on the fringe of a large medieval village. Wasteland near the shore there was colonised by Romany Gypsy encampments during the nineteenth century, then, gradually, others brought huts, caravans, carriages, and anything else that would provide shelter for a day or night or two by the sea. When a local skipper retired, he converted his vessel to a houseboat and moored up on the little river behind the dunes. He started a trend. The local authorities reported thirteen houseboats there in 1924, and worried about sanitation. A lovely selection of old wooden working boats can still be seen. They were hauled up onto dry land and converted into holiday homes long ago. Doors and windows have been inserted into their hulls and extensions have been built around them to provide somewhat strange-shaped accommodation. Nearby, strung out for miles along the dunes and sea bank, there are pre-war timber huts and elegant bungalows with verandas that survived the 1953 flood. There are prefabs that were bought as surplus after the war, and a wide variety of later building types too. My cousins' seafront chalet is a prefabricated accommodation unit that was intended for use in the oil industry. My sister's chalet is a park home with wheels that came from the north of England. My little wooden chalet is in a small complex of identical chalets built in a former orchard in 1966 by the family that still owns the site. Between there and the shore are acres of caravan parks owned by different operators.

It is difficult to imagine a similarly extensive, eclectic mix of accommodation being built, celebrated and preserved at many places inland. At the seaside, however, things are different. The great will to live by the sea, the character of the coastal environment, and the freedom of expression it promotes has produced creativity and pushing at the boundaries of what is normally considered suitable and acceptable.

Increasingly, however, this characterful mix of seasonal holiday homes is being replaced by massive, suburban-type houses built of concrete, cinder block and brick that sell for metropolitan prices. The colourful, carefree, unplanned charm of the place is changing as people and businesses spot investment opportunities, rather than a chance of a cheap and cheerful seaside break. Many places, such as these, that simply sprang up by the seaside continue to be well-loved by residents and visitors alike. Opinions about other historic DIY seaside settlements are more equivocal.

Jaywick in Essex initially developed in a similar way to Humberston Fitties. From 1928 onwards, entrepreneur Frank Stedman leased plotlands on this former salt marsh near Clacton to working-class Londoners, many of whom were from the East End. For a reasonable price these families were able to set about building their own holiday accommodation and property investment. Many of the resulting bungalows and chalets came to be treated as permanent homes. This was exacerbated by a chronic shortage of housing in London after wartime bombing and slum clearance.

Jaywick residents generally resisted attempts for their growing village to be regularised and redeveloped. Only gradually did they get the facilities that most villages and towns take for granted. They waited until 1977 for a mains sewer system, for example. But Jaywick came to be viewed by some as a seaside 'sink estate'. Today, it faces such social and economic challenges that it has become synonymous with seaside deprivation.

The seaside is not always a prosperous and happy place. We might think that living by the coast, with its invigorating and varied environment and all the opportunities that it creates, is consistently pleasant and easy these days. It is true that many coastal towns and villages are very highly sought after and attract the wealthy and their wealth. However, it is also sobering to see how many coastal places are among the most deprived in the country.

The UK Government periodically assesses deprivation in neighbourhoods using various sets of survey data and formal criteria to create an Index of Multiple Deprivation (IMD). The latest IMD ratings were published in 2025. Jaywick once again got the unwanted crown as the most deprived place in England. It has been identified as such four times in a row now, starting with the IMD survey of 2010. Blackpool, which developed solely to provide genteel seaside excursions for the well-to-do and then fun for the masses, tops the table as most deprived town and local authority area in England. It has seven out of the ten most deprived neighbourhoods in the country.[17]

These places, situated in opposite corners of the English coastline, are by no means alone in their difficulties. Colour-coded maps have been produced that depict deprivation in every part of the country. Shades of blue indicate the top four deprivation deciles, with the darkest blue representing the most

17 https://www.gov.uk/government/statistics/english-indices-of-deprivation-2025/english-indices-of-deprivation-2025-statistical-release

deprived areas. There are too many inland areas of deprivation, of course, but looking at these maps it is as if large parts of the English coast is fringed with an icy blue crust, like a chill from the sea. Coastal towns in the north of England are prominent in these unwanted categorisations, but so are some in the south-east. Even the extremely popular tourist coasts of Somerset, Devon and north Cornwall feature places in the lower half of the indices of deprivation.

Too many coastal towns have suffered the same sort of post-industrial decline seen inland, and too many seaside resorts have seen a loss of tourism business and a subsequent loss of purpose. Cheap package holidays abroad and changing leisure habits from the 1970s onwards have greatly affected the viability of many seaside resorts.

Seasonal hospitality work is often poorly paid and there is frequently a lack of alternative employment opportunities. Under-used holiday accommodation is repurposed as cheap, year-round houses of multiple occupation, or temporary social accommodation. Lack of investment in preserving and updating facilities has not helped to retain the appreciation of many formerly beloved places by residents or visitors. There are few things more saddening and maddening than the faded, crumbling grandeur of a once-popular seaside resort.

However, there have been strenuous regeneration efforts in several places, and the better schemes will bear fruit. A 2019 House of Lords Select Committee report on regenerating seaside towns highlighted the role of cultural attractions in reversing decline. It credited the construction of the Turner Contemporary gallery and the refurbishment of the Dreamland pleasure park with breathing new life into Margate. At Folkestone a wealthy social entrepreneur, Sir Roger De Haan, and the establishment of a Creative Quarter has lifted the town. The expansion of universities, with their influx of youth, has made Bournemouth and Brighton much more buoyant and less dependent on income from tourism.

In these east-coast and south-coast places, good connectivity to the capital that can draw in Londoners and their money is also a highly significant factor. Run-down New Brighton on the Wirral has become trendier over the last few years since local entrepreneur Dan Davies began redeveloping the town's Victoria Quarter as a food, leisure and entertainment district. Periodic Government grants for regeneration schemes, such as the recent Levelling Up Fund and Town's Fund, have benefitted seaside towns, along with smaller pots distributed by other organisations such as the National Lottery, Arts Council, and Historic England. Many seaside town authorities have taken steps to maintain or increase their desirability over the years by working hard to attract a combination of commercial interest and public funding.

Other seaside places seemed to have remained sought after for a long time without appearing to work very hard at it. These are the pockets of the coast that show up in healthy light green and white shades on the Indices of Multiple Deprivation maps, rather than a chilly, deprived blue. Average house prices also give a reasonable general indication of the most desirable locations. In 2024, Rightmove identified Sandbanks in Dorset as the most expensive coastal location, as it has been in several previous and similar surveys. The average asking price for a house there was £1,582,331. The adjacent Canford Cliffs was second.

Milford on Sea in Hampshire, Padstow in Cornwall, Budleigh Salterton in Devon and Sandgate in Kent were all in the top ten of average coastal house prices. The latter was the most 'northerly' of the most expensive places. Of the ten least expensive coastal locations, Bootle near Liverpool and Grimsby were the most southerly. If you want to live by the sea, your funds will go further the more north you go.

Incomers buying up coastal properties for second homes is the cause of a lot of frustration and discontent in many parts of the country. In my book, *England's Villages: An Extraordinary Journey Through Time*, I reproduced some of the mixed reactions towards second-home owners in an old Cornish seaside village, around 60 per cent of whose housing stock is second homes.

The contribution of second-home owners to the economy of the village was appreciated by some residents, but others were extremely angry at the way that house prices had been pushed ever upwards, leaving young local families with no prospect of setting up home in their own village. They also highlighted the dwindling of village life and character. Mostly absent semi-residents do not tend to contribute in quite the same ways as permanent residents. The responses of this one Cornish community reflect the experience and attitudes of many coastal communities.

In an attempt to discourage second-home ownership, local councils have been permitted to charge double Council Tax on second dwellings since 2025. The idea is that many second-home owners will sell up, freeing up homes for local families. Average council tax is now over £2000, so an annual council tax bill hike to £4000 per year, or considerably more (around £7000 will not be unusual for the largest properties), will undoubtedly cause some second-home owners to think seriously about quitting. Some resorts have already reported more properties appearing on the market than previously.

However, this punitive measure may well backfire. Second-home owners spend their money in the local economy repairing, furnishing and extending their homes, buying local goods and paying out their money in pubs, restaurants and on a host of other leisure activities, often more lavishly than they do at their main residence, because they are on holiday. Many of the second homes they reluctantly sell will not be snapped up by local families looking for a first home, either because they are too small and not built for year-round living, or too large and too expensive.

House prices in Sandbanks would have to go into free fall before the spacious seaside villas there are remotely in reach as starter homes. It is probable that many seaside second homes will be snapped up by slightly richer second-home owners, or become holiday lets. Time will tell whether the council tax premium and other cost of living increases will build more resilient coastal communities, or simply drive second-home owners and their money away, and result in the appearance of more transient strangers and even emptier seaside homes.

Other trends that affect the popularity of the British seaside are international in nature, and their effects on coastal living are difficult to predict, let alone influence. Covid restrictions prevented people from visiting the coast at times, which hit the seaside economy hard. But it also caused people to rediscover home holidays and the joys of exploring places on their doorstep, which has had a positive effect. Concern about the cost of pollution and climate change does not seem to have dented the demand for international air travel much yet. But who knows how more environmentally conscious, restricted and expensive overseas travel might become in the years ahead?

The protests against mass tourism now regularly taking place in Spain, Italy, Portugal, the Balearic Islands and Canary Islands may have relatively short-term consequences, but they could also have longer-term effects on holidaying choices. All these places have been favourite destinations for vast numbers of British tourists for more than half a century. A decline in the welcome these places extend to visitors may simply drive holidaying Britons elsewhere abroad, or bring them back to home shores.

At the time of writing, Britain is experiencing a heatwave and the seaside is doing a roaring trade. On the Continent, dangerously high temperatures are affecting people's working lives, and inhibiting tourism. Will climate change shift more people towards more northerly holiday destinations, such as Britain's coast?

Such are the varying trends and unforeseen factors that affect visitor numbers, home ownership and business at the British seaside. Whatever the future holds, it is difficult to imagine a time when a short trip, longer break or even quality time in their very own place at the seaside no longer figure in the calendar and aspirations of millions of Britons. The British seaside is an enduring destination, resplendent with natural and built attractions that draw us back again and again, however far inland we live.

CHAPTER 12

OVER THE HORIZON

Runswick Bay, North Yorkshire

The coast is often perceived as marginal territory and therefore peripheral to national interests. From its formation, it has been anything but that. The disappearance of Doggerland, the creation of the Channel, and the completion of an unbroken coastal circuit around Britain undoubtedly had as profound an effect on the development of British society as it did on British geography. The coastline defined Britain as a place distinct from the rest of Europe and its history has been shaped by this most emphatic of physical boundaries ever since. Invasion, migration, trading and cultural exchange have been both facilitated and tempered by travel by sea and contact at the coast.

Bronze Age Beaker folk, people of the Roman Empire, Angles, Saxons, Jutes, Scandinavians, Normans, Flemings, Huguenots, Romanies and many others made purposeful journeys to reach these shores, rather than simply wandering across an unbroken landscape and finding themselves in British territory. They have all brought their own particular influences to an island Britain that nevertheless has remained culturally different from elsewhere.

If there is no sea to cross and no coastline to breach, conflict, exchange and migration tend to be more dynamic and radical than they have been in Britain. Land borders and the regions around them are often more fluid and permeable than sea borders. When we take a good look at the history of countries on the Continent, we are often surprised how arbitrary, equivocal and disputed their boundaries have been throughout time, even in recent history. National borders have carved through ethnic territories, leaving people on both sides historically and culturally attached, but administratively, socially and economically separated.

Imagine for a moment a Britain with no North Sea and no Channel; no coastal borders to separate British territory from Northwest European territories. Imagine a Flemish and Danish-speaking East Anglia, Lincolnshire and South Yorkshire, meeting the solidly English-speaking Midlands somewhere near the River Trent. Would Norman French be the dominant language of the Home Counties? Alternatively, would the western Dutch now speak English with a Suffolk or Norfolk dialect?

It is not so far-fetched. Breton, spoken in north-west France, derives from contact and migration from Britain and is closely related to the Cornish language. Today's English language is itself a mishmash of influences and borrowed words from elsewhere. It is too easy to let the imagination run wild with 'what ifs', and perhaps it is just a lot of old squit to do so.[18] Nevertheless, geography matters.

As much as language and culture might flow more freely around land borders, tensions, flashpoints and invasions can

---

18 Squit is a Norfolk term that means something like 'load of old rubbish' or 'nonsense', for any Dutch readers who want to reconnect with their sometime kinfolk.

occur much more readily. Henry VIII and Elizabeth I could hardly have defended their realms successfully against the Pope's holy wars without the navy and effective coastal defences. The armies of the Catholic states could simply have marched across to join those on these islands who were sympathetic to their cause. If they had been successful, there would have been no English Reformation. Britain might have remained part of the European catholic confederation. Five hundred years of religious, social and political self-determination, with all its consequences for British and world culture, would have been suppressed.

Without the sea moat and huge new investment in the navy and coastal fortifications, Napoleon need not have worried about the vulnerability of his invasion barges and landing his armies on these shores. He too could have marched into Britain, as he did all over Europe. Hitler knew he had to achieve total dominance of air and waves before making the crossing to Britain and storming the coastal defences. His blitzkrieg troops and tanks could not bypass Britain's coast in the same way they had simply gone round the French Maginot Line. Hitler stalled at the Channel and Channel Islands and Britain lived to fight on for the free world.

Britain has not shared the same history of unrelenting invasion, conquest and dictatorship suffered by continental European countries. Consequently Britons perhaps do not feel the warning tremors of impending national instability and oppression quite as acutely as others. We do not feel the same need to bond ever more closely with our neighbours to make sure we all stay good friends. Maybe this is why Britons on the whole have been more ambivalent about belonging to

European federations. We are European, but we are not physically part of Europe.

In his 1914 poem 'Mending Wall', Robert Frost's neighbour tells him: 'Good fences make good neighbours.' In fact he says it twice, for emphasis. It is a proverb or sentiment that has much earlier origins. Britain's coastline has been its fence. Throughout history Britain has welcomed people in through the appropriate gateways, but has also made considerable investments and fought hard to make sure the fence is not battered down by the uninvited.

Britain's coastline on the one hand has provided a useful amount of insulation from its neighbours, intentionally aggressive or otherwise. On the other, it has provided a springboard for seeking out relationships with others. As the poet and clergyman John Donne, a contemporary of Shakespeare, wrote: 'No man is an island.' He might just as well have said that no society is an island. Geographic island reality has by no means prevented the British reaching out and playing global roles. In fact, having no choice but to use the coast and sea to communicate and trade, Britain made a virtue of it.

British mariners, schooled in coastal waters, developed a speciality of venturing out further and further into the world to trade and conquer. The latter mostly to facilitate more trade. The medieval merchants who went back and forth to European countries, and the Tudor, Stuart and Georgian explorers who travelled to all corners of the world, set off in ships built in coastal shipyards. These ships, and those of the navy that protected Britain's trading and other interests across the globe, were world-renowned for centuries. They were particularly dominant as industrialisation accelerated throughout the eighteenth and nineteenth centuries. From the coast, an empire was built.

Ports such as Bristol, Cardiff, Liverpool, Glasgow and London became world ports; cosmopolitan trading hubs for many nations. These places, and the goods imported and exported through them, have had profound effects on Britain's economy and society for two thousand years or more. Britain's major modern trading ports are now largely inaccessible to most people, hidden away behind wire fences and privately owned by multi-national companies such as Peel Holdings and Associated British Ports, but they are no less important today.

Airports may be more visible (and audible) to people, but around 95 per cent of Britain's merchandise trade today is still maritime. The volume of global maritime trade is predicted to treble by 2050.[19] The continuing success of ports such as Felixstowe, which handles nearly half of Britain's containerised trade, is therefore vital to the British economy. Making a seaport such as this function well requires significant investment in road and rail infrastructure far inland. Furthermore, nearly all Britain's digital data exchange with the outside world relies on undersea cables joining the coast, not satellites beaming information from above. So the coast's trading infrastructure looks set to remain as crucial to Britain's economic vitality in the future as it has been at any time in the past.

The coast is rich in natural resources and these have been well appreciated and exploited by people for hundreds of thousands of years. Fish have been a valued commodity as long

---

19 UK Board of Trade, 'Maritime Trade'. A Board of Trade Paper, March 2022.

as humans have been able to whittle a stick into a fish spear, but sea and coast have been harvested for so much more. Shellfish, salt, and seaweed (used for animal feed, fertiliser, and glass-making among other things) were products obtained from near the shoreline. During the eighteenth and nineteenth centuries several British sea ports regularly sent out expeditions to the deep northern seas to capture whales, which were cut up and rendered down for all sorts of vital products. Opportunities to exploit the resources of coast and sea drove the development of coastal communities, and have generated a rich social and built heritage right around the coast.

The Boomer generation may have eaten all the cod out of the North Sea, as comedian Geoff Norcott puts it, so the fishing industry has inevitably changed. With it the character of coastal communities has also changed. Visitors to historic fishing ports today are more likely to see leisure fishing boats and a few commercial crab and lobster boats than fleets of deep sea trawlers. But the seafood industry is still important to Britain. Shellfish exports and seafood processing continue to be economically valuable.

Many Britons still care about fishing heritage and the modern-day industry and this comes to the fore and becomes political when the livelihoods of British fishermen are threatened by quotas, bans and foreign vessels scooping up the fruits of the sea around them. There are even signs that the British public is rediscovering some variety in their seafood diet, either through choice or necessity, after a long period of seemingly ignoring much of what the sea can produce (except cod).

Land, among the most precious of national resources, was

also won from the coast. Coastal drainage and reclamation schemes created some of the most productive farmland in Britain. This work required not only the vision, investment and persistence that has so often manifested itself at the coast, but also a good deal of technical prowess. The extraction of copper, tin, coal and other minerals from the coast and deep beneath the sea also required leaps forward in technology.

The world may have changed and demand for the British versions of these resources has dwindled away, but the British coast still has an immense role to play in harnessing resources for the future. It is at the coast and just offshore that nuclear energy and 'green' (wind and wave) energy will make their greatest contributions to powering Britain forward. The coast will also play a vital part in storing some of the most challenging waste products of progress: carbon dioxide and radioactive material.

In fact, the coast has always inspired and provided a test bed for innovation, from building ever more sophisticated boats and ships to Cornish engines, early aircraft and radar experimentation, and engineeringsolutions to overcome natural obstacles. The Humber Bridge made around four thousand years of tide and weather-dependent Humber estuary ferry services obsolete. When built in 1981, this was the longest single-span suspension bridge in the world. It needed to be very long to straddle the estuary, and very tall to allow ships to continue to pass underneath. It is still one of the longest bridges anywhere in the world that you can cross by bicycle or by foot.

Mighty estuary-bridging endeavours such as this have been augmented by astounding feats of tunnelling. Since the first Blackwall Tunnel under the River Thames opened to road traffic in 1897, a succession of tunnels has been built further towards the sea. There are now proposals for a Lower Thames Crossing, comprising two new tunnels under the Thames Estuary, to bypass the existing congested crossings. It will be an eye-wateringly expensive project, but this ambitious development of coastal infrastructure is considered vital to Britain's economy.

We probably do not think too much about the shipping passing below or above as we cross estuaries, or spare much of a thought for coastal travellers in the past who had it much less easy than we do. But we should count our blessings. Navigating the coast and making a living from the sea has always been hard and fraught with danger. It is no wonder that coastal communities had to be independent, resourceful, tight-knit, resilient and often extremely brave to survive. Saving lives at the coast, despite the roles of national agencies, still relies on people in local communities being prepared to offer helping hands and put their own lives at risk.

If coastal people appeared somewhat rough, lawless and anarchic to outsiders, and indulged in quirky superstitions, customs and tall tales, we should see these traits as bonds that kept them together and kept them going. The faith that one North Yorkshire coastal village once put in a 'hob' (a mythical goblin-like creature) to cure whooping cough, for example, is evidence of their readiness to believe both in the otherworldly qualities of their surroundings and an indication of their desperation. This small, impoverished community had very little assistance to call on in the face of health crises or other times of need, so clutching at almost any straw at all was worth a try.

The coast is an enigmatic and mysterious place, where history merges with legend. Tales of mighty storms, sea creatures, pirates, adventures and smugglers formed at the coast have entered the pantheon of national history and folklore. They have inspired people far inland to seek out their own adventures at the coast or across the seas. The coast has fired the national imagination, and much of what we value, celebrate and even tolerate as part of being British is to be found distilled in coastal communities throughout the centuries.

British people who do not spare a thought for the history and future of their coast, and may not consider themselves to be connected with it any other way, will nevertheless have shared a coastal experience with tens of millions of their fellow Brits: a trip to the seaside. In fact, it is hard to think of another tourism destination and leisure-time choice that is as widely shared by so many Britons. If we have little else in common with strangers we meet, we can safely bet that we have all, at one time or another, enjoyed similar sorts of day trips or holidays at the coast. We all have our favourite seaside places, and those we like less, but we will meet very few people that say they dislike the coast and never visit it, at least once in a while.

Trips to the seaside have been a national institution for around a century and a half. Mention of the coast will prompt almost universal memories of childhood sandcastle building, ice creams, fish and chips (which always taste better by the sea), funfairs and contented exhaustion on the way home. Many people will keenly maintain and renew their acquaintance with the attractions of the coast throughout their lives.

Annually, millions are drawn to the coast as a place of fun

and leisurely retreat from busy inland lives. A Natural England survey in 2020 reported that 73 per cent of children said that the seaside was among their favourite places to visit. The fact that the figure is not even higher is illuminated by other statistics. Cadbury, the chocolate maker, undertook a survey in 2024 that claimed as many as one in ten children had never been to the seaside. Surveys and statistics are not always 100 per cent reliable, of course, but the fact that these findings were presented as something of a wake-up call shows how important the seaside is thought to be to children's formative life experiences and opportunities to extend their boundaries.

The lure of the coast is strong. It has been an aspiration and motivation of many people not only to visit occasionally, but to have their very own place by the sea. Small self-built communities sharing some of the characteristics of Thorpeness, Humberston Fitties and Jaywick have grown up around the British coast over the last century. Old railway carriages, prefabs, converted fishermens' sheds, old boats, redundant military installations and even former public toilets are among the things converted into holiday homes. This level of individualistic creativity in housing development is seldom tolerated inland, but the coast has inspired a different approach to living. Simple, inexpensive accommodation and almost unbelievably luxurious dwellings are still being built wherever demand is strong and development permitted. An influx of incomers has changed the character of coastal communities in many places around the coast over the last few decades, but perhaps it has also helped more of the inland population to better understand and engage with their coast.

The seaside may be largely about leisure, enjoyment and fun

for many people now, but that does not mean it is trivial to the nation's productivity. Far from it. The National Coastal Tourism Academy reported (pre-Covid) that coastal tourism in Great Britain generated a £17.1 billion spend and supported 285,000 tourism-related jobs. The health and wellbeing benefits to society of seaside breaks are even wider and have been recognised for a very long time, though are difficult to quantify and express with statistics. Nevertheless, many people who feel run down and overworked will swear by the restorative effects of a day or two by the sea, just as the privileged few did in Georgian times.

Ancient Rome recognised the vital role not only of plentiful food but also entertainment in keeping its citizens content. The key to avoiding uprisings, it was said, was to offer 'bread and circuses' to the masses. Is it too much of a stretch to credit the increasing availability of seaside breaks from the middle of the nineteenth century with mitigating British social unrest? Britain's industrial workers were able to let off steam or relax at the seaside in ways that were simply not accessible to landlocked populations. They could look forward to and enjoy some time away from the daily grind in a novel, stimulating environment; a place of refreshing new experiences, treats and fun.

Poorer Continental populations that were physically and socially much less connected to a coast could not do that. Discontent was everywhere as countries industrialised and many countries descended into revolution. Fish and chips and funfairs in Victorian and Edwardian Britain may have been the equivalent of grain and gladiators two thousand years ago.

Whether that particular assertion holds water or not, it is clear that the coast has shaped the character of the British people in all sorts of marked and subtle ways; not only people who have lived at or near the shore, but those living far inland too.

A lot of politics, conflict, innovation, culture, and economic and social dynamism has been packed into the geographic periphery of Britain. Much history is made at the coast. Many stories are generated there. Just as rock, shingle, sands, silt, mud and marsh have been deposited and have interwoven to form the geological basis of the coast, so layer upon layer of our heritage is set down and captured in its fabric. It will continue to be. Britain's coast is an endlessly fascinating, never-ending place.

Postscript

I walk across the sand and paddle calf-deep in the gentle surf. The water is not quite as cooling as I expect it to be. It is shallow here and the sea has been warmed throughout the summer and throughout the day. The sun is setting. People have gathered on the sea wall to see the great, glowing disc, now without its fierce heat, sinking into the sea. The sunset casts orange, red and purple streaks across the few low clouds. Finally the last sliver of gold slips below the waves. Tonight, people break out into applause and whoops of appreciation, astounded by the clarity and beauty of the spectacle.

As darkness descends I hear the clinking of glasses, animated chats and laughter from the nearby bar. The faint sounds of rock music and shrieks of pleasure reach me from the funfair along the coast. Strobe lights weave across the sky, and flashing lights whirl round with the taller rides. Across the water I can see the lights of another seaside resort beginning its own night-time transformation. In the other direction, huge wheeling flocks of wading birds that spent the day feeding on the nutrient rich inter-tidal zone, now look for roosts above the tide line.

On the water, crab boats have ridden out on the high tide from port. Their lights are like twinkling stars just above the water. The faint thrum of their engines occasionally reaches the shore. Beyond them the fading silhouettes of container ships slowly and silently make their way down the deep channel and out to sea. Little children are going to bed, sleepy after the excitement of the day. Some people are partying, and others are still working.

The sea will try to steal parts of the coast whether invited to do so or not, but although there is an unusually high tide tonight, the sea wall will easily cope. The caravan parks and camping grounds are safe behind the defences. With care and vigilance, people will be able to enjoy many more years of leisure and business here. I walk from the beach thinking about other coastal places I know, both wildly different and sharing similarities. I think about the stories they tell and the stories they have yet to tell. How are they faring tonight?

Britain's coast matters as much now as it ever has, perhaps more so. Its wellbeing is our wellbeing.

ACKNOWLEDGEMENTS

Thank you to Ellie Carr and all at Bonnier Books for your work in shaping this book. Thanks also to Barry Johnston for his editing, Jitesh Patel and Steve Millership for their delightful art, and Elly James of HHB Agency for her splendid support.

To all those I have travelled with around the coast to make TV programmes, thank you for increasing the pleasure with fine teamwork and good company. Special thanks to Diana Hare (formerly of the BBC), Pam Cavannagh and Dympna Jackson and all at Purple Productions for making *Villages by the Sea* happen in such a joyous way.

To all those at the coast who have taken time to tell me a tale or two, or open their historic homes and places of work so I can have a look around and ponder, my heartful thanks.

Finally, I wish to thank my family for tolerating my absences and making everything worthwhile.

SELECTED BIBLIOGRAPHY

Bellamy, P., Milne, G., 'An Archaeological Evaluation of the Medieval Shipyard Facilities at Small Hythe', *Archaeologia Cantiana*, Vol. 123: pp. 353–82. Maidstone: Kent Archaeological Society, 2003.

Bowyer, M.J.F., *Air Raid! The Enemy Air Offensive Against East Anglia 1939–45*, Wellingborough: Patrick Stephens, 1986.

Brindle, S., *Orford Castle*, London: English Heritage, 2018.

Brodie, A., *The Seafront*, Swindon: Historic England, 2018.

Brodie, A., Sergent, A., & Winter, G., *Seaside Holidays in the Past*, London: English Heritage, 2005.

Brown, I., Burridge, D., Clarke, D., et al, *20th Century Defences in Britain: An Introductory Guide*, Handbook of the Defence of Britain Project, York: Council for British Archaeology, 1995.

Burnal, P., Boschat, S., Mansouri-Robbins, M., & Macolm, A., *The Atlantic Wall in Jersey: The German Fortifications of Jersey 1940–45*, Jersey: Paul Burnal, 2022.

Carver, M., *Sutton Hoo: Burial Ground of Kings?*, London: The British Museum Press, 2002.

Coad, J., *Deal Castle*. London: English Heritage, 2003.

Coad, J., *Dover Castle, A Frontline Fortress and its Wartime Tunnels*, London: English Heritage, 2012.

Cocroft, W., Thomas, R., *Cold War: Building for Nuclear Confrontation 1946–89*, Swindon: English Heritage, 2004.

Colgrave, B. (trans.), *Felix's Life of Guthlac*, Cambridge: Cambridge University Press, 1985.

Connolly, B., *Made in Scotland: My Grand Adventures in a Wee Country*, London: Penguin Random House UK, 2018.

Darby, H.C, *The Draining of the Fens*. Cambridge: Cambridge University Press, 1956.

Darby, H.C, *The Changing Fenland*, Cambridge: Cambridge University Press, 1983.

Delano-Smith, C., Kain, R., *English Maps: A History*, London: The British Library, 1999.

Eastern Daily Press, various editions. Norwich: Newsquest Media Group.

Ellis, S., *Down a Cobbled Street: The Story of Clovelly*, Wellington: Halsgrove, 2012.

Fegan, T., *The 'Baby Killers': German Air Raids on Britain in the First World War*, Barnsley: Pen & Sword Books Ltd, 2012.

Ford, D., *Jersey 1204: A Peculiar Situation*, St Helier: Jersey Heritage Trust, 2004.

Friel, I., *Maritime History of Britain and Ireland c.400–2001*, London: The British Museum Press, 2003.

Gaffney, V., Fitch, S., & Smith, D., *Europe's Lost World: The Rediscovery of Doggerland*, York: Council for British Archaeology Research Report No. 160, 2009.

Garmonsway, G.N (trans., ed.), *The Anglo-Saxon Chronicle*, London: J.M. Dent Ltd, 1992.

Harris, L.E, *Vermuyden and the Fens: A Study of Sir Cornelius Vermuyden and the Great Level*, London: Cleaver-Hume Press Ltd, 1953.

Hegarty, C., Newsome, S., *Suffolk's Defended Shore: Coastal Fortifications from the Air*, Swindon: English Heritage, 2007.

Higham, N., *Rome, Britain and the Anglo-Saxons*, London: B.A. Seaby Ltd, 1992.

Hinman, M., Popescu, E., 'Extraordinary Inundations of the Sea: Excavations at Market Mews, Wisbech, Cambridgeshire', *East Anglian Archaeology Report No. 142*, Bar Hill: Oxford Archaeology East, 2012.

Lochart, A., *Rye*. Hurstbourne Tarrant: A. Lockhart, 1997.

Mattingly, H., Handford, S.A (trans., ed.), *Tacitus: The Agricola and the Germania*, Harmondsworth: Penguin Books Ltd, 1970.

Milton, G., *White Gold: The Extraordinary Story of Thomas Pellow and North Africa's One Million European Slaves*, London: Hodder & Stoughton, 2005.

Newton, N., *The Shell Guide to the Islands of Britain*, Newton Abbot: David & Charles, 1992.

Parker, R., *Men of Dunwich*, Newton Abbot: Readers Union Ltd, 1979.

Platt, C., *The English Medieval Town*, London: Book Club Associates, 1976.

Pryor, F., *Britain BC: Life in Britain and Ireland before the Romans*, London: Harper Collins, 2004.

Research Frameworks Network, *A Maritime Archaeological Research Agenda for England*, 2025. https://researchframeworks.org/maritime/introduction/

Rhodes, E., 'I Do Like to be Beside the Seaside, Part 2' in *The Heacham Newsletter October 2025*, Heacham: Heacham Parish Council, 2025.

Richards, P., *King's Lynn*, Chichester: Phillimore & Co Ltd, 2006.

Robinson, B., *England's Villages: An Extraordinary Journey through Time*, London: Blink Publishing, 2021.

Saunders, A., *Fortress Britain: Artillery Fortification in the British Isles and Ireland*, Liphook: Beaufort Publishing Ltd, 1989.

Shepherd, R., Hinze, V., & Coad, J., *Walmer Castle and Gardens*, London: English Heritage, 2003.

Sherley-Price, L. (trans.), *Bede: A History of the English Church and People*, Harmondsworth: Penguin Books Ltd, 1965.

Story, J., *Lindisfarne Priory*, London: English Heritage, 2005.

Walvin, J., *A Short History of Slavery*, London: Penguin Books Ltd, 2007.

Warren, W.L., *King John*, Berkeley: University of California Press, 1978.

Watson, C., *Seahenge: An Archaeological Conundrum*, Swindon: English Heritage, 2005.

Welfare, S., Fairly, J., *Arthur C. Clarke's Mysterious World*, London: Book Club Associates, 1981.

Wessex Archaeology 'Les Gellettes, Island of Jersey: Archaeological Evaluation and Assessment of Results', Report reference: 74154.01, Salisbury: Wessex Archaeology, 2011.

Williams, P., *The English Seaside*, Swindon: English Heritage, 2005.

OPENING CHAPTER QUOTES SOURCES

Chapter 1: Mattingly, H., Handford, S. (trans., ed.), *Tacitus: The Agricola and the Germania,* Harmondsworth: Penguin Books Ltd, 1970.

Chapter 2: Campbell, J., *Edward Heath: A Biography,* London: Jonathan Cape, 1993.

Chapter 3: Wesley, J. *The Journal of John Wesley,* Grand Rapids: Christian Classics Ethereal Library, 2000.

Chapter 4: Alexander, M. (trans.), *Beowulf,* London: Penguin Books, 1973.

Chapter 5: Collins, W., *Rambles Beyond Railways*; or *Notes in Cornwall taken A-Foot,* London: Richard Bentley, 1861.

Chapter 6: Head, G., *A Home Tour Through the Manufacturing Districts of England in the Summer of 1835,* London: John Murray, 1836.

Chapter 7: Fiennes, C., *Though England on a Side Saddle in the Time of William and Mary,* London: Field & Tuer, The Leadenhall Press, E.C., 1888.

Chapter 8: Rogers, P. (ed), Daniel Defoe. *A Tour Through the Whole Island of Great* Britain, Exeter: Webb & Bower Ltd, 1989.

Chapter 9: Sir Winston Churchill, speech to the House of Commons, 4 June 1940, International Churchill Society, https://winstonchurchill.org/resources/speeches/1940-the-finest-hour/we-shall-fight-on-the-beaches/

Chapter 10: Austen, J., *Persuasion,* London: Thomas Nelson and Sons Ltd, 1950.

Chapter 11: Pearson, F.R., *Charlotte Brontë on the East Yorkshire Coast,* York: The East Yorkshire Local History Society, 1957.

Index